MEN OF 18 IN 1918

Frederick James Hodges

SAPERE
BOOKS

MEN OF 18 IN 1918

Published by Sapere Books.

20 Windermere Drive, Leeds, England, LS17 7UZ,
United Kingdom

saperebooks.com

ISBN: 978-1-80055-585-3.

TABLE OF CONTENTS

PREFACE

THE WESTERN FRONT REVISITED

Some years ago, when my son visited Italy on business, my wife and I accompanied him. This gave me an opportunity to revisit the Somme battlefields of the First World War, where, in 1918, I fought in the British Army against the Germans on the Western Front. As we drove south across France to the Swiss border, we made diversions to villages near Albert which I knew when I was in the trenches from April to August 1918.

I stood in the fields near Mesnil where the Front Line was in April, 1918, where we made the final stand against the massive German Spring Offensive. I thought of the youngsters who had died in these same fields; then so scarred and noisy, now silent and empty save for some women picking up potatoes. I saw how nature, and the farmers, had healed the wounds of this once shell-torn landscape, when only field poppies bordering the trenches and the cry of the water fowl in the lagoons of the River Ancre, spoke of peace. Here in the Ancre valley, many of my older school friends had fought and died in 1916 and 1917. I visited the military cemeteries at Aveluy Wood and Ovillers and found their individually marked graves.

I went through lanes to Pozieres (now entirely rebuilt) and continued to ascend the great Thiepval Ridge which we stormed in August 1918, when my battalion, the Lancashire Fusiliers captured Martinpuich. Dominating the skyline on the crest of the Ridge, there now stands Lutyens' colossal and awesome Memorial to the missing of the Somme battles, 1916-1918. This huge brick-stepped pyramid, pierced by great arches, has 73,357 names carved on its walls.

On our return journey from Italy, I was again deeply moved as I stood in the military cemetery at Neuvilly on the River Selle, where so many Lancashire Fusiliers lie.

I walked slowly past the rows of graves, and came to the grave of Lieutenant R. S. Stott, MC, killed in action 12th October 1918. He was my first Platoon Officer in France. I knelt for a few minutes at his grave.

In the same row was the grave of Corporal F. Lester, VC, who was killed in action on the same day.

As I lingered at the graves of other Lancashire Fusiliers I came to Private Hand's, and remembered his unexpected remark — "Oh Corporal, when is this awful war going to end?" At the time I was fully occupied detailing men for various duties, and had no time to answer his unusual question.

Turning away from the cemetery, I looked towards Inchy, just beyond the horizon over which we had advanced to capture Neuvilly. It was in the streets of Neuvilly that Corporal Lester had won a posthumous VC for his outstanding courage and self-sacrifice.

I remembered how difficult, and how costly the capture of this large village or small town had been, and also how different it was from the trench warfare of the Somme, then many miles behind us.

The village stood on high ground which rose steeply from the far bank of the River Selle, and the windows of the houses overlooking the river valley were heavily sandbagged with loopholes for enemy machine-guns.

Against a determined enemy, our repeated attacks over a period of more than a week, and the enemy counter-attacks, resulted in fierce house to house fighting in which we used Mills bombs freely. I also thought of "Wilky", my fellow corporal, who was fatally wounded by a shell after the battle was over.

At Englefontaine, I tried to identify the farm from which I escorted fifty-eight German prisoners to the small town of Poix du Nord in October, 1918. The countryside here is dotted with small villages — Vendigies-au-Bois, Wagonville and Bousies; several times we were lost in the narrow lanes. I found a rough farm track to Bois de Boustes Farm, which is probably the farm for which I was looking, but so many alterations had taken place since 1918, and I could not be sure.

At Poix du Nord I searched for the arched gateway of the farm to which I led the German prisoners when it was the HQ of the 52nd Brigade. While we were taking a photograph of the gateway a lady appeared from the house into which the old farm buildings had been converted. She invited us to see the alterations which had been made since 1918. When her husband, Dr Martinache-Dupas, returned home for lunch, he pressed us to stay for refreshments and we spent a pleasant time talking to him and his wife, who is also a *Docteur en Medecine*. After leaving them I searched for and found the cattle market where I had handed my prisoners over to the Military Police, and received a receipt!

More memories were stirred at the site of the great Hindenburg Line which the Germans built in commanding positions in 1917, using British prisoners of war. On the 18th September 1918, my battalion captured Gouzeaucourt on this massive fortification and took many German prisoners.

Then we passed through Fins and Rocquigny to the Bapaume-Peronne road, which had been the Divisional Objective. All these places offered exciting memories for me as did Lesboeufs, where we spent time in the military cemetery. I smiled wryly at the rough signpost, Bull's Road Cemetery at the corner of the lane — (Bull's Road was the name originally coined from Lesboeufs by the "Tommies" or "Aussies" of those war days.)

Then we came to Flers, which had very vivid memories of violent scenes long ago, and passing between Delville Wood and High Wood we continued down the great Thiepval Ridge to La Boselle where the Front Line was on 1st July 1916. Before leaving these sad scenes with their horrifying but fascinating memories, I visited several more military cemeteries near Albert and found the graves of more old school friends and battalion comrades.

After this visit to the Somme and Selle battlefields, I began to write some of the events in which I took a small part in 1918, that momentous year in which the British Army, in desperate and bloody fighting, turned the near defeat of March into full and final victory in November.

Although so many years have passed, I find it easy to recall, not only the names of places and people, but also the deep impressions made at the time. The background of those momentous years is inevitably the horror and the devastation of the fourth year of a war which had swallowed up a generation of men on the Western Front.

What I best remember when I recall such sad scenes, which at the time seemed both inevitable and unavoidable, is a generation that accepted every situation with courage and with humour, and above all, with an unshakeable conviction, whatever the situation, that we should ultimately win the final victory.

THE COMMAND STRUCTURE OF THE BRITISH ARMY 1914-1918

Those unfamiliar with the command structure of the British Army as it was during the First World War may find the following of help. A battalion of infantry was commanded by a Lieutenant Colonel, with a Major as his second in command. The Adjutant and the Medical Officer held the rank of Captain. The Intelligence Officer, Machine-Gun Officer, Signals Officer and the Quartermaster were Lieutenants, and there was a Regimental Sergeant-Major, known as the RSM. Each of the four companies of a battalion was commanded by a Captain, with a Lieutenant as second in command. There was a Company Sergeant-Major, the CSM and a Company Quartermaster-Sergeant, the CQMS.

The four platoons of a company were each commanded by a 2nd Lieutenant, who was always addressed as Mister. A Platoon Sergeant was second in command. The four sections of a platoon were led by a Corporal or a Lance-Corporal. There were 8 to 12 men in a section, 40 or so in a platoon, 180 to 200 men in a company, and 750 to 800 men in a battalion.

A brigade comprised three battalions and was commanded by a Brigadier-General. Three brigades made a division, and this was commanded by a Major-General. Two or more divisions were in a corps, commanded by a Lieutenant-General. Various numbers of corps composed an army, of which there were five. These were under the command of Generals Allenby, Plumer, Byng, Rawlinson and Gough. The Commander-in-Chief was Field Marshal Sir Douglas Haig.

In 1918, it was no longer possible fully to replace the heavy casualties sustained in 1916 and 1917, and reorganisation of the British Army was necessary. To achieve this the four infantry brigades of a division were reduced to three, and the four infantry battalions of a brigade were also reduced to three. By this reorganisation the number of infantry battalions in a division was reduced from sixteen to nine. This reorganisation was completed by 4th March 1918, only two weeks before the German Spring Offensive, and following the further heavy casualties sustained in that offensive, ten divisions were reduced to cadre strength and were no longer operative.

INTRODUCTION TO WAR

BORN TO DIE, THE STORY OF A GENERATION

When the Great War broke out in August 1914, the young men who had been born in the 1880s and 1890s were just the right age for it. Not only were they the right age, they also had the right spirit, having grown up in the traditions of the British Empire.

Their education and upbringing had taught them that war was a glorious and honourable service; that it was manly and heroic to die for one's country. Consequently, at Kitchener's call they rushed to join the Army, and his original call in August 1914 for 100,000 men, ultimately resulted in more than 3,000,000 men leaving civilian life to join the Army, the Navy or the Air Force.

Thus from 1914 to 1918, a whole generation of men was willingly caught up, with few exceptions, into a highly traumatic experience, though at the time those men would not have so understood their war experiences. Those who served on the Western Front, though living under constant stress, experienced a degree of male comradeship and solidarity and total dependence upon one another which civilian life never knows. The Line was their home and its defence their responsibility; it was their world. That other world, nicknamed "Blighty", which they had willingly left, depended on that solidarity which is born and maintained under fire.

At home, the casualty lists grew ever longer, and every city, every town and every village was affected. Many were the homes saddened by the arrival of a telegram as the succession of battles during 1914, 1915 and 1916 and 1917 literally ate up a generation of men. These, Britain's best young men, were sucked into a vortex of endless and often unprofitable slaughter. This unskilled butchery on the Western Front never ceased, yet the Front scarcely moved from the autumn of 1914 to the spring of 1918. The dead were buried every day, if they could be reached, or found; the wounded returned from hospital and when battalions relieved one another, they took over the same old familiar trenches, dug-outs and strong points which they had occupied before.

Yet, even in 1917, after three long years of war, as boys reached the age of eighteen, they still enthusiastically chose war and wounds and death, fearful only that the war might end before they could play their part in it.

"ALL OVER BY CHRISTMAS"

When the Great War commenced, in August 1914, I was a schoolboy aged fifteen at the local Grammar School — The Northampton Town and County School. Suddenly the town was full of soldiers — the Welsh Division arrived by rail and were billeted in the homes of the local inhabitants. At my home, we had two who shared a bed and had their meals with the family.

On the racecourse, near my home, there was tremendous military activity and we Grammar School boys, on summer holiday, spent all our time there. There were huge ration dumps in and around large marquee tents; large heaps of freshly baked loaves; whole cheeses and the carcases of animals were being cut up on trestle tables erected on the grass near the tennis courts. Most of the soldiers wore their smart blue dress uniform; only a few had khaki. They were Territorials, popularly known as "Saturday Afternoon Soldiers" who went to camp annually for a week.

All along the St. Georges Avenue border of the racecourse, drinking troughs were set up with water from the mains for the hundreds of horses and mules. Wooden stables were erected on the football pitches; army farriers were shoeing horses; mules were being broken in, and bugle calls and trumpet calls became a familiar sound from Reveille to Lights Out. Long columns of men, wagons and guns began to move through the town, often holding up all the traffic and giving the civilians a legitimate excuse for being late for work. Young Welsh soldiers began courting Northampton girls and some eventually married and settled in the town after the war was over. One of them, named Williams, became Mayor of the Borough.

No one had the least idea of what was really involved by Britain being at war with Germany, and the prevailing mood was often expressed by the phrase "It will be all over by Christmas."

One man knew better. Lord Kitchener, the hero of Khartoum, realised from the beginning that the war would last three years or more.

KITCHENER'S NEW ARMY

There was an immediate and enthusiastic response to Kitchener's call for 100,000 men to sign on for "three years or the duration". Half a million enlisted in three weeks and began training in civilian clothes; no uniforms being available for many months. Many towns and cities quickly raised battalions, such as the Accrington Pals, the Bradford Pals, the Grimsby Chums and many such battalions. There were the Public Schools battalion, the Boys' Brigade battalion, the Railway Pals, and for those who were officially too short, a Bantams battalion — one of my friends joined the Bantams and soon came home on leave wearing three stripes and a crown as a

15

CQMS (Company Quartermaster-Sergeant).

At Northampton, a well known and popular local and international rugby footballer, Edgar Mobbs, immediately left his business and rushed off to London to apply for a Commission. At thirty-two he was told he was too old, though possessing the physique of one in a thousand. He came back to Northampton and at once set about raising a Corps himself. Four hundred rallied round him including footballers, artisans, business and professional men. Only 264 passed the medical test and were enlisted in what was at first known as Mobb's Corps, together with many other men recruited from the county, and 175 in Peterborough. On 14th September 1914, the Northampton contingent paraded in civilian clothes; caps, bowlers, straw hats, many carrying macs on their arm or shoulder.

They then marched to the Castle Station to entrain for Shoreham, where they lived in tents and trained on the beach. By the time they went out to France as the 7th (Service) Battalion, Northamptonshire Regiment, to take part in the Battle of Loos, Edgar Mobbs had risen from Private to Major. He later commanded the battalion and was awarded the DSO. He was killed in action on 31st July 1917, in the Ypres Salient.

At the end of the summer of 1914, so many young men had suddenly left civilian life to train as soldiers that there was a great demand from employers for replacements. A number of boys including me, left the Grammar School prematurely for this reason. I started work in a local office, though I had expected to stay at school for several more years.

THE GLAMOUR OF WAR

From the outbreak of war and throughout 1915 and 1916, my older school friends were joining the Army or the Navy or the

Royal Flying Corps. Sometimes one came home on leave in uniform or in Hospital Blue. One of them who had joined the RFC flew very low over the Grammar School football pitches one Saturday afternoon and waved and grinned at us. "Look!" we shouted to one another as the plane swooped over us, "Look! It's old Nutter Beech." And someone shouted "How about a ride, Nutter?"

Then one day I was with a group of old school friends near my home when we met R. B. Hincksman, who had been a master at the Grammar School during my time there. He was on leave in the uniform of King Edward's Horse, a Canadian Force in which he had served before he became a schoolmaster. He told us how he "had had the good fortune" to get back into his old Unit — even as a humble Trooper.

These and many other exciting and glamorous encounters with old friends made us as "keen as mustard" to get into uniform and play our part in the war. One day, a group of ex-Grammar School boys stood outside my home, exchanging news about who had joined what. We knew that Nutter Beech, Beavan Pitt, Sid Hanafy, Les Wooding and several others had joined the Royal Flying Corps, but the vital question was — HOW did one get in?

Les had been home on leave in the glamorous uniform — double-breasted tunic (and spurs!) of the Royal Flying Corps. He told us that before he was accepted as suitable for training as a pilot, he had to ride a horse and drive a car round a field; two things he had never done before. Now he was learning to fly! We were thrilled.

Other items were exhaustively discussed — Norman Beale, one of my friends, had told me that he had been promised a Commission in the 7th Northants, as soon as he was nineteen. Someone else said that L. J. Urquhart, one of the young

Grammar School Masters, who had taught us, had been killed at Loos while serving as a 2nd Lieut, in the 7th Northants; and someone else said that Ormrod, another Grammar School Master, had been wounded.

"So has Noakes", I said, "he's full of shrapnel, I've talked to him!" 2nd Lieut. Noakes, one of our school friends, had turned up one day in Hospital Blue, on crutches and his arm in a sling, from the Battle of Loos. Several of us had ringed him round and plied him with questions as he stood with his back to a wall near the racecourse. He told us he was "full of shrapnel", all down one side, head, shoulder, arm, thigh and leg. We were thrilled! In our eyes, the boy we had known at school, was a war hero. It is amazing to me how attractive all this information about the war was to under-age boys; we were fearful that the war might end before we could get into it. "One thing was certain" we all agreed "we must, we *MUST* be fit, so that we would pass A1 when the long awaited day came."

CONSCRIPTION!

By early 1916, most young men had volunteered for and were serving in the Armed Forces and the British Army was now flexing its muscles for further action. In 1914, it had consisted of 100,000 very well trained Regulars who, at the outbreak of war had been augmented by the Territorials.

These volunteer amateur soldiers, having had regular weekend training and an annual camp, naturally felt superior to Kitchener's recruits, whom they described as Kitchener's Mob. As trained "Terriers" they not only felt superior; they sometimes expressed their feelings, in a good humoured way with much laughter, by singing a parody of a well-known popular song of those days…

"THE GALLOPING MAJOR"

Hi! Hi! clear the way, here comes Kitchener's
Army.
Hi! Hi! never say die! here comes Kitchener's
Army.
When they get to the Front, they'll drive the
enemy "barmy"
Hi! Hi! clear the way, here comes Kitchener's
Army.

The Territorials had originally signed on for home defence hence the name, Territorial. Some of them wore a metal clasp on the chest, inscribed "Imperial Service"; this indicated that they had also volunteered to serve abroad. Eventually, of course, most of them did.

In 1915, the Derby Scheme was introduced. It was sponsored by the well-known sporting Earl, Lord Derby, who invited all men up to the age of forty-one, married and single, who had not yet enlisted to register for service. This voluntary registration very quickly became a call-up, in fact, it was virtually conscription. This was quite a shock to some of the married men! Britain thus had four classes of soldiers; the Regulars, the Territorials, Kitchener's New Army and the Derby Scheme men. In February, 1916, it was announced that conscription was to be introduced officially on March 2nd, thus making a fifth class of British soldier.

We had always known that the countries on the European mainland conscripted their young men for various periods of military service, and were thus able to mobilise large armies when war threatened — but NOT BRITAIN! The saying had always been — "One volunteer is worth two conscripts". Consequently, the very word Conscript was anathema to Britain's young men. We had been brought up to think of war as a kind of sport, and of course we all knew that an amateur was better than a professional. (This theory was later tested in the Somme Battles of 1916 onwards, when our best amateurs were matched against Germany's professional conscripts.)

In February, 1916, the Official War Posters made a last appeal to the volunteer spirit with this slogan —

WHY NOT MARCH TOO? DON'T WAIT UNTIL MARCH 2

Bert Griffin and Wally Gross were two of my closest friends; I saw them every day, but not in the last week of February 1916 — they disappeared! No conscription for them! Their sudden disappearance caused quite a sensation, for they were only seventeen and eighteen, and their parents were asking all of us who were their friends if we knew where they were. None of us knew; they had kept it a close secret, but eventually we learnt that they had gone to London to enlist in the Gordon Highlanders. Unfortunately for them, Griff was accepted and put on a train for the long journey to Aberdeen, while Wally was rejected because he was not tall enough. Wally, however, was very powerfully built and had excelled in sport at school, so he went along to the Crystal Palace to join the Royal Naval Division. He was accepted and trained as a naval gunner. He served as a gunner on a merchant ship and had an exciting adventure in an encounter with a German U-boat.

About four or five months later, Griff came home on leave from Catterick Camp in Yorkshire, wearing the kilt of the Gordons, which dazzled us all still more. I was standing outside my home talking to him, when we saw Wally Gross approaching in his naval uniform. Suddenly he saw us, and as Griff said, came rolling up the street like a ship in full sail with a strong wind behind it. They ran to meet each other and thumped each other and grinned, while I delightedly listened to all their adventures since they were parted in London.

A few days later, Griff and I were strolling on the racecourse, when we saw approaching us a young officer in the double-breasted uniform of the Royal Flying Corps; it was another old Grammar School friend, Beavan Pitt. We ran to meet each other, and after a very perfunctory salute between Griff and Beavan, we started to discuss old school friends and what had happened to them. It was a lovely summer day and we sat on the grass near the cricket pitches and talked for an hour or more. We recalled the events of our schooldays, especially the last Annual Boxing Competition for the Paget Cup, which had taken place in the School Hall on 26th March 1914. Pitt and Griffin had taken part in the Lightweight Competition and had fought each other in the semi-finals, and Griff had been beaten in the final. All these events now seemed so long ago. We did not realize that it was the last time we were to see Beavan; he was shot down a few months later on the Western Front. (Later, I heard that, tragically, he was hit by our own artillery.)

The war had now been going on for two years, the First Battle of the Somme was claiming the lives of many of our school friends: Hanafy, Nightingale, Pitt and Grose as young officers in the Royal Flying Corps, and many others as Subalterns in the Infantry. The Welsh Division had left Northampton and the racecourse was occupied by troops of a Midland Division, mostly young soldiers of about nineteen years of age. In Abington Park too, near the lakes, young soldiers lived in bell tents, training all the week and thronging the paths and gardens of the park on Sunday.

One Sunday afternoon, I too was walking with my friends around the large lake near the spinney in Abington Park. Noisy groups of young nineteen-year-old soldiers met and parted from other groups as they strolled round the lake. As is usual when such groups break up and part, there were last words, final jokes and witticisms, and one young soldier, as he left a group, waved to them and said — "I shall be 'kicking up the daisies' by then". There were roars of laughter at this prediction although it was only too tragically possible.

OFFICER OR PRIVATE

By the spring of 1917, only two of my friends were still in "Civvy Street", and we three would become eighteen in June and July. We discussed the question of applying for a Commission in the Army, but this had one snag; we would need to get our call-up at the age of eighteen deferred for three months. So "Bumper" Wells and I cycled ten miles to Stow Nine Churches to see the Rector, who was said to be some sort of agent or to have some influence with the Inns of Court Officers Training Corps. We had tea with him in a very lovely octagonal room on one of the corners of the rectory, which had leaded windows overlooking a beautiful garden. We discussed the matter fully and he confirmed that we would need to apply to the local tribunal and obtain deferment for three months.

I also went to see my old headmaster, Edward Reynolds, and he gave me a letter recommending me. He was very sad about the grievous losses already sustained among the school staff and its scholars. Of the staff, in addition to Urquhart, Hincksman had been buried alive in a dug-out, Badcock, Cooke, Ormrod and White were serving as officers in the Army, also many of Edward Reynold's best scholars, who had won scholarships to Oxford and Cambridge, had been killed.

THE NORTHAMPTON SCHOOL CADET CORPS

I also obtained a certificate of my service in the Northampton School Cadet Corps, which had been formed in the Spring of 1913, and was affiliated to the Northamptonshire Regiment.

Two Companies had been formed; A and B. A Company was officered by Captain Sopwith, Lieut. White and Lieut. Urquhart. B Company by Captain Hughes and 2nd Lieut. Richards. These five were all masters at the school. The four House Captains had chosen the best 24 boys in each House for A Company, which thus had a strength of 96 Cadets, and 18 boys from each House for B Coy. B Company, with 72 Cadets, was a reserve to fill vacancies in A Company.

When the lists went up on the school notice-board, I saw that I had been allocated to B Company. I was only fourteen and could expect nothing else, but it was "worth a try", so I approached my house captain, T. H. Bryant, who was to be a Sergeant in A Company. "Oh well", he said, "I'd rather have someone who is keen than someone who isn't; I'll get you transferred." So I became one of the youngest boys to wear a khaki uniform in A Company. I suspect that my real motive was the glamour of the uniform — B Company wore football kit!

In our brand new khaki uniforms we drilled with carbines in the school playground, or in the school hall if it was raining. R. B. Hincksman and a Sergeant Bayes of the Northamptonshire Regiment soon licked us into shape, and also trained the NCOs in squad drill. We had a Field Day in Abington Park and were taught to move in the new "extended order" designed to reduce casualties, and we learned to carry out these orders by whistle and by hand signs.

In September 1913, I had been one of the Guard of Honour supplied by the Corps at the ceremonial unveiling of the

Memorial to King Edward VII at the main gate of the Northampton General Hospital.

The NCOs of the Cadet Corps were the school prefects, and when the war began in 1914 they became officers in the Army or the Royal Flying Corps. Many of them were killed in early actions, and later many of the younger boys were also as the war continued. The War Memorial in the school lists the names of ninety-four who were killed.

ENLISTMENT

Eventually, Bumper Wells and I decided not to apply for deferment in order to try for a Commission. On 13th March, 1917, at the age of seventeen years and eight months, we went to the recruiting office and offered ourselves for military service. There we met another old Grammar School friend, Winter, a tall broad shouldered youngster who was also anxious to get "fixed up". We were duly attested in the office of a local solicitor, Major A. E. Ray, who was the Recruiting Officer, No. 1 Sub-area, 48th Regimental Division.

At our attestation, we held a bible in our hand and swore to defend with our lives, King George V, his heirs etc., etc., and were transferred to the Army Reserve until we reached the age of 18. We received a day's pay, one shilling; and one day's ration money, one shilling and nine pence.

Then we were medically examined at the Northampton Barracks and were classified as "fit for general service as soon as trained". The medical officers who examined us visibly "brightened up" when we appeared before them with our chests bare. As we entered the room, I heard one of them say "Ah, now these three look more like it!" No doubt, by 1917, they had become accustomed to older men, unfit men and men who had been sent to them for re-classification after recovering from wounds, and the sight of three young men who were "raring to go" must have been refreshing to them.

My friends and I had been quite determined not to be classified as anything but A1 when we joined up, and so half a dozen of us had gone into strict training during the past winter. We went for long runs through the country lanes outside the town, and we formed a boxing club and spent two evenings a week boxing in a room in one of the local shoe factories. J. B. C. Knight (Jimmy) was the strongest of us physically; a good punch on the jaw from him when we had the gloves on made the room spin. His stamina on our six or seven mile long runs always amazed me, for I was always good at cross country running. When, after five or six miles, most of us were beginning to flag, Jim seemed to turn on extra power so that I had great difficulty in keeping up with him as he literally bounded up the last long hill from Buttocks Booth, and sped downhill into the town. He joined the Royal Flying Corps and was killed in Egypt while I was serving on the Western Front.

TRAINING FOR WAR

OUR MILITARY SERVICE BEGINS

The age at which young men were called up for military service had only just been reduced from eighteen years and nine months to eighteen years, with the proviso that they should not be sent on active service until they reached the age of nineteen. We were therefore due to be called to the Colours in July 1917 and due to go on active service in July 1918. However, in the Spring of 1918, when the great German offensive of 21st March was threatening Amiens, Paris and the channel ports, all young men in training who had reached the age of eighteen and eight months, were very hurriedly sent to the Western Front to reinforce the badly depleted battalions who were stemming the German advance.

My two friends were a few weeks older than me, but as we very much wished to be together, I reported at the barracks with them when they were called. This was no problem; my papers were soon produced, added to theirs, and then for an hour or two we remained together through all the formalities of being embodied in HM Forces. At the very end of all the paperwork, and just before we were kitted out in our uniforms, we were told that Bert Chapman was to go to a Training Camp at Luton, while Bumper and I were to go to Tollgate Camp at Dovercourt, near Harwich. Our protests were ignored, and Bumper and I did not see Chapman again until after the war. Bumper and I were put into a party of nine which marched to Castle Station in charge of a Corporal of the Northamptonshire Regiment, who had several wound stripes on his sleeve. He regaled us with tales of his experiences as a

"First Bayonet Man" in trench raids on the enemy. The nine were myself and Bumper, four others from Northampton, Crouch, Swain, Thompson and Whitehead; the other three were Tim Costello from Guilsborough, Jim May from Towcester and Wally Beale from Brigstock. (Of these nine, Whitehead and Beale were killed; Crouch lost a leg; and Wells, May and Costello were wounded.) At Euston, nine young men from Acton joined our party, brought there by a Sergeant in the Middlesex Regiment who handed them over to our Corporal. Three of them, Harvey, House and Wenderleish (a Jew), were refined, well-educated boys; three were of the rough tough type, Gordon, Pelly and Norris; and the other three were harder to classify on sight. One was another Jew named Hotcha; one was a very tall youngster named Fox; and the third was Turner, who later won a Military Medal.

Gordon was a huge youngster with a great barrel of a chest, a bullet head, a beefy face and very narrow eyes. His hair was black, short and bristly. Pelly and Norris seemed to be his jackals; Norris looked as if he was capable of anything so long as it was not lawful. This first impression was confirmed when he later smashed all the lights, broke the luggage rack and cut off the window straps in the carriage of a train in which we were travelling to Dover.

Pelly had a more open face, but was evidently prepared to back them up in any trouble they caused. We had no trouble with them while we were in charge of the Corporal on the train to Dovercourt, but I could see that they had given the same impression to my friend Bumper Wells, and to Tim Costello, with whom I exchanged glances.

UNDER CANVAS AT DOVERCOURT

At Dovercourt Station we formed up and marched to the

Battalion Headquarters where we were inspected by an old Colonel who wore Boer War ribbons.

After an orderly room sergeant had taken various particulars, we were handed over to a very young sergeant, who marched us to Tollgate Camp about a mile up the road where we were taken to a marquee tent and began to assist with its erection on the long wet grass of a field near a farm. When the tent was up we left our kitbags in it and were taken to a barn where we were given an empty mattress each and told to fill them with the straw in the barn.

Then we went to another farm building where we were told to pick up three long wooden planks and two very low trestles, which were wide enough to accommodate the three planks. Loaded with our filled mattresses, planks and trestles, we returned to the marquee tent and began to set up our beds in the wet grass.

By this time it was raining again, and Gordon, rather than go outside, proceeded to urinate on the grass in the tent. Immediately Costello called him a dirty B—, and told him to go outside. For a moment I thought he would strike Costello as he scowled at him and said "Oo do you fink you are?" His two jackals moved to his side, and Bumper and I lined up with Costello, but for the moment no blows were struck. It was plain that Gordon, whom his jackals called Basher, was very proud of his nickname, and he certainly looked very capable of living up to it.

My friend Bumper, whose name was actually Arthur Wells, was nicknamed after a well-known boxer because of his physique. Bumper was shorter than me, but was very broad shouldered, and had very long arms and slightly bowed legs, which seemed to impress Gordon, Pelly and Norris. He was

28

not, actually the tough type, but I felt sure that Gordon and his supporters thought he was.

After a few days we were moved to bell-tents pitched round the periphery of the parade ground, and so for the time being we were no longer in close contact with Basher Gordon and his mates. Months later the trouble flared up again between the Acton boys and the Northampton boys when we were all together again in an army hut in the huge Clipstone Camp near Mansfield.

Basher Gordon used to return to the hut drunk after an evening in the pubs in Mansfield, and was often in a fighting mood, when he would boast and swear and challenge someone to fight him. Then he would be sick on the floor and stagger to his bed and snore. One evening when he was boasting about his prowess with his fists, Whitehead challenged him to a proper fight with seconds, and rounds of three minutes. Whitehead was a tall, raw-boned, long armed boy, and a good deal tougher than any of us had thought. He gave Gordon as good as he received for six rounds, until Sergeant Thorogood came into the hut and stopped the fight. I think Basher Gordon was glad that he did.

ARMY TABLE MANNERS

At Tollgate Camp our meals were in the cowsheds of the farm, and when the bugler blew "Cookhouse" we all had to line up in the farmyard. Here the sergeant cook numbered us off in batches of sixteen; he had an eagle eye for anyone who lined up for the second breakfast after having had the first. It was a challenge to some boys to try to defeat him but it was no use; he came along the double line of boys, barking — two, four, six, eight, ten — out you! Somehow he never missed! We took our places at rough wooden trestle tables set up in the cowsheds. On each table were four large white basins and a basket with sixteen pieces of bread. Table manners were non-existent; each soldier immediately grabbed a piece of bread and an orderly filled the large basins with hot tea from a bucket. Each basin was for the use of four; two each side of the table, and when they were empty we shouted for the orderly to fill them again. Lifting the heavy basins filled with a couple of pints of hot tea was quite a balancing act as well as a feat of strength.

ARMY HAIRCUTS

One of the Acton boys, Harvey, had very fair hair, which he wore long and swept back from forehead to neck. As soon as the Sergeant-Major saw him with his cap off, he ordered him to go and get a haircut. Harvey went, as ordered, to one of the barns in the farm, where his hair was cut off — all of it — with horse clippers! We did not recognise him when he returned to the tent; his head seemed to be half the size it had been. After this, Ernie Smith, one of the Northampton boys, who had been a barber's boy, cut hair at two pence a time.

Harvey was a refined boy, well educated but with a slight stutter. I had several conversations with him several months later when we were waiting our turn to fire on the range up on the moors near Clipstone. The first time we came under enemy fire in the trenches in France, he went to pieces; face pale and limbs trembling as the shells burst. He was sent down the line with shell-shock and I never saw him again.

ARMY TRAINING

On our first evening at Tollgate Camp, after making our beds and sorting out our kit, some of us decided to go for a stroll. We walked out of the camp, past the sentry at the gate of the parade ground, and then we met a soldier who was wearing a long rubber mackintosh. Not realising that he was our Company Sergeant-Major since there were no badges of rank on his mac, we asked him if this was the road to take for Dovercourt. "No!" he roared. "THAT'S the way for you, until you are issued with your leather belts. EVERYWHERE outside this camp is out-of-bounds to you until you are properly dressed."

Our platoon sergeant was Sergeant Newton, a very experienced soldier and a very firm disciplinarian; he had been wounded several times on the Western Front. Another platoon sergeant was Sergeant Thompson, who had been so badly wounded in the back that he could never wear a full pack. The physical training sergeant was very fond of telling us that he was the only man in the British Army who had had a German bayonet in his throat; and had survived.

Sergeant Roe, who sometimes trained us, was a Northampton man and there were several Northampton boys apart from the nine and Ernie Smith. Two friends, Dunmore and Ablethorpe had managed to stay together at their call-up.

Our company commander was badly disabled by a wound in his skull; he had a small metal plate fixed over the hole. He took no part in our training and only came on parade to take the salute and then handed over to his second in command. All the company officers were men who had been wounded and were partly disabled.

On our fifth day at Tollgate I was made a section leader, and had to call the roll of my section when we fell in on parade. No stripes were given at this very early stage in our military career, and later in our training when they were, it was given to Ernie Smith, who took it down when we arrived in France.

On August 3rd we marched to Harwich General Hospital to be vaccinated; and the next day leather belts were issued to us. They were absolutely new, just bare leather, and we were told to buy a tin of Kiwi polish and keep polishing them until they looked "like the sergeant's".

TRAINED MEN AND RECRUITS

After about a week at Tollgate Camp, we went into the farmyard one morning to line up for breakfast, and found that during the night, hundreds of sunburned youngsters had returned from leave. They were referred to by the NCOs as the trained men. Orders would be given — "Recruits will fall in on the parade ground; the trained men will go to the large barn for a lecture on the Mills bomb."

Later, when we had this lecture, we learned from the bombing instructor that the Mills bomb, named after its inventor, was "a cast iron segmented body, filled with ammonite, which was exploded by a fuse of fulminate of mercury, etc." Then we were taken to the bombing range and taught to use them in sandbagged slit trenches. The Mills bomb was the size and shape of a lemon, with deep-cut grooves, so that on detonation it would form shrapnel. It had a spring lever which was curved to the shape of the bomb and was held in place by a split pin through a lug at one end of the bomb. When the split pin was withdrawn with one hand, the fingers of the other hand held the curved lever in place until the bomb was thrown. Five seconds later it exploded.

THE GRADUATED BATTALIONS

There were several other military camps in the Dovercourt-Parkstone-Harwich area, where many thousands of eighteen-year-old boys were being trained in the various young soldiers battalions. The boys were graduated according to age; each of the companies in a battalion being composed of boys whose age was within a few weeks of each other. Bumper and I became friendly with a boy named Bennett, a well-educated youngster who came from Bedford. Then it was discovered that Bennett was a week too young to be in D Company, and he was transferred to E Company, and was henceforth known as Babe Bennett.

From our parade ground at Tollgate Camp we could see the boys' camp at Parkstone on the coast, and though it was a mile or more distant, the boys there often shouted and waved to us. There were also at Parkstone many thousands of youngsters who were being trained in the Royal Navy. One day when we were marching along the road to Parkstone Quay, we met a thousand or more of them, also out for a march, in their Naval caps and blouses and bell-bottomed trousers. Compared with the boy soldiers, who by now had done a great deal of squad drill and ceremonial marching, their performance was poor, their marching was ragged and we made some very uncomplimentary remarks as they passed.

FURTHER ARMY TRAINING

Everyday we had a period of physical training, which became progressively stiffer. We started to have daily runs along the road to Manningtree. Many of the boys had evidently never run long distances and were soon winded, while Bumper and I, who had been in strict training, easily led and outdistanced everyone. About the middle of August, we had a battalion sports day, when the five companies competed in running, jumping and relay races.

Then in addition to our leather belts, other leather equipment was issued and we were taught how to assemble it, how to fold our greatcoat to fit neatly into the pack; how to keep it all clean with leather polished and brass sparkling. We then commenced route marches, first in skeleton order, then progressively to full marching order. Towards the end of August we had a brigade stunt with other battalions and also "Night Ops." which we thought were a bit of a lark. There were also several German Zeppelin raids at night, when we left our tents and took refuge in trenches dug around the parade ground. This gave us a taste for sleeping outside, and for the remainder of our time at Tollgate Camp we slept under the stars whenever it was fine. One night, many of the tents were blown down and we got rather wet.

During our two months at Tollgate Camp we also had much musketry instruction in preparation for firing on the range. We also marched to the General Hospital at Harwich to be inoculated. We were given forty-eight hours off physical duties, and attended lectures on various aspects of weapon training, and had medical inspections while our arms were sore. By the end of September, the July intake of boys were no longer raw recruits; we had been welded into very smart soldierly platoons, and were inspected by the Brigadier General at a ceremonial parade of drilling and marching.

CLIPSTONE CAMP

On 28th September we went by train to Clipstone Camp, near Mansfield in Nottinghamshire. This was a huge hutted camp accommodating 60,000 men; it had named roads, cinemas, banks, post offices and military police! It also had many YMCAs, canteens and churches of all denominations. Everything was in wooden huts. One could walk for miles in the camp and get lost. We discovered that there were thousands of boys training to be machine-gunners. One of these was an old school friend named Tom Price, who had joined the Machine-Gun Corps at the same time that we had joined our Young Soldiers' Battalion, the 53rd YS Battalion, Bedfordshire Regiment; we now wore the Bedfordshire cap badge.

While we were here we "fired our course" on the ranges up on the moors, some miles from the camp. The weather was cold during the fortnight in November in which we marched daily out to the moors, and there was often a strong wind. It was not good weather for marksmanship, especially when firing at 200, 300 and 400 yards range with bayonet fixed to our Short Lee Enfield rifles. The light was often bad too, and although I had hoped and expected to pass out as a marksman I had to be content with being classified as a 1st Class Shot. These little things were important to us youngsters; a marksman could wear crossed guns in brass on his tunic cuff!

We now had different officers and NCOs. We took our meals in our own hut and were responsible for its cleanliness. Every day one of us in turn was orderly man for the hut and fetched the coal for the stove from the coal yard, cleaned the windows, dry-scrubbed the floor, and scrubbed the collapsible tables with soap, and water; we became quite domesticated! We also had many kit and foot inspections, and, in turn were put on ceremonial guard for periods of twenty-four hours. While we were at Clipstone Camp we had a number of route marches, first as a battalion, then in a Brigade Group. Towards the end of our time at Clipstone Camp we also had a grand field day, and had a hot meal from travelling cookers.

There was a light railway from the camp to the town of Mansfield, and in the evenings thousands of young soldiers were to be seen, walking round the town in groups, laughing and talking until it was time to catch the last train back to camp. There was no rowdiness; the Military Police kept a very strict eye on us; not a button could be left undone.

While we were in Clipstone Camp we were issued with new box respirators and were marched to the gas chambers to test them in chlorine and other gases.

On 28th November we went home on six days leave; this was the only leave that I was ever to have during my twenty months service in the Army. We returned to camp on 3rd December, and I did not see Northampton again until February 1919.

COLCHESTER

On 12th December, we entrained for Colchester, and on arrival, we were immediately put into quarantine. We were told that Spotted Fever had broken out in the camp we had just left. We did not know what the disease was, and it sounded fairly harmless, but I have learnt since that its official name is Meningococcal Meningitis, or Cerebral Spinal Fever, and that it causes inflammation of the membrane surrounding the brain. In 1950 I spent six weeks in a Military Hospital near Oxford where, at one end of the ward, half a dozen serving soldiers were being effectively treated for this disease with regular injections of penicillin. This disease was greatly feared before the discovery of penicillin because of the risk of an epidemic. Characteristically it attacks children and young adults who are living in close proximity as we were. Hence the swift action by our medical authorities in December 1917 to put us into quarantine. We were locked in wooden huts, except for parades and training. These huts reeked of disinfectant and parades were welcomed. We bought various things such as writing paper, razor blades, chocolate and cigarettes, from the YMCA hut by handing money and a list through a window to boys who were not in quarantine. Later, when all danger of infection was over, we moved into one of the old regular army barracks, which were brick built with stone stairs to the upper floors. Each block was named after a famous battle.

In the town, the local churches and chapels vied with one another to supply us with free notepaper, tea and coffee, cakes and sandwiches. We sometimes toured the various church halls to see which was the best. I realise now that their interest was more than generosity to youngsters away from home; no doubt they were also concerned for our spiritual welfare. I was given a new testament, and carried it until I was demobilised.

SPECIALIZED TRAINING

On 17th December, I was sent, with others to the brigade signal school to start training as an army signaller. We began by learning the morse code. Our instructor was a young corporal recovering from a wound received on the Western Front with the Lancashire Fusiliers. I was paired with a boy named Seabrook, with whom I alternately made and received messages in morse. At first we worked in a hut with a buzzer, and later we made signals out of doors with army signal flags which we washed and ironed.

Training, including several long route marches, continued for seven weeks. Then we handed in our flags and returned to our companies, and for a fortnight marched each day to the rifle range. Here we were employed as butt markers, swinging the huge targets up, marking the shots, lowering the targets and repairing the shot holes with patches and a pot of paste. There was a field telephone from the butts to the firing positions, controlled by officers at each end, and while we were up on the top from our trenches a large red flag was displayed. We all enjoyed swinging up and down these huge targets for the troops who were firing their course in musketry and marking the score bull's-eye, inner, outer or waving a flag when it was a washout.

On 20th February, we returned to the brigade signal school to continue our training by commencing station work on the golf course, where in brisk breezes our flag wagging became quite competent.

REGIMENTAL RIVALRY

Colchester is a town with a long military history and at the time was full of soldiers of many regiments. Strict discipline was enforced both in the many barracks and in the streets of the town by the military police. There was also great rivalry between the regiments in their turnouts for guard duty at the gates to the various barracks, and at church parades. On Sundays there was special cleaning of buttons, brass and leather equipment before the big church parade to the garrison church. Battalions competed in appearance and marching to the church, as the regimental bands played stirring music.

BILLETS IN NORWICH

On 25th February, we went by train to Norwich, and on arrival were billeted in homes. This was a new experience after bell tents, army huts and regular army barracks. Four of us were billeted at the home of Mrs Holt, a widow, in Bury Street: 44,243, Private F. J. Hodges, 44,244, Private A. T. Costello, 44,224, Private W. Beale, and 44,240, Lance-Corporal R. House.

I was good friends with Tim Costello, Wally Beale and Bob House, and we were pleased to be together in such a comfortable billet. Mrs Holt gave us the front room downstairs for our kit, and the front room upstairs in which there were two double beds. We were not used to beds, or bedrooms, and at first could not sleep, but the next Sunday we overslept.

Every evening there was a roll-call in the street at 9 p.m. and another at 7.30 a. m. On Sunday, 3rd March, we were still half asleep in bed, when we heard the sound of troops in the street outside. Someone said — "Oh, its only the roll-call, someone will answer our names for us." Then, to our horror, we heard the command "Move to the right in fours, right!" and as we leapt out of bed and rushed to the window, we saw the company marching off to church parade. We dressed hurriedly and went downstairs. Soon there came a rat-tat-tat at the front door, and there stood the Company Sergeant-Major with an escort. We were marched, under military escort, to one of the large three storey houses in Unthank Road and handed over to the guard.

We spent the day and night in the cellar, sleeping on bare boards. The next morning we were marched, again under escort, through the streets to Company Headquarters. Bob House, as a lance-corporal, was not shut up in the Guard Room cellar; he was left in our billet under open arrest with another lance-corporal to guard him and brought to us when we were charged. We were marched in, under escort, in front of the company commander, and the charge was read and we were asked if we had anything to say in our defence. Then the company commander said it was too grave a charge for him to deal with and we should have to go before the commanding officer of the battalion.

Eventually, we were again marched in, this time before the CO, the charge was again read out, and after hearing our defence (or excuses), the CO gave us each seven days CB (Confined to Barracks).

DISCIPLINE FOR DEFAULTERS

My further training as a signaller commenced the same week on 4th March, so I had a hard time. I was at the signal school all day and then I and my fellow defaulters had to answer all the bugle calls for defaulters through the evening, and scrub floors, clean dozens of metal washbasins with sand, and run errands for the guard on duty. I had no difficulty in sleeping, and I had a salutary fear of not hearing the bugle call.

WASHING UP FOR THOUSANDS

At Norwich, all our meals were served in the large Drill Hall, several streets away from our billets. After a meal, the sergeant cook would order the boys at one of the long trestle tables to do the washing-up. I suppose most boys have assisted their mother or sisters with the washing-up after a meal, but it was a new experience to wash up for thousands.

The washing-up squad took off their tunics, rolled up their shirt sleeves, and filled large galvanised wash-tubs with hot water from the kitchens. This was always a public performance: the local housewives lined the iron railings around the yard of the Drill Hall, and were very amused. The boys always entered into the fun, swapping humorous remarks with the ladies, as some boys washed the dirty plates, dishes, pots and pans; and other boys dried and stacked the plates; and others carried them back to the tables in the Drill Hall.

ADVANCED TRAINING

During the next few weeks, our training in the Signal School became more advanced, and we also went on several very long marches with the Sussex School of Signalling, a Brigade Group where we met boys from other Boys' Battalions. We also tested our gas masks for tear gas.

Then, very suddenly, all training came to an abrupt end.

"MEN OF 18 IN 1918"

On Sunday evening, 24th March, in the streets of Norwich, a rumour began to spread among the young soldiers who thronged the pavements of the city. It was that our troops in France were retreating, and that we youngsters were to be drafted to the front without completing our training.

On Monday morning, 25th March, the rumours proved to be true; at the early morning roll-call, as we paraded outside the billets, we were told officially. The situation on the Western Front was so grave that all those who had reached the age of eighteen years and eight months were to be drafted to the Front immediately. My age was eighteen years and eight months on 18th March, and so I was eligible.

We signallers reported for the last time at the Sussex Signal School, handed in our flags, and said goodbye to our instructors. We returned to our companies, where all training had also ceased, and we spent every moment of the day in long queues, being kitted out for the Front. We put on our best khaki and handed in the tunic and trousers we had been wearing. In great excitement, we queued to have our bayonets dulled and our rifles inspected by the armourer sergeant. We marched through the town to the gas school, and queued up to pass through the various gas chambers and tunnels for a final test of our gas masks.

Everyone was happy and full of youthful high spirits, and that evening, when at last we were free, we all went down into the city centre where many thousands of excited youngsters of eighteen laughed and talked as we milled round the city. We already wore coloured ribbons — red, yellow, green, blue, etc. around our service caps, to distinguish the many young soldier battalions in that area. Now we added to these, red, white and blue ribbons which we bought at Woolworths, trimming our uniform caps across the front above and below the cap badge and making rosettes at each side. I was quite good at this and was in great demand.

As we roamed the city centre in large groups, the military police who would normally stop us for any infringement in our dress or behaviour, now took no action. Authority was being tolerant and unusually friendly; our own officers were very friendly and informal as they stood chatting to us as we waited again next morning in long queues for boot repairs. They seemed … or was it we, who now suddenly seemed to be a race apart. We were now bound for the Front, from which they had returned with wounds, to train us.

My platoon officer always wore a brown kid-glove on his left hand; or rather, the hand of his artificial arm. He gave us some friendly advice about active service on the Western Front, and at times seemed almost envious of our opportunities. He said "They say 'Jerry' is still coming over in massed formation; you lads will have wonderful targets; make the most of your opportunities."

GENERAL MOBILISATION

On 27th March, we marched to the railway station and entrained for London and forty-eight hours leave prior to departure overseas. At Cambridge the train was stopped and we saw that the platform was lined with Military Police. The situation on the Western Front was now so grave that a General Mobilisation Order had been issued. This meant that all men on leave or proceeding on leave were to return to their units at once. We returned to Norwich and marched to the drill hall at 11 p.m. for some hot soup, and then returned to our billets.

Preparations continued for our departure overseas, and Easter Sunday, 31st March, found us not at a church parade but at the gas school once again testing our new gas masks in several gas chambers. Later, we were marching up Unthank Road, when suddenly I was very surprised, but delighted to see my mother and father.

They had come to Norwich to see me before I went to France. I found them lodgings in a nearby street, and they stayed until 3rd April, my mother's 53rd birthday. She, in common with all mothers of sons in those days, had very good reasons to feel worried about me. George Dunmore's two older sisters also made the difficult train journey from Northampton to Norwich before we left for the Front. It was the last time they were to see him; he was killed by a sniper's bullet.

THE GENERAL'S ADDRESS TO US

On 4th April, there was a big ceremonial parade in one of the city parks where the many thousands of youngsters in the young soldiers battalions were assembled. After a grand ceremonial march past a general, we stood in long ranks, our breath condensing in the cold air and our young pink faces glowing, as we waited expectantly for the general's farewell address before we left for the Western Front. Every eye was directed to the lone figure of the elderly general on the dais as he began to speak.

> "You men," he began, and then paused as he surveyed our eager young faces, "I know, of course, that you are only boys of eighteen … I know that you have not completed your training... however, you are now to proceed overseas at a very critical time, and you have to play the part of men. You all

know that a great battle is going on at this moment on the Western Front. On 21st March, the Germans launched a tremendous attack; they have broken through our fortifications; they are being continually reinforced; in fact, they are attacking in massed formation. Their objective is Paris and the channel ports, and... THEY HAVE GOT TO BE STOPPED. You young men are NEEDED at the Front... without delay. I know that you have not completed your training, but I trust, indeed I am sure that the training you have had in this Division will stand you in good stead. You have all fired your course with the rifle, and some of you have learned to use the Lewis gun. What we have taught you on the ranges, you have now to put into practice at the Front, and from what I hear, there is no lack of targets there! Good luck to you all."

He then descended from the dais, and proceeded to inspect us at close range, walking along the many long lines of boys drawn up, and occasionally stopping to talk to a few who appeared to him to be exceptionally young or small.

OVERSEAS TO WAR ON THE WESTERN FRONT

EMBARKATION

On 5th April, in full overseas kit, we marched through the streets of Norwich for the last time … to the railway station... for London.... for Dover... and for the War!

This draft of eighteen year olds was exceptionally large, and attracted a large crowd in the street leading to the railway station. The pavements were crowded, especially near the entrance to the station yard. The majority were women, some no doubt our landladies from the many streets in which we had been billetted. Others were probably housewives who had often enjoyed watching the boys washing-up for thousands in the yard of the large Drill Hall. Today they were in a very sober mood, many of them in tears as they watched the long column of four march proudly past in full overseas kit. Some shouted "Good luck lads," others wept as they waved, and one woman shouted "Poor little beggars, they are only boys. Fancy sending them to the Front to die for us."

The grave situation on the Western Front was beginning to sink into the public mind; in fact, any attempt to conceal it by propaganda at this hour of crisis was useless.

My feelings as we marched past the Military Police at the gates of the station yard were a mixture of patriotic pride and embarrassment at this public display of feeling. I could not, or rather did not want, to show emotion or to be affected by other people's feelings. Two days earlier, when saying goodbye to my parents at this same railway station, I had felt the same. My mother had clung to me and begun to weep. I remember it was her 53rd birthday, and she said "If you don't come back —". I just squeezed her and kissed her and broke away, saying "Don't worry mum, I shall come back." Then I hurriedly left the station.

It was difficult in those days of the British Empire for boys to show emotion whatever we felt inside. We were trained to "keep a stiff upper lip", and maintain discipline in all circumstances.

It was evening when we arrived at Dover and marched up the steep hill to the castle. After mugs of hot tea and sandwiches, we bedded down on blankets on the floor of the castle, but were awakened about 4.30 a.m. and ordered outside. After tea and porridge we were soon marching down the winding hill to the quay, where we boarded a paddle steamer.

Lifebelts were issued as we went up the gangways, and soon the old boat, a cross channel steamer, was full of men; decks, stairs, passages, all crowded with soldiers in full equipment. During the crossing we were accompanied by a Royal Navy cruiser and two or three destroyers which circled us; while overhead several aeroplanes flew to and fro to spot any German U-boats. The excitement among the boys was intense.

When we reached Calais, after several hours we disembarked and marched to a base camp where we were lined up in a very long single row. We were then counted off into groups destined for different battalions. Friends who stood in line next to one another were parted by a hand and an order, and marched off to different Regimental Base Headquarters. These were bell tents in a long line, where particulars were taken, and to our surprise, new regimental numbers were given to us. My number was changed from 44243 to 57043.

In this peremptory way, I and about 300 others suddenly became Lancashire Fusiliers, while some of our friends became

Manchesters or Duke of Wellingtons or East Yorkshires. As one humourist said, "They can't put us into a Scottish Regiment unless they give us kilts!"

While we were waiting to be interrogated, I saw several of our young NCOs drop their stripes. One of these was a tall well-built youngster, who, while we were training had been made a lance-corporal. He had been sent on a Lewis gun course, after which he had been made up to full corporal. He had just started to instruct when we were sent overseas, but now he was looking very sorry for himself. Then he began to unpick the stitches of his corporal's stripes and pull them off. Then Ernie Smith said to me "I can't keep this stripe now that we are going into the trenches. I'm going to take it off." So he did.

During this brief period at the Base Camp there was constant activity until quite late at night. We joined a very long queue for a brand-new groundsheet/cape, and it was quite dark when we queued for 120 rounds of small arm ammunition. This made us realise that training days were over. We were going to kill and be killed. Fred Ablethorpe, usually a thoughtful, refined boy, said to me "Well, now they've given us all 120 rounds of ammo, I intend to use it, and shoot as many of the Bs as possible before I'M killed." I too was thrilled as I realised that we boys were going to face death or wounds for our country. I said to Ablethorpe "We've GOT to STOP THEM whatever OUR fate." We accepted the fact that our young lives were no longer our own in this crisis, and that our country expected us to sacrifice them. I felt no fear. The grave situation overwhelmed personal fear.

THE NEW LANCASHIRE FUSILIERS

None of our old officers had accompanied us from Norwich;

they were all either partly disabled or recovering from wounds. Our old company sergeant-major had escorted us so far and now he said goodbye and good luck to us. When all the paper work of our transfer to the Lancashire Fusiliers had been completed, the documents were entrusted to Corporal Croot, a very self-assured youngster who had trained with us. This lively ginger haired youth, who like all of us was not yet nineteen, marched us off very confidently to some railway cattle trucks which were marked "Hommes 40, Cheveaux 8".

THE BASE CAMPS

We travelled for many hours by rail in the cattle trucks from the base camp at Calais to others at Boulogne and Etaples, and then on, as far as the line went, to the railhead at Canaples. This track ran between military camps, military hospitals and military cemeteries, and our top speed was about five miles per hour. There were innumerable and inexplicable stops, sometimes for five minutes, and sometimes for half an hour. During these halts some of us walked along the track and talked to the engine driver, a soldier in the Royal Ordnance Corps. On one occasion he gave some of us hot water from the engine boiler to make tea; we thought this a great lark and we also tried to buy some eggs at a farm, but after crossing a field and getting to the farm door, we heard a toot-toot from the engine, saw the long train start again, and had to chase after it. It was not difficult to catch up with the train and there were occasions when it travelled so slowly that some of the boys got out and walked beside to stretch their legs.

After passing more camps near Boulogne, the train jogged along to Etaples — always known by British troops as "Etaps". Etaples was the British Army's main base, and it literally sprawled for miles and miles and miles! As we jolted through miles of railway sidings, we passed thousands of army huts, bell-tents and marquee tents. The latter were tented hospitals marked with the Red Cross. There were sand dunes with the sea breeze blowing the long coarse grass, and innumerable huge army dumps of war material for every conceivable purpose.

We also passed by an enormous military cemetery, where as far as the eye could see, thousands of small white crosses stood, row after row. There were also prisoner of war camps behind barbed wire fences, and a mile long stretch of hutted camps for newly arrived drafts of infantry during their training in the "Bull Ring".

WE AVOID THE "BULL RING"

We had all heard a great deal about the famous, or infamous "Bull Ring", at Etaples, and were pleased that the urgent need for us at the front precluded the usual training given to troops before they were sent up the line. We had heard from older soldiers who had passed through Etaples on their way to the Front that the so-called training was harsh and brutal. I had heard more than one man say that the instructors were men who had not been up the line themselves and were professional boxers and footballers who were dodging the column. At the time that we boys avoided the "Bull Ring" we did not know what was true and what was only old soldiers' gossip, but a book has been published which amply confirms all that we boys heard about the brutality and persecution by the "Canaries", the permanent staff instructors who wore yellow armbands.

The book, entitled *"The Monocled Mutineer"*, confirms that they were the worst type of bullies imaginable, and gives a vivid picture of the misery of life during the period of training at the base. The drafts of men from England, who had disembarked at Calais or Boulogne were marched from Boulogne by the "Canaries" who continually bawled at them. On arrival at Etaples, they were confined to the mile long row of infantry base depots, with no passes into the town of Etaples. Routine was reveille at 5 a.m., a scanty breakfast and then a four mile march in full kit to the "Bull Ring" on the beaches, where everything must be done "at the double" — running and charging on sandhills where it was difficult to walk let alone run.

The "Canaries" bawled at them continually as they climbed over obstacles, through barbed wire, in and out of trenches, uphill, downhill, running and stumbling in the soft sand, scrambling up again to the shouts of "Get a move on!" They had to charge with full pack, rifle and bayonet at dummies of German soldiers hanging from gallows in this mile long series of assault courses staked out among the sandhills.

This training lasted for at least a week and sometimes longer. It is not surprising that eventually, in 1917, a mutiny broke out which lasted six days, with the authorities powerless to stop it, and the "Canaries" and "Red Caps" (military police) of this huge base camp fleeing for their lives. It was mutiny by men who had survived the battles of Arras, the Somme and Ypres and Passchendaele; mutiny not against their officers but against those who had humiliated and persecuted them — the hated "Canaries" and "Red Caps".

Few of the troops at the Front knew about the mutiny at the time. It was suppressed by bringing two battalions of men back from the Front, replacing the camp commandant and making terms with the ringleaders for much improved conditions — better food and passes into town. Very few people knew at the time, least of all the French army which had a much bigger mutiny to cope with, or the Germans, that more than 100,000 men had been immobilised in the vital week before the start of the Passchendaele Offensive.

The leader was Private Percy Topliss (The Monocled Mutineer), a deserter from his battalion who used many disguises and assumed many ranks from corporal to colonel, sometimes wearing an officer's uniform and a monocle. He was sentenced to death, but made a daring escape, swimming the river to freedom, and returned to England posing as a medical orderly looking after wounded men. He continued his brazen impersonations as a decorated and wounded officer or a senior NCO even after the war ended, and was the leader of a petrol racket, selling army petrol to civilian firms during the rationing period. Eventually, he was hunted by armed police, shot dead near Carlisle and buried secretly at Ullswater.

Many years later when my wife and I were visiting our son in Vancouver, I was talking one day to a friend about our experiences in the Great War. He had also served on the Western Front, with the Canadians. When I asked him if he had heard of the mutiny at Etaples... "Heard of it!" he exclaimed. "I was there, on the Iron Bridge over the river where it all began." So I told him about the book — *"The Monocled Mutineer,"* and how he was shot dead by British police in a ruthless nationwide hunt for him.

Many police officers were armed with Lee Enfield rifles, and stood at crossroads outside towns. They stopped all cars as they searched for Topliss. I saw one armed police officer, a very unusual sight in those days, standing in the centre of the crossroads near my home in Northampton.

ON OUR WAY TO THE FRONT
At Calais we had each been paid five francs, the amount being

entered in our pay books, but it was of no use to us on this long, slow journey to the Front. We were also issued with a new groundsheet-cum-cape, and, what WAS of great interest to us — 120 rounds of SAA (small arm ammunition). This personal possession of such a large quantity of ammo excited us; we were used to having SAA doled out to us by our sergeant as we lay in the firing position on the firing ranges, where there was always the very strictest discipline. There, every round had to be accounted for, but now, we all had 120 rounds, and so, as soon as the train moved well away from Etaples, there was some rather reckless firing by some of the boys at various objects in the fields or at doors of farm buildings.

Like the civilian population at home, we boys had no idea of what the Western Front was really like, or of the conditions we should find there. Much that we had read in the press had glamorised the war and our gallant troops, although we took this with a pinch of salt, knowing that there could be very little glamour left by the spring of 1918. Despite this, we were full of the excitement of youth; we were actually on our way to the Front! We had not the least idea of its size, complexity or dangers.

Actually, the Western Front was the most gigantic system of trenches, barbed wire, sandbagged strong points, dug-outs and duck-boards that had ever been constructed. It stretched 400 miles from the Belgian coast to the Swiss border, and its defences, on both sides, were many miles deep. Millions of men, British, French and German, had dug, filled billions of sandbags, maintained these huge fortifications and had lived and died in them for the past three and a half years.

Now it was our turn! How excited we were! How naive, young and inexperienced!

In my cattle truck was an old soldier returning to his unit, which was the 10th (Service) Battalion of the Lancashire Fusiliers; the battalion which, in a moment of time, had also become mine. This "old sweat", Brandon, wearing the 1914 Star ribbon on his tunic, had been watching our boyish tricks and our naive enthusiasm with a great deal of interest. He grinned at us and said "When 'Old Jerry' sees your lovely pink young faces in the line, he'll say 'Mein Gott! New troops! Rat-tat-tat-tat-tat-tat-tat!'" Then, looking us over with a fatherly eye he said "I expect you kids will DO and I must say, they've done you proud with those brand-new groundsheet-capes, you'd better hang on to them tight out here, or somebody is likely to win them off you." Later, 8807 Private H. Brandon, was under my command when from August onwards, I was in charge of the regimental police. The long slow journey began to get boring and some boys, including Pelly and Norris climbed on to the roofs of the cattle trucks and started firing again. Then the train passed through a tunnel and they returned to us, coughing and grinning, with black faces. We were also very thirsty, and extremely pleased when at last the train reached the railhead at Canaples.

THE OLD TENTH

At Canaples, we were met by a company quartermaster sergeant of the 10th Lancashire Fusiliers. We were wearing steel helmets; he was wearing a service cap, and our eyes went instantly to his cap badge, to see what the LF cap badge was like. Someone asked when we should be issued with cap badges, but he laughed and said "You won't be needing them at the moment". How right he was; instead of cap badges we were issued with sacking covers for our steel helmets; this was to stop them shining in the moonlight. We had had our bayonets dulled in Norwich with black enamel for the same reason. Our thirst for information was insatiable, and by questioning the CQMS (Company Quartermaster-Sergeant) and some storemen who were unloading various stores from the cattle trucks, we found that the 10th Lancashire Fusiliers were part of the 52nd Brigade, together with a battalion of Manchesters and a battalion of the Duke of Wellingtons. We also learned that this 52nd Brigade was a part of the 17th Division, which in turn was part of the Vth Corps, which was now the right flank of the 3rd Army.

The 3rd Army was commanded by General Byng, familiarly known to the old soldiers as "Bungo". It was inevitable that we now called ourselves the Byng Boys. (At the Alhambra Theatre in London, and on tour in the provinces, many of us had seen Andre Chariot's "Bing Boys", with George Robey and Violet Lorraine singing — "If you were the only girl in the world, and I was the only boy".)

From the railhead at Canaples we marched in the rain, proudly wearing our new groundsheet-capes. We must have looked very new, and we began to feel it too when we arrived at some tents in a wet field, which were being erected for us by the survivors of the Old Tenth, always known by the real Lancashire lads as T'owd Tenth. We realised that our training days were over... this was IT! We also realised we had much to learn, and listened attentively to any tips about life in this strange new world. These survivors of the Old Tenth had only just come from the forward area of the Line, their numbers reduced to less than a hundred very tired, dirty, unshaven men, whose faces showed the strain of the past fortnight. Many years later, I learned what they had been through, when reading Major-General Latter's History of the XXth. The Lancashire Fusiliers, 1914-1918. The 10th (Service) Battalion was formed in Bury on 6th September, 1914. They moved almost immediately to Wimborne, Dorset, and after training in that area they embarked for France on 15th July 1915.

When the Great German Spring Offensive began on 21st March 1918, the 10th (Service) Battalion, now a part of the 52nd Brigade of the 17th (Northern) Division, were manning trenches in the front line near the uncompleted dry Canal du Nord at the perimeter of the Flesquieres Salient. The four Divisions holding this twelve mile long perimeter were an outpost line in the Forward Zone which would not be reinforced and would inflict maximum casualties on the expected German attack. When the German plan to "pinch out" the Flesquieres Salient at its base, began to succeed, a fighting withdrawal became inevitable, resulting in heavy casualties and encirclement in some areas.

The German artillery bombardment began at 4.45 a.m. when 6,000 guns on a fifty mile front from north of Arras to south of St. Quentin opened fire with gas and HE shells, while trench mortars burst all along the British front line. At 9.45 a.m. the German infantry attacked in thick fog. Six waves were repulsed by the Lancashire Fusiliers, but the Germans broke through in two very strong thrusts north and south of them.

To maintain a continuous line, the 52nd Brigade were ordered to withdraw during the night to the previously prepared defences at Havrincourt. On 23rd March, the Lancashire Fusiliers withdrew to a position west of Havrincourt Wood, and on the 24th the fighting withdrawal continued, first to the Red Line, north-east of Rocquigny and then to east of Le Transloy on the Bapaume-Peronne road.

They retired again to Flers under great pressure from the Germans, who succeeded in cutting off some of A Company, taking prisoners including Captain A. J. Barrows, MC, who was wounded. Eventually, at 7 p.m., six officers and about 200 other ranks reached Flers, where German patrols constantly attacked, but were driven off. On 25th March, further fighting withdrawals were made to trenches east of Martinpuich, then to Courcelette and Pozieres. On the 26th the retirement continued to Mealte, Dernacourt and Henencourt, where Captain J. B. Wood, D Company, and others were encircled and captured. On the 27th the much depleted battalion reached Senlis and then positions east of Millencourt.

From 28th March, the Lancashire Fusiliers manned a front which had been stabilised in old trenches west of Albert. On 2nd April, they were relieved, and the battalion, much reduced in numbers, by casualties and encirclement, marched to Warloy Baillon and then to Havernas. Casualties were seven officers and 227 men and several hundred had been taken prisoner. By 5th April, the casualties in the 5th and 3rd Armies totalled 164,000 and 100,000 had been encircled and taken prisoner.

On that day, 5th April, the eighteen-year-old boy soldiers left Norwich, and on the 6th they landed at Calais and were rapidly transferred to the battalions which had suffered severe casualties. Then they were transported in cattle trucks to the railhead at Canaples. Those who had been transferred to the 10th Battalion of the Lancashire Fusiliers then marched, in the rain, to Havernas where they met the survivors of the "old tenth" as they called themselves.

Our young, pink, cheerful and eager faces were a complete contrast to the grey worn and weary faces of these veterans, who had fought a retreat. We looked with awe at them, men whose clothing was so muddy, so torn and stained; but whose rifles were so clean. They looked at us with a mixture of pity and amusement, knowing that very soon our clean round baby faces would be lined and dirty too.

I JOIN "A" COMPANY

As we stood in the rain, a young officer came on the scene, accompanied by a corporal and a bugler. He ordered the bugler to blow the call for company sergeant-majors — a bugle call not very often heard. In a few minutes one CSM, one sergeant and two corporals lined up in front of the young officer. I noticed that two of them had cut the skirt off their overcoats, and I was slightly shocked to see that all of them badly needed a shave. In a few minutes we were split up into four parties and taken by the four NCOs, who marched us off to join our respective companies.

I was transferred to A Company, the only company still having a company sergeant-major; an Irishman named Doolan. He was a regular soldier, one of the very few of the original British Expeditionary Force who had survived to this stage of the war. Soon he had us putting up some bell-tents in the rain. He quickly sized us up and promised us a treat when we had finished. "Now then, me bhoys," he bawled, "who could drink a nice cup of hot tea?" Some of us rushed eagerly forward, to be told to go and scrounge some dry wood from somewhere — "And I don't care where ye git it, me bhoys, and THEN, we'll all have that nice cup of hot tea!" We thought he was a "Gem", and set about carrying out his orders with good humour; we asked him endless questions, to which he responded with equal good humour. We were conscious, and he realised too, that we were new boys in a strange new world.

QUALIFICATIONS

After a night in the rain-sodden tents, we paraded for inspection, and were closely questioned about our training. As we stood in line, a young soldier questioned each boy in turn.

As he neared me I wondered what his rank was, as I could see no stripes on the sleeve of his tunic. When he reached me I saw the single pip on the epaulettes of a private soldier's tunic, and I realised that he was an experienced active service officer, which was a new type of officer to me. Remembering many school friends who had become officers, I was glad to see this long overdue dress innovation which reduced the very heavy losses incurred by officers being singled out by enemy snipers.

This had been inevitable when they wore a distinctive uniform with a collar and tie and a Sam Browne belt. In the 1916 battles of the Somme, the officers were quickly picked off. This young officer was cheerful, ruddy of face and full of go. "Now then" he said, as he reached me, "I want one or two more Lewis gunners, has anybody else handled a Lewis gun?" I told him I had been trained as a signaller, and Jim May, next to me said, "I haven't completed the course, sir, and I haven't got my badge, but I know how to fire a Lewis gun." "I see," grinned the young officer, "you mean you haven't killed anyone yet." There was a dutiful laugh from the rest of us, and then he said, "Oh well, you'll do, in fact you'll all have plenty of opportunities to kill 'Jerries' very soon; he's still coming over in masses looking for trouble, but we'll give him a bloody nose."

THE OLD TENTH REFORMED

I remembered that my platoon officer in Norwich had also said "'Jerry' is still coming over in massed formation". The general who inspected us had said that the enemy objective was Paris and the channel ports, and "he has got to be stopped". When we arrived at Calais, we had seen the news posters of the *Continental Daily Mail*, which declared in bold black letters — FOCH SAYS AMIENS SHALL NOT FALL.

Now, here we were, being hurriedly organised and prepared to take part in the defence of Amiens.

Further reinforcements arrived; they included the remnants of a Battalion of the Loyal North Lancashire Regiment, which had been almost wiped out and was not being reformed. There were also some men and NCOs from a cycling battalion, and about a score of older men who had been combed out from the Army Service Corps. Four young officers, straight from England, also arrived. One of them, 2nd Lieut. Stott, became my first platoon officer in the 10th Lancashire Fusiliers. Three or four men who had just been discharged from hospital after wounds, were also put into No. 2 Platoon of A Company with me. One of them later showed me the wound in his back, which had only just healed and was red and tender.

A Company was reorganised so there were a few old hands in each of the four Platoons of about forty to forty-five men. The four sections of No. 2 Platoon each had ten to twelve men; the Lewis gun section was led by Lance-Corporal Unsworth, and the other three sections were led by Corporal Croot, one of the eighteen-year-old boys; and by Corporal Hobson, a regular soldier; and by a young lance-corporal named Walsh, always known for some reason as "P" Walsh.

As we lined up for inspection in the reorganisation, two real old sweats came hurrying along and were put into No. 2 Platoon. Their names were Pearson and White; both had previously fought in the line, been wounded several times, and after long service in the trenches had been given softer jobs at a ration depot. Now they had been recalled to their battalion for further duty in the trenches.

MY "OLD BILL"

Pearson, who wore the ribbon of the Military Medal and three wound stripes, came and stood next to me. Although he was nearly twice my age, I quickly became friendly with him, and later in the trenches, he was my Old Bill (the well-known character in Captain Bruce Bairnsfather's wartime cartoons). I asked him many questions and always took his advice. Pearson was a short, sturdy little man, with a hare-lip and a cleft palate which affected his speech. He always referred to tins of Machonachie, which was a meat and vegetable ration sometimes issued, as M and We. He would say "Werry good ration is M and We; now as for them tins of pork and beans, I say, where is the pork?"

Later, after Lance-Corporal Singleton became my section leader, I asked him how Pearson won his medal. "Before my time" he said, "but if I know anything, Pearson wouldn't know WHY they gave it to him, he's pretty thick." This was the outward impression Pearson gave to most people, but I thought he had a very attractive personality, and some six months later I discovered that he possessed an artistic talent which no one would suspect him of having. One day he was sorting out the contents of his haversack, and to my surprise, he produced a small flat metal box containing water-colours. This was indeed a rare sight on the Western Front.

When I said, "Do you paint, then?" a happy smile spread over his ugly face as he said, "Ave a look at these then," and from between two pieces of stained cardboard tied with string, he produced ten or a dozen lovely little water-colours of country scenes which he had painted in various French and Belgian villages behind the front. When I told him that I enjoyed painting in water-colours, he said, "Well, Corp., I don't show these to many blokes, they wouldn't understand, would they?"

PERSONAL ACCOUNTS OF THE RETIREMENT

Another attractive personality in No. 2 Platoon was Lance-Corporal Unsworth, the Lewis gun section leader, into whose section Jim May had been put. He was a youngster of about nineteen or twenty, but aged by his war service, and quite imperturbable when we were under fire. I was talking to him one day in the trenches when he astounded me by asking me in his thick Lancashire dialect "Art tha wed, la'ad?" I had to ask him to repeat his question several times, and was very surprised when I finally understood what he meant. Me? married at eighteen?

As we new boys got to know the old hands better, they told us some of their experiences during the retreat, which incidentally, our officers always insisted must be referred to as a retirement. When the German Offensive opened on 21st March, the 10th (Service) Battalion of the Lancashire Fusiliers was in the front line at Havrincourt, many miles to the east (i.e. farther forward) of where we now were.

Havrincourt and Gouzeaucourt were on the famous Hindenburg Line to which the Germans had withdrawn in March 1917, to shorten their line and thus need fewer troops to man it. Later Gouzeaucourt was recaptured by the 10th Lancashire Fusiliers in September 1918, during our offensive.

UNCLAIMED LETTERS

We boys learnt much about the retirement when a batch of letters arrived from England. A lance-corporal mounted an old water tank in the farmyard and shouted "Letters". A crowd quickly gathered round him.

As he called out the names, very few of them could be claimed; most were addressed to men who had been killed or wounded or were missing. As the lance-corporal called out the name, he was told by the survivors of the Old Tenth "He's missing", or "He was killed at so and so", or "He was wounded, I think...."

I mingled with the crowd and listened to the gossip, and learned quite a lot. The post started them talking, and I heard how they had come out of the retreat with only one Lewis gun still effective, used by a lance-corporal who had been recommended for the Military Medal.

I looked with awe at this man who sat at a stable door on a box, calmly splitting wood with his bayonet, for a fire which several other men were trying to start in an old bucket with holes punched in it. The idea was to scrounge some water from somewhere, never an easy task, and make some tea. I heard about the officer who had led some of them through the gardens of a village in the hands of German troops, who had penetrated right behind our front during the retreat. They had lain low waiting for darkness and then the officer and the lance-corporal with the only remaining Lewis gun had safely found a way through gardens and orchards.

Others told me of the stand they had made at Havrincourt until the Germans had been almost up to them, and were passing them on the flanks. One man, Morris, said to me, "I bolted out of one end of that trench while 'Jerry' was coming in at the other, they nearly got me!"

There were many questions from the boys, some of whom wanted to know whether it was better to "go over the top" or to make a stand in a trench while "Jerry" came over. Most of them said that they had enjoyed being in a trench and shooting him down for a change after all the other occasions, especially during the British Somme Offensive, when they had been the target. All this gave the boys much food for thought and discussion among ourselves.

UNOFFICIAL RATIONS

We were also told about the disorganisation in the daily distribution of rations; how often nothing got through from the usual sources. Many were the gleeful stories about the abandoned YMCA and Church Army and Expeditionary Force Canteens; and about all the cigarettes, chocolate, cafe au lait, biscuits and other items of food which the retreating troops scrounged.

Although we had then heard first-hand a great deal about what happened to the 10th Battalion of the Lancashire Fusiliers on 21st March and during the retirement, the full story of that massive German Spring Offensive had yet to be told. Historians now call it the 2nd Battle of the Somme, and can now give a perspective totally unknown to the men involved at the time.

AN OFFICIAL ACCOUNT OF THE 2nd BATTLE OF THE SOMME

The German attack began on 21st March 1918, on a front stretching from north of Arras to south of St. Quentin. This fifty mile stretch was held mainly by the British 5th Army under General Hubert Gough, with the 5th Corps of the 3rd Army under General Byng being also heavily engaged on the 5th Army's left flank. Roughly two-thirds of the fifty mile front under General Gough was undermanned following an extension of the British front southwards to take over more line from the French Army.

Between Arras and St. Quentin, sixty-three German Divisions were used in the initial attack on a forty-three mile front. The attack was held for a time at Arras, but there was a complete breakthrough south of the Somme at Havrincourt and Gouzeaucourt where the defenders were thin on the ground. Gough had only fourteen divisions in the line, and few reserves at his immediate disposal.

Gough's troops could not be relieved while the battle lasted; indeed it has been said that they were tested, as an Army, to the point of destruction. Despite this, it is also a matter of history that General Hubert Gough was made a scapegoat, and was removed by Field Marshal Douglas Haig from the command of the 5th Army.

The attack was expected, even the date was known; German prisoners who were captured near St. Quentin on 18th March gave the date as 21st March, and on 20th March, British raids established the certainty of the attack on the morrow. The German artillery bombardment began at 4.45 a.m. and was the most concentrated that had ever been experienced. Nearly 6,000 guns opened fire along a forty-three mile front with both gas and high explosive shells. Trench mortars burst along our front line while the shells roared overhead to burst on our artillery positions and ammunition dumps.

For two hours the battle zone was systematically plastered, gun positions, battery headquarters, road junctions, casualty clearing stations, machine-gun posts, communication trenches, all were systematically and accurately pounded. Then this devastating barrage began to creep back to our front line, rising to a climax at 9.35 a.m. when the German trench mortars came into action again. At 9.45 a.m. the German infantry, who had been specially trained in infiltration tactics, advanced in wave after wave through a thick white ground mist, even fog in places.

Visibility was only forty feet; gas masks were worn on and off all day; telephone wires had been cut by the shelling. The enemy had overwhelming superiority in the number of men available, and they had been trained to probe and penetrate every weak spot. Massive reserves were available to follow through every gap. Special reconnaissance parties sent back news of progress, and storm groups, armed with automatic rifles, machine-guns and light mortars pushed on through weak spots, leaving any surviving defenders in the British strong points to be dealt with later by waves of infantry.

By nightfall forty miles of front, most of it held by Gough's 5th Army, had been broken; German troops in some places had even reached the British guns by their ruthless skill. This massive and well-planned attack, which had been organised by the German Field Marshal Ludendorff, was reinforced every day by fresh troops.

When the Russian Front disintegrated into revolution and the Peace Treaty of Brest-Litovsk was signed in 1917, the German High Command had been able to transfer a million men and 5,000 guns from the Russian Front to the Western Front. Ludendorff had 192 Divisions at his disposal, and by the evening of 22nd March, Gough's third line of defence was broken between Vaux and Beauvais. General Byng, of the 3rd Army, readjusted his line, but the rearguards were attacked by continuous assaults and the retirement continued.

Gaps in the line were skilfully exploited by thrusts, and the Germans forced the passage of the Crozat Canal and entered Ham. By the evening of the 24th March, the British had been forced out of all the villages between Bapaume and Peronne as far west as Longuval. There were heavy losses on both sides, but the Germans always had unlimited fresh troops, while the British had by now come to the end of their resources in the area of battle.

On 25th March, the enemy was still pressing with all his strength, forcing the British to retire on the whole fifty mile front. General Byng's 3rd Army retired to the line of the River Ancre, and by the 26th March, the right flank of Byng's Army, the 5th Corps, was firmly anchored near Bray-sur-Somme, ten miles south of Albert. The 4th and 5th Australian Divisions, and a New Zealand Division, were hurriedly brought south to block the way to Amiens, the vital road and rail junction only ten miles behind the Front. The Germans, in their probing, discovered a gap between Beaumont Hamel and Puisieux and broke through to capture Colincamps, but the New Zealand troops, who had just arrived, drove them out again.

During the night of 26/27th March, the Germans entered the town of Albert and Aveluy Wood while the British held Beaumont Hamel, Mesnil and Martinsart overlooking the River Ancre. Many British battalions had ceased to exist as distinct units, having lost all their officers. Most of the men who had survived attached themselves to groups led by whoever could do so, and eventually these groups of haggard British troops, after holding on in shell holes, ditches, cellars — any position available, were organised into composite battalions. These often had to fight their way through the masses of German infantry which still continued to infiltrate and surround every point of resistance.

The British Army had undoubtedly been badly mauled; casualties by 5th April were 164,000 and 100,000 had been taken prisoner by the infiltration method of encirclement. Nearly 1,000 guns had been lost; many having been blown up by their crews just before they retired to avoid capture.

THE NEW BOYS' BATTALIONS

Eventually, many remnants of battalions were amalgamated and reinforced by boys of eighteen sent out from the Graduated Battalions in England before completing their training.

These hurriedly formed battalions, composed of boys of eighteen, and young inexperienced officers of eighteen and nineteen, and a leavening of older men and officers, then relieved the hard pressed groups still in contact with the enemy. There was no clearly defined Front as there had been for the past three and a half years; each company of these new battalions took over a section of a very disconnected front line, and endeavoured to join up with the companies on either flank.

It was a completely new situation for the "old hands" who had been accustomed to a regular "going up the line" and relieving another battalion in the old familiar trenches and strong points. For more than three and a half years, no attack by British, French or German armies had moved any part of the 400 mile long front more than five to ten miles, and then at great cost. Now, a great gap had been torn in it, and Amiens with its vital road and rail systems was still threatened.

After the war I met Duncan Campbell, the well-known Scottish evangelist, when he was visiting Northampton. He had enlisted in the Argyll and Sutherland Highlanders in 1916, and had been a machine-gunner at Passchendaele in 1917. Then in April 1918 he was suddenly transferred to the Cavalry Corps.

He told me that the situation in front of Amiens was so grave on 12th April 1918, that two cavalry charges were made to drive back the advancing German hordes while the ragged line of infantry dug in. He was severely injured in the first charge, and picked up by a trooper of the Canadian Horse returning from the second charge, who took him to a Casualty Clearing Station.

Although General Gough's 5th Army and the Vth Corps of General Byng's 3rd Army had been forced to retire, overwhelmed and exhausted, they were not beaten. Their morale was intact and the new Boys' Battalions, though inexperienced, brought an injection of youthful spirit. This then was the situation when I and my friends joined the battle hardened survivors of the 10th (Service) Battalion of the Lancashire Fusiliers and were welded together with them into a part of the plug in the great gap in the Front.

TOUTENCOURT

On 10th April, my battalion now reorganised, marched to Toutencourt. As we went we could hear in the distance the rumbling of the guns at the Front. It was like a distant thunderstorm, and the boys wanted to know how far we were from the Front Line. The old hands said that it was further than a day's march.

The village of Toutencourt was relatively undamaged and there were still a few civilians living there. In Toutencourt Wood, bordering the village, we found some bell tents already erected. Previous occupants had dug out the soil in the tents to a depth of about eighteen inches and had stacked the excavated soil round the tent walls. The tent pole thus stood on a pyramid of earth in the centre of the tent, somewhat restricting the space for our feet. After taking possession of the tents, we strolled through the wood to the village, and passed a roadside shrine where jars of water with flowers stood. One of the boys said that it was called a Calvary and that we should probably see many of these in France as it was a Catholic country. We stopped to talk with the old Roman Catholic priest who was strolling down the street in his long black coat which reached almost down to his ankles. On his head he wore a large black shovel hat.

The following day, 11th April, Field Marshal Sir Douglas Haig, Commander-in-Chief, British Armies in France, issued his famous..

> ... SPECIAL ORDER OF THE DAY
>
> *TO ALL RANKS* — Three weeks ago the enemy began his terrific attacks against us on a fifty mile front. His objects are to separate us from the French, to take the channel ports and destroy the British Army. In spite of the most reckless sacrifice of human life, he has as yet made little progress towards his goal. We owe this to the determined fighting and self-sacrifice of our troops. There is no course open to us but to fight it out. Every position must be held to the last man; there must be no retirement. With our backs to the wall and believing in the justice of our cause, each one of us must fight on to the end. The safety of our homes and the freedom of mankind alike depend upon the conduct of each one of us at this critical moment.
>
> *D. Haig, FM*
> *C in C, British Armies in France.*

When this was read to us, we boys were thrilled, and also pleased to be in a battalion with such a fine spirit whose confidence in ultimate victory was unshaken. The survivors had fought every day in their retirement from Havrincourt to the position at Mesnil, near Aveluy Wood where the enemy was now being held by other troops. Now, after rest, and reinforced by the Byng Boys, the battalion was returning to Mesnil.

GERMAN DISILLUSIONMENT

The German Army had also suffered; first by the enormous

casualties sustained in their mass formation attacks, and secondly and more seriously, they had suffered a great psychological blow.

The spirit in the British Army was excellent despite our great losses, and the WILL TO WIN was as strong as ever. Morale in the German Army however quickly sank when during their rapid advance to the British rear area, they discovered a land, which to them, was flowing with milk and honey, compared with their own supplies.

Like the retiring British troops, the Germans looted the abandoned canteens. From the French Estaminets they took Vin Blanc and Cognac. They also took from the British dead, real leather boots, real leather jerkins, and rubber ground sheets which they had not seen for years. The initial intoxication due to this marvellous loot, after years of privation and substitutes, was even greater than that from the wine.

However, the deeper psychological effect of discovering the enemy was so much better fed and equipped than themselves, was DISILLUSIONMENT. They realised that the reputed effect on the British economy of their U-boat campaign was false, and when the plunder was exhausted a great reaction followed.

Propaganda and strict censorship deceived them while the Front was an inviolable wall of partition, but the breakthrough revealed the truth that the enemy possessed greater material resources.

ENEMY BOMBS

During this first visit to Toutencourt Wood we foolishly lit some fires of brushwood in one of the clearings. The fact that previous occupants of the bell tents had excavated soil and stacked it round the tents should have warned us, but we were inexperienced. On the second night these fires attracted the attention of the enemy and German planes flew low over the wood and dropped bombs. We all took cover in the tents, lying down close to each other as the bombs whistled down and exploded. I lay next to Pearson.

Soon there was a cry for "Stretcher-bearers!" and we all wondered who had been injured; then when the bombing ceased, we found, to our surprise, that the bombs made very small shell holes. Our sergeant told us that they were a new type of bomb which exploded on impact, and were thus very effective against troops. After this experience all fires were forbidden.

ARMY BATHS

It was while we were in Toutencourt Wood, from 11th to 14th April, that we had our first experience of an Army bath house. In France, the troops in the forward area had no chance, as we later discovered, to have a wash and shave. Here, just behind the front, the opportunity to have a bath and a change of underclothes was irregular and infrequent.

We were marched some miles to the bath house and sat down in a field to wait our turn with other troops of various battalions. These bath houses were rough sheds with corrugated iron roofs, and were divided into several compartments. Outside was the little boiler house which heated the water. We queued up to enter, and in the first compartment we rapidly undressed, throwing our underclothes into large wooden crates. We bundled our tunics, trousers, puttees and boots and handed them through a trapdoor into another compartment. Naked, we passed into the bath section, which had a concrete floor with a drain in the centre and overhead a number of one inch diameter pipes with small holes drilled in them.

The corporal in charge of the bath house gave the order to the man outside at the tap of the boiler "Turn 'er on, Bill!" A thin trickle of lukewarm water began to splutter down on to us from above as we stood in close proximity, twenty or thirty at a time, endeavouring to create a lather with our small pieces of army soap. By the time we had succeeded in washing about half of our bodies, we heard the order "Turn 'er orf, Bill!"

Protesting loudly, we passed into the next section, where we were given a towel and a set of underclothes. Our platoon sergeant was a large man, and he struggled hard to get on the shirt issued to him. Standing with it stretched across his hairy chest, the sleeves ending just below his elbows, he wrathfully demanded to know if they thought he was a "something" pygmy.

The lance-corporal issuing the underclothes, not knowing that he was a sergeant, began to be equally rude and blasphemous. Then the sergeant tried to put on his socks, but as the heel was only about five inches from the toe, this was impossible. Exploding with wrath, he demanded a larger outfit, and, as the "lance-jack" had by this time realized that he was dealing with a sergeant, he got it.

My own change of underclothes was of a reasonable size, but of a quality very much poorer than those I had discarded, which were of excellent quality. When I tried to put my trousers on, I found that they did not fit, and in the pockets I found someone else's possessions. Eventually, I found the man who had been given my trousers and tunic, and so got them back. Finally, after another battle to get my own boots and puttees, I emerged from the bath house somewhat exasperated. When everything had been sorted out we marched away, and soon began to perspire as we slogged along at a fast pace to Toutencourt Wood.

PESTS AND DISEASES

That night we began to be bitten by the lice which had been stimulated by the warmth of our bodies, and we realised that the "clean" underclothes issued to us at the bath house were infested with lice and their eggs. The official attitude to lousy troops was, to say the least, peculiar — it was a military offence to be lousy! I have often wondered since why none of us complained, and have also wondered what would have happened if we had!

A few weeks later, when we were in trenches near the ruins of Bouzincourt, some of us had our shirts off one sunny afternoon and were busy cracking "chats" with our thumbnails. Without any warning our major, the second in command of the battalion, whom we rarely saw, came along the trench. When he saw what we were doing, he exclaimed — "Good God! the men are lousy!" We all stood at attention respectfully and said nothing, but when he had gone we asked one another what the old fool thought we could do about it, except kill 'em.

However, we had misjudged him, for he obtained some flat irons and arranged for them to be heated in the ruins of a cottage in a wood behind our trenches. That night, we were sent, in twos and threes, very much enjoying the opportunity to stretch our legs, to the ruined cottage among the shattered tree stumps, where we took off our trousers and ironed the eggs in the seams. Outside, the war flashed and grumbled as usual while we ironed our underclothes too. We regarded this little outing as a great lark, and henceforth thought of Major Forwood as a type of kind elderly uncle. I expect he was about forty!

For the rest of the war I do not think I was ever entirely free from lice, and I found this a great trial. On more than one occasion I rubbed the skin of my legs just below the knees until I was sore and bleeding, and then I had to ask the corporal at the First Aid Post to treat them. He always scolded and lectured me as he put on a vile smelling ointment and bandaged the sores, reminding me and warning me of the military offence of being lousy.

The Army authorities had the same peculiar attitude towards men who suffered from trench feet through spending many days and nights in cold muddy and even flooded trenches. "Why had they not kept their feet warm?" "Did they not know that it was a 'crime' to get trench feet?" "If anyone else gets trench feet, he will be put on a charge." Then our platoon officer would be told "There must be more foot inspections" — he must see to it! *He* would be held responsible if there were any more!

There was one malady which sometimes occurred among the troops in the trenches for which the authorities could not blame them; it was an abnormal rise in temperature which the troops called "trench fever". I have since discovered that the medical officers did not know what caused this, but they always called it PUO for Pyrexia (Fever) Unknown Origin.

My doctor in civil life used to write GOK in his notebook in reference to some of his patients. It meant God Only Knows what is the matter with them.

The troops had another well-known description of a certain condition which they humorously called DUG-OUT DISEASE. This malady was liable to occur after a man had spent some days and nights in a dug-out without facing any danger. It was easily cured when the patient was given a spell on the firestep during a period of enemy activity, or by a trip into no man's land to mend the barbed wire in front of our trenches, or, better still, to go out with a patrol and toss a few Mills bombs into "Jerry's" front line.

UNDER ENEMY FIRE AT FORCEVILLE

On 15th April, the battalion marched to Forceville, which was then under intermittent shell fire from the enemy artillery. We were halted in the main street and after we had fallen out, I with about twenty others went into a farmyard through an arched gateway. This farmyard was surrounded by farm buildings of various kinds, and some of us entered a stable and put our rifles and equipment along the back wall, thus booking ourselves a place to sleep, assuming of course, that we were to stay the night there. Then we walked along the street to the edge of the village on the enemy side, to find out what there was to be seen in that direction.

About fifty yards beyond the last houses there was a battery of British heavy guns, which began to fire. We watched the recoil of the guns and tried to see the path of the large shells in the sky. We were only boys, curious to see all there was to see, but we were behaving like a crowd of tourists, and one of the gunner officers told us to disperse so that the enemy observers should not see a crowd of men and retaliate. So we returned to our farmyard and some started to write letters, but Private Pearson and I went for a walk towards the centre of the village.

On this first of my short visits to Forceville, Pearson and I came to an area where there was a large space between the houses, as if rubble had been cleared away after previous shell fire. Burning in the centre of the cleared ground was a fire which gave off an acrid smoke. This fire Pearson called an incinerator, and displayed a lively interest in it.

"You never know what you might find in a place like this," he said. "Look at these!" He picked up some small paper packets which had been dumped in a heap near the incinerator. "These are soup powders, jolly good to put in our 'bull stew'." I was not impressed, but he assured me that they were alright, so I pocketed half a dozen packets; but I never dared to use them. Just then there was a whining sound which grew rapidly louder, and then a shell burst among the adjoining houses. It was my first enemy shell and I had an instinctive impulse to return to my billet in the barn, as if I had been caught out without my mac or umbrella when it started to rain.

However, as more shells whined over and burst indiscriminately here and there, I realised, that from now on, one place was as safe as any other. So, accepting enemy shells as one of the everyday facts of life in this new world to which I had come, I returned with Pearson to our farmyard stable. We stayed the night there, and I slept well despite the various noises off. In the morning when we went outside to look for somewhere to wash, all we could find in the farmyard was a large square galvanised water tank, about four feet by five feet, containing some dirty water. We scooped the worst of the scum off and washed ourselves there, and on several later occasions we used the same tank, and I believe, the same water apart from any rainfall. At the time we boys thought this was very primitive, but there were very few farmyards in France which had a water tank, and often we washed in a stream or a ditch. Once I washed in a puddle of rainwater.

NON MILITARY DUTIES

Although the village was within range of the enemy guns, it was not badly damaged and during the next few months we spent several short spells there between periods in the line. On one of these occasions I was one of a party of men who were told to report to the Town Major.

Like other Town Majors, he was a disabled officer who had been given a soft job, administering various things in a rear area. He told us to go through the village and look for Army rum jars, which were evidently in short supply. So off we went, exploring the village houses and farm barns for rum jars; one wondered what next they would find us to do.

We wandered through the rooms in the deserted houses which had once been homes; downstairs there were clothes hanging on nails behind the doors, utensils of all kinds in the kitchens, religious pictures and crucifixes on the walls. Upstairs, there were beds, made and unmade, more clothes, hats and shoes. We felt like burglars who had been given permission by the police to ransack these homes, some of which had the front or side half blown out; others had a broken roof sagging into the street. We were successful in our search, and carried twenty or thirty rum jars back to the Town Major; received his thanks, and then returned to our more military duties.

MORE ADVICE FROM THE OLD SOLDIERS

After breakfast, we paraded outside in the street and our platoon sergeant told us to put our gas masks in the alert position; this was on our chests with a string round our chests to keep it firm. Then he marched us to an orchard and soon had us crawling about in the grass, and then rushing forward for about twenty or thirty yards, and then down again. "Now lads," he said, "we shall soon be going up the line, and you will soon be manning a front line trench or a line of connected shell holes." He then proceeded to give us some tips about life in the trenches. "Now lads, when you are on sentry and you begin to think you can see something out there in no man's land, settle the matter by having a look. Get your mate to cover you while you creep out very quietly to see what it is that is worrying you. Ten to one it will be a tree stump or a bush waving in the wind. Now if you don't go you'll get more and more windy, so go and have a look-see. One other thing — never, NEVER, answer a call from the enemy trenches, and of course, never strike a match for a smoke without getting under cover."

Another experienced soldier whose advice we heeded was Corporal Hobson, my first section leader. He had served in India with the Regular Army when, as he said, "soldiering WAS soldiering". Corporal Hobson wore the crossed flags of a signaller above his stripes and he told us how he had used the heliograph in India, flashing messages quite incredible distances from the hills across the valleys. I told him that I had been training to be a signaller when we were suddenly sent to France with our training only half completed. I asked him why he was not a signaller with the Lancashire Fusiliers, and he asked me what my number was, and when I told him 57043, he laughed and said, "What do you think my number is?" It consisted of only three digits and he was very proud of this, being a survivor of that small elite pre-war British Army who had known the wartime generals when they were battalion officers. "Pooh," he said. "Who wants to be a signaller with this lot?"

In this area immediately behind the Front, many new trenches were being dug by thousands of German prisoners and Chinese labourers, under the supervision of the Royal Engineers, and we were taken several times during our short stay at Forceville to deepen them or dispose of the soil excavated. New trenches on the uplands were difficult to conceal from the enemy reconnaissance planes because of the chalk which was excavated. There was ceaseless activity in the air during daylight from both British and German aircraft, and all troop movements to and from the Front took place at night.

TRENCH WARFARE, APRIL TO AUGUST 1918

(Stemming and containing the Great German Spring Offensive)

THE MEN OF 18 GO UP THE LINE

After two days at Forceville, the time came for our first tour of
the line. Going up the line eventually became a matter of
routine to us as orders were given to "Fall in", usually in the
late afternoon or in the dusk of evening. Then followed
various inspections, by section leaders, by platoon sergeants,
platoon officers and finally by the company commander. This
first trip up the line was so thrilling that it has left impressions
I am still able to recall after many years.

We did not know what to expect, and so we noticed every
detail as we set out from Forceville in the dusk of that April
evening. At last, after all the checks that we had 120 rounds of
SAA, a full water-bottle and iron rations (a tin of corned beef
and thick, hard army biscuits), and after all the inspections and
last minute adjustments, the order was given by Captain
Sankey, our Company Commander. "Move to the right in
fours, by platoons. Right! Quick march!" and we were off. We
were moving into an area where enemy shelling could be
expected, and so there was a hundred yard gap between the
platoons.

There were about forty men in each platoon, mostly boys of
eighteen. My platoon officer was 2nd Lieut. R. S. Stott, a tall
well-built youngster of nineteen or twenty; a public school
type, used to taking responsibility. He led us out of the main
street of Forceville, through a gap between the houses, and on
to a field track which led up to country similar to English

downs. In front, the darkening sky was lit up by flashes of light and distant verey lights. Soon daylight faded completely, but Stott knew the way; he and one of our eighteen-year-old lance-corporals had been up to the front the previous night to make arrangements for the takeover of our particular bit of the front. This turned out to be some battered trenches and shell holes in front of Mesnil, a ruined village between Englebelmer and the enemy occupied Aveluy Wood.

Suddenly the dark countryside was brilliantly lit up when a battery of our field artillery fired a salvo as we were passing their gun pits. This unexpected flash and roar, so close to us, made us wonder for a moment if we were still alive! Ahead we could now see the flares going up and realised that this was the Front. Corporal Hobson told us they were German flares; he said we didn't use our verey light pistols very often; no need to while Jerry was sending up his flares. These German flares were always known to us as Flaming Onions; they shot up into the dark sky, six or seven, eight or nine, I could never resist counting them, in a string, presumably held up by a small parachute, until, after hanging in the sky, they went out one by one and then up went some more strings.

We were getting used to the gun-fire and eventually passed beyond our field artillery and came to a deserted trench which we leapt over without difficulty. Then we heard the drone of an aeroplane engine; the plane was flying very low and we saw its dark outline plainly as it flew towards us. Corporal Hobson said, "It's alright lads, it's one of ours." Whether it was or not, I shall never know. What I do remember is the bombs exploding, and all of us trying to take cover in the deserted trench. In our enthusiasm for safety, poor Corporal Hobson was hustled and trodden on, and was heard to say "I thought I'd brought some MEN up the line, not a lot of scared kids."

This remark was very effective, and we were soon on our way again.

THE RESERVE LINE

Soon after this incident, Mr Stott led us off the Downs and on to a main road in a cutting; we scrambled down a steep bank and crossed to the other side of the road, and here we halted for about ten minutes. Traffic was heavy and a long column of horse transports passed close to us; so close in fact that one lad near me had his rifle butt broken by the wheel of a passing limber. We lads were shocked to see a rifle broken; in England an incident like this would have been the subject of an official enquiry.

It would probably have resulted in punishment, but here, in a forward area, Corporal Hobson merely said, "Don't worry, lad, you can easily get another rifle when we get to the trenches!"

Just before we moved on, enemy shells began to burst along the bank down which we had scrambled on the other side of the road, but apparently no one was hit. Then Mr Stott led us back on to the Downs, and soon we came to a trench which was very sparsely manned by a few steel helmeted men. This was evidently a reserve line, but we boys noticed that the sentries stood in pairs.

GERMAN ATTACK EXPECTED

At this point, before we had crossed the reserve line, we heard the sound of horse hooves behind us. Out of the darkness came a man on a white horse, he reined in his horse and called for Mr Stott. It was Captain Milne the Adjutant; bending down from the saddle, he gave Mr Stott some instructions and then rode off in the darkness to find the other platoon leaders. Mr Stott gathered us together in a group and told us "No reliefs of the battalions in the line can now be attempted. The Germans are now carrying out trench raids at many points right along the front and a full-scale resumption of their offensive is expected at dawn."

Our orders were — "Dig in and prepare for the dawn attack." Mr Stott led us forward to a newly dug section of trench that had been excavated to a depth of about 18 ins. to 2 ft. and told us to get busy with our entrenching tools. We took the tool from its leather case hanging from our belts, and drew out the handle from its holder next to our bayonets and began to dig. None of the boys had ever used their entrenching tool during our training; no doubt we should have done if our training had been completed. Not far in front of us there were some battered trees and tree stumps, the remains of a wood, and as I dug I imagined the enemy advancing through them when it was dawn.

With only our entrenching tools we could not hope to dig a proper trench, and so we concentrated on digging a small pit each and stacked the soil in front. At dawn, a tremendous barrage of machine-gun fire broke out all along the front, and we boys imagined our machine-gunners mowing down the Germans as they advanced in mass formation. We wondered how many would get through to us as the machine-gun barrage went on and on and on, but after about twenty minutes it began to get less intense and eventually the front settled down and became comparatively quiet. Evidently the expected resumption of the German spring offensive was not to be made today after all; the boys had mixed feelings about this.

We spent part of the day in these uncompleted trenches, doing some digging, and then we were moved to a place where they were deeper and we would be concealed from enemy aircraft. Our rations arrived and were distributed, and as soon as it was dark we resumed our march to the trenches. I remember marching down a sunken road with gun pits dug into the bank and covered with large tarpaulins under which we glimpsed a few gleams of candle-light as the gunners moved in or out. This sunken road led downhill, turning and twisting, and when we finally emerged on to a field track we came to a ruined sugar-beet factory with a chimney full of shell holes; someone said that it looked like a tin whistle!

Sugar-beet factories were to become a common sight to us, and were often used as map references by the British troops. At first I used to wonder why so many of the French villages had a sugar-beet factory; an unfamiliar sight to boys reared in Britain, where at that time, the bulk of our sugar came from sugar-cane from our colonies. Later I learned that it was because Napoleon had encouraged the beet sugar process when the British blockade had cut off the raw sugar supply from the West Indies.

Mr Stott halted us near the ruins of the sugar-beet factory to await the arrival of the guide from the battalion we were relieving; no doubt the factory had been used as a map reference when he made the arrangements for the relief.

While we were waiting, the two old soldiers, Pearson and White, moved off the track into the shelter of the broken chimney-stack to light cigarettes. As soon as Mr Stott saw the light, he pounced on them. "Put that light out! You bloody fools! You two ought to know better; we're just behind the front line." Then the guide approached silently out of the darkness and spoke a few words to Mr Stott, who told us to follow him as quietly as possible, no talking, and break step (meaning no sound of marching men).

MESNIL

The sense of expectancy grew among the boys as we quietly scuttled along what had once been the main street of a village, and on past the low ruins of some houses and a church with part of its tower still standing. We became quite familiar with the ruins of this church during the next few weeks for several reasons. Although the church was so badly damaged, the cracked and crumbling spike of stonework which had once been its tower still provided the German gunners — being on their skyline — with an excellent target on which to range their guns. In daylight, great clouds of fine stone dust rose from the rubble surrounding the stump as their shells burst. The shell scarred road through the village continued up a gentle slope and over the brow of a hill and then down into a valley at the bottom of which the River Ancre, a tributary of the River Somme, flowed near Aveluy Wood.

THE TRENCHES

As we left the last of the wrecked houses behind us, we realised that now everything of life as we had known it, was behind us too. We had now arrived; the war was just ahead, where the German flares were whooshing up from their front line. The muddy road, pitted with shell holes full of water, began to slope more steeply downhill, and as we crept quietly down it, we were very conscious of being exposed. In fact, this road, in daylight, was in full view of the German trenches.

On our right, a low grassy bank gave us partial shelter as bullets from a German machine-gun began to whip past and over us. We arrived at a trench; it was dug across the road and was quite shallow, but as we stepped down into it and turned right, and off the road into the bank, we found that the trench deepened. It twisted and turned every ten yards or so, and in some places enemy shells had reduced the trench to shell holes. We crowded along it in single file, and it became very congested with Lancashire Fusiliers moving in and men of the Royal Naval Division struggling to get out. Eventually, no one could make much progress, as men wearing full equipment, struggled to pass each other. Then an officer looms up in the darkness; he is above us on the top, and outside the trench. I think it was Lieut. Drummond, the Second-in-Command of A Company.

THE FIREBAY

Somehow he got men moving again, and about half a dozen of us, all new boys, turned left out of the trench and entered a small trench which, in the form of a sap or firebay, had been dug parallel to the main trench, on the enemy side. This little trench, relatively undamaged, was a short section about twenty feet in length and it had a dead end. We youngsters — Whitehead and Wenderleish, Reg Thompson and Jim May, Turner and I — settled in and took possession.

Our little trench was about six to seven feet deep and was dug in crumbly soil and chalk; previous occupants had dug out small holes in the side and we used these as cupboards for small items. We took off our equipment and leaned our rifles against the muddy wall and waited for further orders. However, in the confusion we had apparently been forgotten as we were now separated from Corporal Hobson and the rest of the platoon.

UNDER ENEMY FIRE

After some time, it began to get lighter and we began to take a few peeps over the top towards the German line. We could see very little; long coarse grass and barbed wire and some pieces of broken wood, one of which was only about three or four yards from our parapet.

Whitehead, one of the Northampton boys who had joined up with me, thought that the piece of broken wood could be used to light a small fire and boil some water in one of our billycans to make some tea. He proposed to crawl over the top and get this piece of wood — how inexperienced we were! Several of us tried to dissuade him, but someone bunted him up and over he went and quickly returned safely with the coveted piece of wood. Within minutes, a salvo of shells burst near us; then another and another; clods of earth, pieces of chalk, stones and pieces of metal whizzed through the air. We cowered in the bottom of the trench and by some miracle, no one was hurt, except by some of the stones, one of which bruised my upper arm.

CUT OFF

Then a shell roared down almost on top of us and burst with a roar at the junction, the entrance to our little private trench, effectively blocking it and completely cutting us off from the rest of the platoon. When the shell fire ceased — it lasted about ten minutes — we began to take stock of ourselves and our equipment. Wenderleish, the young Jew from Acton, said "Look! my equipment; my pack with my overcoat; they are all buried under all that soil and chalk. What shall I do?" They were indeed; the soil and chalk were four or five feet deep at the junction.

At this point, an officer, passing along the main trench, heard us talking, and said to us from the other side of the obstruction "What the 'blank blank' are you fellows doing in there?"

We could only see his steel helmet as we replied, "We've been here ever since we arrived, sir."

"And you'll jolly well have to stay there now until it is dark again," he said.

He didn't know that we had been the cause of the shelling and we didn't tell him. We worked on the obstruction with our entrenching tools, and eventually managed to excavate Wenderleish's equipment, but we did not dare to throw any of the soil out of the trench. Then Corporal Hobson found out where half of his section was and helped us to get back into the main trench. He soon found some work for us to do.

MY FIRST RATION PARTY

In trench life there is always much to be done between dusk and dawn since very little can be done in trenches which are under constant enemy observation during daylight hours. Besides a constant watch by double sentries on the fire-step, there are rations to be fetched and repairs to be made to the trench. Sentries are changed every two hours, after which they are available for other duties during the next four hours, before another two hours duty on the fire-step.

On this my first night in this close support trench in front of Mesnil, I was sent back to the village with the ration party. There were about a dozen of us led by an NCO through the trenches to the shell-pitted road which led to the village; where in the crypt of the ruined church, Jock, the company cook, made tea and stew in a thick fog of smoke. How he avoided being suffocated by the smoke of his fire still puzzles me. As I was a tall youngster, the NCO gave me the job of carrying hot stew in a metal container which I wore on my back like a pack, with my arms through straps.

It was heavy and I could feel it warming my back as I trudged carefully back through the deserted village and down to the trenches with the stew sloshing about inside the container. Fortunately the metal container was provided with a close fitting metal cover, otherwise I should have been scalded! Incidentally, never again during my service in the trenches did I see, let alone use such a contraption, or indeed ever again have hot stew in the trenches.

Back at the close support trench, the rations — soup, bread, cheese, jam, margarine, cigarettes were divided between the sections. Then I heard Pelly and Norris talking about the graves of French civilians in the churchyard, and was horrified to see them showing to other boys some rings that they had taken from bodies which had been exposed by enemy shelling.

THE FIRST CASUALTIES

Then we heard about Lance-Corporal Fox, Lance-Corporal Willard and Private Waite; all three had been killed together by the deadly blast of a trench mortar which had burst in or near the front line. Some of the boys in my platoon had been down to the front line trench to fetch their bodies, and had just returned to us after carrying them on stretchers to Mesnil for burial.

These first casualties among the boys were an example of what has been described as the crazy arithmetic of war. I knew the two lance-corporals well and I thought sadly of their parents, who probably had not yet even heard from them since we came up the line. What sad news for them.

TRENCH MORTARS

We had all heard the big explosions down in the front line, about one hundred yards in front of us, and Pearson, whom I had adopted as my "Old Bill" of Bruce Bairnsfather fame, had already told me that the big bangs were trench mortars. "Nasty things!" he said. "Worse than shells." I asked him what their range was, and he said that they were always being improved … if you could call it that.

Trench Mortars were always known as "Toc Emmas"... jargon readily understood by me as a signaller trained in the morse code. The toc emmas were usually fired at us during the night at Mesnil, and I soon agreed with Pearson that most men feared them far more than they did shells. They were so unpredictable, and so devastating when accurate. Sometimes one could hear the small explosion as they were fired from the German positions, and then we might see a small red spark, like a lighted cigarette moving through the dark sky; but one could never judge correctly where they would fall.

The blast of a toc emma was deadly, apart from all the flying pieces of hot metal, and so the trench mortar was a weapon which was very unpopular with infantrymen. Even our own Stokes Mortars always attracted vicious enemy shell fire.

(During our next tour of the line, our Stokes Mortars fired over us from a trench behind us. Some fell short; nearer to our trench than the German front line. One didn't explode, fortunately for us, and one whooshed over my head as I stood on the fire-step, burst with a roar like doom about thirty or forty yards ahead, and several pieces come whirring back over my head. One of these was a curved band of metal about twelve inches long which could have decapitated me; I recovered it later from behind our trench.)

TRENCH REPAIRS UNDER FIRE

Here in these battered trenches in front of Mesnil, there were no communication trenches connecting our close support trench with the front line ahead of us or the reserve line behind us.

It was impossible to dig any because ever since the British retirement on and after 21st March, the Germans had occupied all the high ground of the great Thiepval Ridge, and their artillery observers were able to see every movement outside our trenches. Consequently, all the repair work to our trenches was done at night, for if a spadeful of soil was thrown out of our trenches in daylight, it drew shell fire. Yet continual repair of our trenches was required, so it must always be done at night and with as little trace as possible.

So the chalky soil had to be shovelled into sandbags and then lifted up to men on the top, who quickly shook out the contents into the nearest shell holes while other men with spades covered all the chalk with brown soil.

We worked in gangs, taking it in turns to fill sandbags in the trench or empty them out on the top. The work in the trench was cramped and arduous, and on top it was sometimes quite exciting when enemy machine-gunners traversed the front while we crouched in a shell hole.

The German machine-gunners were experts; sweeping our parapets very skilfully, and sometimes suddenly switching the deadly spray of bullets back again when they thought we felt it was safe to start work again.

THE JACOB'S LADDER TRENCH

The following night an officer, an NCO and about twenty men were sent as a working party to another part of the line to do some repair work. We followed Mr Stott, our platoon officer, along the trench to the left, until we came to the road from which we had first entered the trenches. Crossing this road, which led downhill to the German front line, we entered another trench which extended diagonally down the valley of the River Ancre. This hillside was of course exposed very clearly in daylight to the enemy occupying positions up on the high Thiepval Ridge. The trench, well known to the British infantry as the Jacob's Ladder trench, descended the valley of the River Ancre, and had been dug at a series of levels which were connected by the Jacob's Ladders.

These sections of trenches were very deep so that men could move about in daylight without being seen by the enemy, and as we came to the end of a section of trench there was a wooden stair or ladder which we climbed to a small platform. Then we descended a longer ladder, actually wooden steps wider than a ladder, down to a section of trench at a lower level, and so on to another level and to another and another. We were, of course, very much encumbered by rifle, spade or pick, sandbags or pieces of timber, but we new boys were thrilled and excited by another new experience of night life on the Western Front.

THE RESERVE LINE

After four nights and days in the close support trench, there was a reshuffle of the platoons, and my platoon moved back to a reserve line near the village of Mesnil. There was not even a trench here; just a farm ditch along a hedge. As we sat in it one evening, the front suddenly began to wake up; machine-guns began to fire on our left and it quickly spread to our own front. Our Company Sergeant-Major, not Doolan, but another man newly arrived among us, ran forward to a low ridge about fifty yards in front of us. Then he waved us forward and pointed to some freshly dug shallow pits, which we quickly occupied. He said, "I don't know what is happening, but we are in a better position to fire from here if Jerry is thinking of coming over."

This is it, I thought, and selected a good position in one of the pits. I made sure I had "one up the spout" and also took out several clips of cartridges from the canvas bandolier in which they were issued at the base. Then we waited and wondered what was going to happen; was this the resumption of their big offensive, and if so, would they come in massed formation? We had become quite used to machine-gun fire; both ours and Jerry's; but on this sunny spring evening, Sunday, 28th April, with the front for miles on either side of us waking up, our machine-gunners, firing from behind us, put a curtain of fire over us as they swept the German positions. There was no shell fire but the noise of thousands of bullets sounded like swarms of angry bees flashing over us as we waited. The machine-gun barrage continued for about a quarter of an hour and then stopped as suddenly as it had begun. Eventually it was clear that Jerry was not paying us a visit this time, and we returned to our ditch.

WATER PARTY

While we were in this reserve position, some of us were sent back one evening to Mesnil to fetch water in petrol cans. A corporal, whom I did not know, took about six of us back over the ridge, past the broken houses and shattered church, not far from which was the roadside well from which we obtained the water. I was not impressed by the behaviour of the corporal, who took shelter in the ruins of one of the houses when a few shells began to burst, while we lowered a bucket on a rope for water.

We had filled the petrol cans and had started back to the reserve line beyond the village, when we heard a low flying aeroplane coming towards us. Then we saw it, flying very low as it came over the brow of the low ridge between us and our trenches, and then, suddenly, we were under fire. It was all over in a few seconds; we saw the black crosses on the wings as it flew right over us. We dropped the petrol tins of water and ran; I did not attempt to take cover — there was no time for that. Instinctively, I ran towards the plane as it roared over us, and I was very quickly out of the German pilot's gunsights.

It was a miraculous escape; I saw the soil spraying close to me as the machine-gun bullets struck the ground. None of the others were hit either, and as the German pilot circled round to return we all took cover in the ruins of the houses. After watching the plane circle round once or twice and then return to the enemy lines, we recovered the petrol tins and returned safely to our ditch on the outskirts of the village.

THE FRONT LINE

After four days and nights in the reserve line, we moved on 30th April, during the night and very quietly down the road past the close support trench, and then on for about one hundred yards to our front line. This trench, being further down the slope of the River Ancre valley, was dug in almost pure chalk. When it was wet it plastered our uniforms and our hands and faces so that we were as white as millers, and when it was sunny we used to beat the chalk out of our clothing in clouds.

Here we were at last in the front line; I had often thought of the front line as the spearhead of the war; the climax of all the organisation behind it. Now I was experiencing the reality; a roughly dug trench on a slope visible to the enemy; cut off from our own close support and reserve lines.

The next afternoon, I was on sentry alone in one of the chalky firebays; the front was strangely quiet; so quiet that I felt as if I was the only man in this section of our front line.

I sat on the chalky fire-step with my back to the parapet; my rifle and bayonet between my knees. The sentry I had relieved passed on to me a small mirror, about two inches square, which was fastened to his bayonet by a small bracket. I had never seen such a thing before, and never used one again, but I clipped it on to my bayonet and soon began to try to use it. I felt that I was not much of a sentry if I was not observing something, but I could see very little when I raised my rifle and bayonet so that the small mirror was just above the parapet. In fact, all I could see in no man's land was the long coarse grass and glimpses of our barbed wire.

I ATTRACT ENEMY FIRE

Evidently the sun glinted on the mirror and attracted the attention of the German artillery observers, for in a matter of minutes — no more than three — a salvo of German shells burst on and near our front line. Soil, chalk and stones slithered into the trench near me; stones rattled on my steel helmet and a piece of shell thudded into the trench close to me. I wished I had not been so keen to use the mirror, but when a jagged splinter of metal whammed down on to the fire-step within reach of my hand, I foolishly picked it up and instantly let it go — it was hot and burnt my fingers.

I was all alone in the firebay, and when I walked round the corner to the adjoining bay, I found three boys playing cards, and another one writing a letter. The boys were getting used to shell fire or adopting a fatalistic attitude; there was nothing one could do about it anyway, but I did not tell them that I had been the cause of this latest little outburst of hate from Jerry.

Jerry was certainly doing his best to maintain his ascendancy, but to little effect, for as I passed by the little funk hole dug in the chalk where my platoon sergeant sat, we grinned at each other and he said, "That's reet, la'ad, ta'ake no'a no'a'tice, Jerry'll geet fed oop sooner or la'ater."

PATROL INTO NO MAN'S LAND

At night sentries were posted in pairs for a period of two hours, which we spent peering into the dark scene in no man's land. Mostly it was boring but sometimes hair-raising when we thought we could see figures moving "out there". It was much more interesting and exciting to go down into the valley towards the River Ancre on a patrol with Mr Stott. He was a hefty youngster, and as half a dozen of us followed him along the trench and climbed up over the top, his steel helmeted bulky figure in a trench coat loomed large in the starlight.

He held a huge Service Revolver in his right hand as he led the way slowly and quietly over the shell-pitted ground to our listening post. We all took turns to man this all night, two at a time.

This listening post was on our right flank about fifty yards beyond our front line towards Aveluy Wood which was occupied by the enemy. Mr Stott questioned the two boys manning the post and told them we were going on towards the German outposts which were believed to be manned at night, and were this side of Aveluy Wood. We then followed Mr Stott quietly down the valley until we came to a strong line of barbed wire. We boys wondered whether it was "his" or "ours". Then we lay motionless in the rough grass for a few minutes, listening. Mr Stott whispered to Lance-Corporal Walsh, and they went on through a gap in the wire to have a look-see.

After an age, probably only about ten minutes, they returned to us and led us along our front for about 150 yards. (Word had been passed along our front line that an observer patrol was out in front.) When the German flares went up and turned the dark scene into a brilliant "limelight" scene, we all stood quite still, petrified like statues as we had been told to do before we went out. This jogged my memory and reminded me of some TABLEAUX VIVANTS illustrating SCHUMANN'S KINDERSCENEN in which I and my older sisters had taken part at a Church Concert when I was only five years of age, and had to stand still.

During our sentry duty in the front line we had often heard, down in the valley, the quacking of ducks and the cries of other wildfowl; now we had been nearer and had seen some of the channels and lagoons where they lived. On this our first patrol, we saw no sign of the enemy and we returned safely, breathless with excitement, to our own front line.

TRENCH RAIDS

It was not until June that we began raiding the German outposts down in Ancre valley; our night patrols and listening posts having confirmed that they were occupied only at night. In the daytime, the German front line was on the other side of the River Ancre at Authuille and Ovillers, which were not captured by us until August. At night the Germans manning their outposts used a pontoon bridge to cross the river, and later, in August, we used it in our big attack.

"P" Walsh took part in a raid in June and brought back two German prisoners from the German outposts. He was awarded the Military Medal and promoted to full corporal.

As time went on our raids increased; the policy was "Give him a bloody nose", but I think now that it was also to blood us; to prepare young inexperienced boys for the time when they would take the offensive, not only in trench raids, but in a big attack on a wide front.

The boys were now getting used to the routine of trench life, and the many and various duties and activities of the night hours, when all the work is done. At night, when double sentries were posted, it was customary for one man to stand on the fire-step and for his mate to sit on the fire-step at his feet. This gave each sentry a rest from the continual eyestrain of staring into darkness, but this practice was forbidden after a German raid on our front line. The German raiding party crept very quietly up the valley, crossed our front line between two sentry posts without being seen and then circled back on to two of our sentries. The man standing on the fire-step was wearing a woollen cap comforter, probably knitted by his mother, to keep warm in the trenches on a cold night. This Balaclava helmet is very comfortable to wear on a cold night, but, it covers the ears, and so the boy heard nothing until the German raiders attacked him and his mate from behind! After their bodies were found, an order was issued that no woollen cap comforters were to be worn by sentries during their two hour spells of duty. "If you are cold, you'll KEEP AWAKE."

THE CO AND THE BRIGADIER-GENERAL

One very cold night before the order was issued, I was standing and my fellow sentry was sitting on the fire-step. He was one of the older Lancashire lads. We heard voices in the next firebay, and the old soldier said to me "Now la'ad, this'll be CO mecking his rounds; CHALLENGE him!" Wishing to show keenness as a young soldier on sentry in the front line, I thrust my rifle and bayonet forward aggressively as two officers came round the corner of the trench traverse. "HALT!" I shouted. "Who goes there?"

It WAS the Colonel, followed by the Brigadier-General, an unusual honour!

The Colonel stopped very suddenly as he found my bayonet within a few inches of his throat. "Alright, alright!" he said, pushing my bayonet to one side with his hand. "Don't challenge so loudly in the front line!!" They passed us, very warmly clad in British Warms and thick woollen scarves; their bulky figures seeming to fill our firebay as they squeezed past us and then disappeared round the next traverse. As their attendant runner followed them, my fellow sentry, the old soldier, grinned at him and said "Ee' la'ad! when th' two of 'em coom'd ra'and corner of traverse, th'e loo'oked like cuppie gree'at bears wi' all tha't on!"

WORKING PARTIES

In addition to duty on the fire-step at night, there were ration parties and various working parties; no one could sleep between the stand-to at dusk and the one at dawn. Working parties usually went to another part of the line or to a reserve position to dig a new trench, the outlines of which had been marked with white tapes by the Royal Engineers.

One night some of us were led by one of our young officers to the edge of a wood well behind our trenches, and there handed over to a corporal of the Royal Engineers, who showed us where to dig. We could not dig freely until we had done some work with pickaxes among the roots of trees and bushes. Eventually, we began to dig more easily, and I got busy throwing up soil with my shovel. Next to me was a Lancashire lad, a miner, who said to me "Ee'h la'ad, THAA best work wi pick an' let me 'av t'shovel; tha'a canst na'a throo as mooch wi' t'shovel as arh can wi' tayspoon!"

SNIPER AT WORK

As we moved at night on these working parties, we sometimes used trenches or sunken roads, but often had to follow a field track across ground which offered no cover. Here we sometimes saw crudely drawn notices "Keep moving here" or

"Keep down here" or "Watch out — Sniper at work".

One of my Northampton friends, George Dunmore, was killed instantly by a sniper's bullet while crossing an open space, and his close friend, Fred Ablethorpe, had the sad task of writing to his parents.

BACK TO CLOSE SUPPORT

We had now been in the line twelve days and nights, and although we had not had a proper sleep we felt quite fit. The only chance to sleep was during the day, usually in the afternoon when for some reason enemy shelling was not so likely, perhaps because the Germans too were resting.

In the early evening, Jerry usually shelled us for half an hour or so, and then as darkness fell we were all busy again.

On 3rd May, another platoon relieved us in the front line, and we moved quietly back to the close support trench, and spent another four days and nights. Every morning, at dawn, and every evening, at dusk, right along the western front, the word was passed along "Stand-to!" We all ceased whatever we were doing and cleaned our rifles. Mud was the constant problem in the trenches; boots and puttees, trousers and the skirts of tunics were plastered with mud. Faces, too, were often muddy and food was eaten with dirty hands.

All this was excused, but the rifle and bayonet, the "bundook and spike", must be clean at all times. After cleaning our rifles we wait for our platoon officer's inspection, opening the breach and placing our thumb nail in it so that he can get a reflected light from it as he looks down the barrel. Then as he passes on, we close the breach, put one "up the tunnel", apply the safety catch, and wait for the word to be passed along "Stand down".

Occasionally, at dawn, a neat rum ration was issued, which made our throats smart, but it warmed us.

ENGLEBELMER

Our next move was to a reserve line near Englebelmer between Forceville and Mesnil to deepen and improve some new trenches. Although the German spring offensive had now been contained, the British positions were in poor condition and continuous efforts were being made to improve them. By day we worked on uncompleted new trenches where it was possible to avoid enemy observation, and otherwise at night. The road into the village was screened from enemy observation by camouflage netting which the Royal Engineers had hung from the trees and tall poles.

This camouflage consisted of rolls of wire netting to which had been attached small pieces of canvas, dyed various shades of green, brown and yellow. I made several visits to Englebelmer; mainly to try to find water, which was always in very short supply. The villagers had evidently left in a great hurry a few weeks before; food and clothing were still in the houses; the fields cultivated, and the hedges and the ditches were in good order. The scene was still rural and comparatively peaceful and very different from the war scarred area at Mesnil and beyond, where the 1916-1917 battles of the Somme had destroyed all signs of peace and natural beauty.

One wet night I was in a working party carrying heavy trench mortar shells from the transport limbers in a sunken road to one of our TM Battery sites. Part of the track was very muddy, steep and slippery. More than once I slid for several yards hugging the large mortar shell to my body and holding it by the fins.

TEN DAYS' REST

On 7th May, we went back during the night to Forceville, and next day we marched to Archieves in daylight, which was pleasant. On 9th May, we marched still further away from the front to Talmas, a large village in the back area. In this area behind the front, large gangs of Chinese who had been recruited in Canton were employed as labourers. They wore pale blue overalls and the strangest hats I have ever seen on men, they really were fantastic — unbelievable! They had tall crowns and large brims; were made of thick felt-like material and were unshapely. The incongruity of these individually shaped Chinese village-made hats, and the Western-style standard factory-made overalls on these grown men, made them look quite grotesque, ridiculous. As we marched along the road where they were working, they all stood aside, leaning on their long handled shovels and they all, without exception, beamed happily at us as we passed.

Their job was to shovel the mud off the roads and stack it in long banks at the road side; there was certainly plenty to shovel on these small country roads now carrying heavy military traffic. Some of our older men had seen all this before, and as the Chinese stood by the roadside, grinning from ear to ear, all kinds of lurid and blasphemous jokes in "Pidgin" English were exchanged. They were the most primitive men I have ever seen, but apparently happy with this menial task.

These Chinese labour companies were under the control of elderly British officers and partly disabled British NCOs. At night they were locked up in hutted camps, behind barbed wire, patrolled by British sentries.

REST, REORGANISATION AND RETRAINING

Our first tour of the trenches was over and now we could

catch up on sleep, clean our equipment and ourselves, and get our boots mended, and write a few letters. The Byng boys had now been "blooded" and had matured considerably in only a few weeks. Any deterioration in our physical appearance was more than compensated by a maturity of spirit and a calm acceptance of new, unfamiliar and everchanging surroundings. We had joined the Lancashire Fusiliers as inexperienced half-trained Boy Soldiers, full of high spirits and immature enthusiasm. Only a month later, we had learned to face and accept the prospect of death or wounds, and had rapidly evolved a new philosophy of life and death, amid the whine and crash of high explosives and the noisy clatter of machine-gun fire. The massive German spring offensive had been contained but the cost was 300,000 casualties, of whom almost all were infantry, and many were the boys of eighteen.

Fresh from the noisy battle area, now a distant rumble, one was profoundly conscious of peace in this quiet village of Talmas. Instead of the man-made desolation was the fresh live beauty of nature. Instead of a dreary vista of muddy trenches and ugly shell holes, barbed wire and tree stumps, one saw live trees, lush grass... and flowers! Instead of the sickly-sweet smell of unburied mules and cordite fumes, the scents of village life... from a baker's oven, from flowers in a garden and from hay being stacked. Instead of the sight of bodies and stretcher-bearers and the sound of pain, there was the sight and sound of a hen and chicks crossing the road. Here was nature apparently unaware of and unaffected by the blight of war only a day's march distant.

CENSORSHIP

In Talmas, we were joined by more men, received pay twice (15 francs and 20 francs) and bought whatever was available.

We obtained free notepaper and envelopes from a YMCA hut, and wrote home. Envelopes were not stamped, but we wrote OAS (On Active Service) on them. They were collected by a lance-corporal and taken to our officers unsealed. After censorship they were returned to us for sealing and despatch. Often some words or sentences had been obliterated with lead pencil. Once my platoon officer told me to rewrite my letter, and to say "Nothing, absolutely nothing which could be of value to the enemy." I had said nothing that could possibly be of use to Jerry, now miles away from us, even if he had the privilege of reading my letter to my mother. However I just said "Yes Sir", and obediently rewrote my letter.

GREEN ENVELOPES

Sometimes we could, while on active service, put our letters into a Green Envelope, which were made of strong buff coloured paper with green printing which stated...

I swear on my honour that this letter contains no information that could be useful to the enemy; only personal and family matters.

The envelope had to be signed, with our Regimental Number and Rank. Then we were permitted to seal it ourselves and it was not subject to censorship, except for a certain proportion, which were opened at the base as a random check.

The "Poor Bloody Infantry", as we were known, and proud to be called, always accused the ASC (Army Service Corps) of taking all the strawberry jam and the green envelopes. After I was demobilised, my brother-in-law, who had served in the ASC told me that he always used green envelopes. "There were plenty," he said, "in his Unit!"

"Oh yes," I said, "I believe that! There were plenty for the ASC because you reserved them for yourselves, like the strawberry jam and the 'Woodbines', by theft!"

SECRET CODE

Before I went to France, I had agreed on a code with my mother so that I could tell her what part of the front I was serving on. Albert was the first name I gave her, by a slightly heavier pressure of my lead pencil on the letter "a" in a word, then an "l" in another sentence and so on. Albert had been captured and occupied by the Germans on 27th March, during the first week of their spring offensive.

Albert had been the hub of a network of roads leading to the battle zone, and a railway linked it with Amiens, fourteen miles away. Now only one of the four roads which used to lead to our old front line, the one which runs northward to Auchonvillers, was still in our hands. The other three, leading to Authuille by way of Aveluy Wood, the State Highway northeast to Pozieres, and one to Fricourt, were all now in enemy hands. Albert was very well known to the British troops, for many tens of thousands of them had marched through it on their way to the trenches. They had passed the famous church of Notre-Dame-de-Bribiere, a shrine for the Virgin of Albert, which had at the top of the church tower, a large gilded statue of the Virgin with the Infant Jesus outstretched in her arms.

The church was a prominent target for the German gunners. In 1915 a shell had exploded at the base of the statue bending the iron rod to which it was fixed. The statue leaned over at an angle which was below the horizontal and the Virgin appeared to be diving into the Square below. Hundreds of thousands of British troops had seen this precarious looking statue, and a legend had grown that if it fell, the war would end in our defeat! Rumour had it that the Royal Engineers dealt with this remote possibility, by strengthening the support to which the statue was fixed.

On arrival home in 1919, I found that my father had a map of the British front, and that he and my mother had been marking my progress all the way from Albert to Berlaimont. My mother also asked me questions in her letters which she knew I could not answer, so I used to put two kisses if the answer was "yes", and three kisses if the answer was "no". In this way army censorship and the lack of green envelopes was overcome. Letters from home were very precious to the boys, and were read, reread and shared.

BACK INTO THE LINE

Before returning to the trenches our boots were mended. They often needed new steel tips on the toes and heels on active service. One day I went to the "Cobblers Shop", a barn, and took off my boots for repair. While I was waiting I walked to the other end of the barn where several army tailors were sitting cross-legged on a long trestle table. One of our Company Sergeant-Majors came in, took off his tunic, removed the brass crown on the cuffs, and said "Sew on some Sergeant's stripes". He had just heard that another CSM had returned to his company after recovering from a wound, and, believing him to be senior in service as a CSM, wanted to reduce his own rank.

On 19th May, we left Talmas and marched to Lealvillers, a small village near Forceville; and then during the night of the 20th we went back into the line, passing through Acheux and Mailly-Maillet, to take over trenches in front of Auchonvillers. This second tour of the line began, as usual, when the command was given "Company to parade — outside, in battle order".

We were inspected and checked, and then set off for the front by platoons. The platoon officer was leading and the platoon sergeant was at the rear. We went first along field tracks, then along a sunken road to a main road, which we had to cross. At this crossroad, well known to the enemy artillery, we had to run for it in small groups, as enemy shells burst — "Wait! wait! — *Now!* — fast as you can."

The front here had a much greater depth than at Mesnil. Eventually we entered a communication trench, and commands were passed back from man to man "Wire overhead"... "Mind the wire"... "Duck under here"... "Sump hole on right"... "Hurry here"... "SNIPER, keep down!" Then it was "Mind this bloke" as we step over a dead man. (Who is it?) Then at last we met some of the men of the battalion we were relieving, and our long trek along the communication trench became more tiring as we squeezed past each other, all wearing full equipment. We continued to pass messages backwards and forward.

AN OLD CONFUSED TRENCH SYSTEM
We trudged on, past Battalion HQ with dumps of Mills bombs in wooden boxes with rope handles, rolls of barbed wire, iron stakes, boxes of ammo and petrol cans full of water.

During a relief, if the enemy gets wind of it, he shells the trenches with "whizz-bangs", a very unpleasant type of shell (4.2 calibre) with a fuse which causes the shell to burst without any warning. We used to say that a whizz-bang seemed to burst before it arrived, there being no warning whistle or even the final whoosh, as in the case of a 5.9 shell. Going into or out of the line could be more dangerous than being in it.

Ahead, the Germans were, as usual, sending up strings of Flaming Onions which hung temporarily in the dark sky.

At last we reached the trenches we were to occupy. The trench system at Auchonvillers was very confusing; old battered 1916 trenches being criss-crossed with more recent ones. The old trenches were grass grown and shallow, having been blown in during the 1916 battles. One of these was held by us at one end and by the Germans at the other. Another obvious danger was that Jerry could creep through the long coarse grass growing between his positions and ours and throw hand grenades into our trench. Small parties of men were sent out with hand sickles to cut down the long grass in front of our trench!

GOOSEBERRIES

My old section leader, Corporal Hobson, had been given a soft job in charge of an army bath house while we were at Talmas, and his replacement was Lance-Corporal Singleton. He was not a regular like Hobson; there were very few of them left at this stage of the war, but he had been in France for several years. He surveyed our section of trench and then showed us how to make barbed wire gooseberries to strengthen our defences.

We fetched reels of barbed wire, and under his instruction we made gooseberries by cutting off lengths of barbed wire and joining the ends to make a ring about four feet in diameter. We then fastened the rings together in the form of a globe, scratching our hands in the process, but nevertheless enjoying this new experience. Then we carried them along the old grassy communication trench which led straight towards the German front line, thus making a barrier which we hoped would prevent the enemy from getting close enough to bomb our end of the trench.

When Singleton was satisfied that Jerry could not creep up and attack us without warning, we explored round to see where we were in relation to the other sections. Our platoon officer, we discovered, was using a little dug-out, just room for one, dug in the chalk in a short cul-de-sac trench leading from our trench, which we now presumed was the front line!

Previous occupants of the section of the line had dug into the sides to make small dug-outs into which a man might crawl and lie down. I tried several for size, but could not find one big enough to stretch out fully, and in any case we had few and short opportunities to rest. Indeed I had little sleep during this tour and spent my free time amusing myself by carving faces with my jack-knife on some of the rounded pieces of pure chalk which littered the trench.

Every evening during Jerry's regular bombardment of the area with HE, someone would be hit; some men moved to another part of the trench system; some remained where they were; it was a matter of opinion which was the safest spot. Apart from the shelling there were other reasons why this area was not a safe position to hold, and later some of us were sent out into no man's land during the night to strengthen the barbed wire in front of our trenches.

RIFLE GRENADIER

While we were here my platoon officer gave me a box of rifle grenades and some special blank cartridges. He also gave me a metal cup to attach to my rifle in place of my bayonet, which I put back in its scabbard on my belt. This cup held a rifle grenade, which was the familiar Mills bomb with a short metal rod screwed into its base. During our training on the range, we had fired a few out of the metal cup by a special blank cartridge, while holding the rifle at an angle with its butt on the ground.

I was not pleased about being the platoon's rifle grenadier, because the blank cartridge made the barrel of the rifle filthy, and I knew this would be no excuse if my platoon officer found my rifle dirty when he made his twice daily inspection. I also disliked having no bayonet on my rifle in the front line, and when, a few weeks later, I was put in another platoon with a different officer, I reverted to rifleman.

THE POIGNANT CHARM OF NATURE

Actually, I never had any occasion to use these rifle grenades. One day I picked a bunch of red field poppies from the old grassy trench and put them in the metal cup attached to my rifle. They quickly wilted in the hot sun, but in any case I don't think the idea would have appealed to my officer if he had seen them. Most of the boys and men I was with apparently found no pleasure in flowers, but I was acutely conscious of them growing there in the midst of all that manmade destruction. Only field poppies and a few other wild flowers, but the persistent charm of nature in such conditions during that period of May, June and July, 1918, was more poignant than it had ever been before in my life, or since.

That spring and early summer, I was often conscious of the great contrast between the man-made ugliness and horrors of the war torn countryside, and the fresh unchanging harmony and beauty of nature. Certainly I have never lived so close to nature since, nor been so acutely aware of life. Between the wrecked villages, the crops lay ungathered, and nature, uncontrolled by man, was a riot of scent and colour; oats and barley mingled with blue cornflowers and red poppies, with the song of a lark in a blue sky. This contrast was almost too much to be borne.

In our daily lives in towns and cities, we live with our senses half asleep, but in those fields near Albert, where for nearly four years, death reigned, I was never more alive. Even at night, when on sentry under the stars, which I seldom noticed when living in a town, I was intensely aware of the orderly arrangement of the stars compared with the disorderly scene all around.

AN UNFORGETTABLE VILLAGE

Mailly-Maillet is a village I shall never forget; I never saw it in daylight until to my great delight, I revisited it in 1965.

During those weeks in the trenches at Auchonvillers we often passed through it, always at night, on our way to and from various working parties and ration parties. Like many other villages in the forward area, its houses were very badly damaged by shell fire.

It was always an eerie place, even when things were comparatively quiet, and we usually hurried through, heads down and best feet forward as enemy shells burst in the street and among the ruins of what must have once been a very nice village. There was a long high wall, quite impressive in the moonlight, on one side of the street. This enclosed the grounds of a large chateau, and was pierced in very many places with large holes caused by shell fire.

I used to wonder what the seigneur would say if he could see what had happened to his beautiful chateau, extensive grounds and gardens and the protecting high brick wall. On one of our working parties, when enemy shells were bursting with loud crashes in the street flanked by the high wall, our officer led us through the village by the back ways and gardens, and I had a good view in the moonlight of the smashed and broken chateau gardens, greenhouses, statues and summerhouses as we hurried through the tree stumps. Yes, Mailly-Maillet is for me an unforgettable place!

RATION PARTIES

Every night in the trenches, whatever else we had to do, a party of men, in the charge of an NCO made the long trek through winding trenches to a sunken road or to the back of a wood, where the company quartermaster-sergeant and his men dished out the rations.

Our rations were brought up every night from the horse lines, which were usually in a wood or a deserted railway station. To this conglomeration of wagons, limbers, horses, mules, tents and stores, the Army Service Corps brought up supplies from their larger depots, still further behind the front. Sometimes the CQMS's party would be caught by enemy shell fire and there were casualties to men, horses and mules. Then the sickly-sweet smell of dead mules would be wafted by the wind to our trenches until someone could find time to bury them.

When the rations had all been dished out, the ration party, loaded like mules with sandbags full of loaves, cheese, jam, tobacco, cigarettes and matches, tins of bully beef and Machonachies, made the long trek back to Company HQ. The sandbags were tied in pairs and slung over the back and chest, and with a petrol can full of water in one hand and a bundle of sandbags in the other we were sometimes overloaded. At Company HQ the rations were divided between the four platoons, and after that between the four sections in each platoon.

CASUALTIES

Casualties may occur at any time in a forward area; not only when Jerry was really straffing us, but sometimes when the occasional stray shell happened to catch someone. At first I was rather shocked by the casualness of some casualties. One day a man came along the trench and as he passed he said, quite conversationally "Howarth has just been killed — got one all to himself; his officer wants another servant; any of you fancy the job?" Another day Corporal Wormleighton was killed in like manner; a direct hit by a 5.9 shell — it seemed more casual than a road accident.

Casualties were inevitable; with millions of men engaged in not only the great battles, or the countless minor ones and the trench raids by either side, but also in the normal everyday occupation of a section of the line.

In the great battles at Loos, Neuve Chappelle, Arras, Ypres and the Somme, hundreds of thousands of men were killed or wounded, but EVERY day of the war, men died. A battalion which occupied a so-called quiet sector and carried out no raids, usually lost about twenty men during a tour of duty.

When we relieved another battalion and asked "Have you had many casualties?" the answer might be "Oh no, about a dozen, very quiet here, but you want to look out for his snipers." All these dozens and twenties added up, along the whole length of the western front, to thousands. Although they contributed nothing towards winning the war, they were necessary to hold the line and to prevent us losing it; it was as simple as that!

Now that the supply of replacements was at last recognised as limited, in an effort to cut down casualties the front line was thinly manned, and one hundred yards or so behind the front line was the close support trench, from which a counter-attack could be made, if ordered. Further back was the reserve line with company HQ, and still further back the battalion HQ.

The front line soldier knows nothing outside his own section of trenches; he can never take a good look "over the top" in daylight. He never gets an overall perspective of the battle. He knows that if Jerry attacks, or even raids, the front line troops are all expendable during the period in which various HQs behind him sum up the situation and make a decision.

THE SAP

One day, Sergeant Mercer, our platoon sergeant, came along the trench and told our section leader, Lance-Corporal Singleton, to move his section to another part of this confused system of trenches, where, he said, there was a sap we could use. At the time I didn't even know what a sap was, but as he led us to it, Singleton was very pleased indeed, gleefully chortling "Will you move your section along to a sap?" "Indeed I will! This way to the sap, lads."

The trench in which the sap had been dug was in much better condition than the section where we had been; the sap itself had obviously been dug some time before by the Germans into the side of the trench and deep down into the pure chalk. Since the enemy had dug it, it was facing the wrong way for us with the two openings in the rear wall of the trench. They were about four feet high and three feet wide and led down a shaft at about forty-five degrees, with roughly made steps cut into the slope, which led about twenty-five feet to a very dark chamber.

It was about twenty feet by seven or eight feet, in pure chalk. The walls and ceiling glistened with moisture in the candle-light, which was the only light apart from the daylight which filtered down the two shafts. Singleton and some of the boys were pleased to have the sap, and of course it gave us protection from enemy shell fire, but I found the place cold and damp and very uncomfortable. I could never sleep in it when it was my turn to lie down for a few hours, and, I also had an uneasy feeling that one could easily be trapped there. Indeed this was exactly what happened about ten days later when Jerry came over on a very savage raid. Looking back now to the confused trench system we were holding, and certain events which preceded the raid, I remember a night when I was one of the sentries on the fire-step, peering into the shadowy scene in front of us, and the Germans began to call out to us. Their front line was probably about 100 to 150 yards away, so it was difficult to hear someone calling "Tommee! 'allo Tommee!" and once I thought I heard a voice say "Come on over, Tommy." I said to my fellow sentry "Stand up, listen to this! Did you hear that? Did he say come on over, Tommy?" I got down from the fire-step and went along to Sergeant Mercer's little dug-out to tell him what was going on. He said "Ta'ake noa noatice, la'ad, and doan't answer. Just keep a sharp loo'k out, and fire if you see ANYONE coming over — ther's noa patrol of ours out thee're to'neet, la'ad."

WIRING IN NO MAN'S LAND

During the night of 29th-30th May, I was chosen to be one of about a dozen boys who were sent out with a sergeant I had not seen before, to strengthen our barbed wire defences. The sergeant climbed out of the trench first and then gave us each a hand up into no man's land. I sensed that he was nervous by the perspiration on his hand. I wondered how I was supposed to feel if he was nervous. I realise now that previous experience of wiring in no man's land would tend to make one dislike and fear it, for one would never get used to that job.

Incidentally, we boys had no training or experience of what to do. Some heavy reels of barbed wire and some screw pickets were handed up to us, and then we moved off quietly into the darkness until we came to our wire, which was badly broken by shell fire and obviously needed strengthening.

"Now" whispered the sergeant, "if he sends flares up, don't move". We started to screw the iron pickets into the ground with our entrenching tool handles, and then I started to roll out some barbed wire from the heavy reel, trying not to make too much noise.

Then several flares whooshed up from the German lines, turning the dark scene into daylight or rather limelight. "Stand quite still till the flares drop; they can't see us unless we move," said the sergeant. I hoped it was true! We stood petrified until they slowly sank down to the ground and the darkness enclosed us again. "Now, get a move on, but don't make a noise," said the sergeant. It was an impossible order, but we did our best. More flares went up from the German line and once a machine-gun traversed the front, but the bullets passed over us. Then, I heard my name being called. A voice from our trench called softly, "Send Hodges back." The sergeant told me to return to our front line, which I did, very thankfully, and curious.

When I reached our front line trench I found my platoon officer, 2nd Lieut. R. S. Stott, waiting for me, and as I scrambled down into the trench, he looked up at me and said, "Is that you Hodges? Have you ever been on a gas course?"

"No Sir," I said.

"Then off you go at once to battalion headquarters, and report yourself to the RSM." Hurriedly collecting my rifle and equipment and a few personal possessions from a hole in the side of the chalky trench, I made my way through the seemingly endless twists and turns of the trenches which led to BHQ. I reported and was told to wait and eventually about a dozen of us, NCOs and men, were sitting waiting in a trench near the BHQ cookhouse, from whence there came a mouth watering smell of frying bacon, which was all we were to have.

OFF TO THE GAS COURSE

It was nearly daylight before the senior NCO, Sergeant Hastings, was given the warrants and papers connected with the various courses we were going to attend. He then led us back through more trenches until we finally emerged from cover and began to follow a field track to a distant village. We were spotted by the German artillery observers in their captive balloons strung out like sausages in the sky above their front. Shells began to burst near the track and several times we had to wait, but had no casualties and safely reached the shelter of the village, Beaussart.

In the main street we passed several French gendarmes who were arguing and gesticulating with a group of Frenchwomen and old Frenchmen. These civilians had evidently returned to their village with their possessions on a handcart; but from what I heard of the argument, they were not to be allowed to stay. When we reached Acheux, our transport lines, Sergeant Hastings gave me my papers — I was the only one for the Gas Course — and told me to try to jump a lorry to Raincheval, which was then the railhead. There, he said, "You must report yourself to the RTO" — (Railway Transport Officer).

I walked a long way through the back area, feeling hot and hungry, and whenever I passed other soldiers they called out to me from their bivouacs or gun-pits "Are you going on leave, chum?" All leave had been stopped when the German offensive had started, and everyone was hoping that it had restarted. Once I stopped to talk to some artillery men who were cleaning their guns and their cook gave me some hot tea and a hunk of bread and cheese.

At last, after several lifts in army 3-ton lorries, which were a wonder in those days of horse transport, I reached Raincheval and reported to the RTO. His office was a railway truck in a siding well away from the station, which was sometimes bombed by German planes. British girls in ATS khaki uniforms were boarding army lorries as I arrived; they were being taken to their camp, well away from the threat of enemy bombs.

The RTO examined my papers, gave me a chit to obtain some rations, and told me that there was only one train a day to Abbeville, and it had gone. He said — "You can sleep on the station platform and catch tomorrow's train."

THE YANKS

It was here, on 2nd June, that I met my first Yanks; I was to see many more during the next week or so. The back area was full of them, unloading vast quantities of stores of every description; there were large dumps everywhere. They were doing physical training in large squads, and marching in full kit, and what a lot they carried! Every man was loaded like a pack mule, and they even had a spare pair of boots hanging from their heavy packs. I wondered how long it would be before they realised that they couldn't possibly carry that lot when they went into action. I heard later that their rifle proved unsuitable; it was heavier than ours and longer, and had an aperture foresight. They were later issued with the Short Lee Enfield with the V foresight and the British bayonet before they went up the line.

I was impressed by their physique, their freshness and vigour; they looked brand new compared with we British troops. Not only were they bigger men and stronger physically; they were all about the same age in mid-twenties, having all been drafted. British soldiers, after nearly four years of war, were then composed of about 25 per cent war-worn older survivors, and 75 per cent youngsters of eighteen and nineteen.

Despite their smart new officer type uniforms, the Americans looked inexperienced, and on active service against tough experienced German troops, they obviously had much to learn.

After collecting my rations I sat on the old wooden railway station platform and ate my bully beef and army biscuits. Three or four huge well-fed Yanks regarded me with good-natured amusement. "Say, Tommy," said one smiling fair-haired giant, "Can you eat that hard tack? Is that all they give you?" I began to feel the poor relation as I compared my mud-stained uniform with their quality clothing. I even wondered if I could persuade them to give me some louse-free underclothes, such was my discomfort; but like all other lousy British soldiers, I would have felt ashamed to admit that I was lousy — officially, it was my fault!

One of them showed me his wonderful wrist-watch, with luminous hands and numerals, and told me proudly how many jewels there were in it, and, that it was stainless! Another produced some American paper money; real dollars, which he kept in a real pigskin wallet, and explained to me at great length and in the greatest detail, how the paper was made of real fibre.

He told me it was not like your English pound notes, nor this despicable French money, which was just dirty little bits of poor quality paper. "Can yer beat it!" he said, "they wouldn't cash an Abbeville five franc note in Amiens!" They were certainly very proud of their country, and I found them exceptionally friendly and enjoyed my first encounter with our new allies.

My next experience with American troops was in September after I had been promoted to corporal, and appointed Battalion Gas NCO. A battalion of them were brigaded with the 52nd Infantry Brigade for experience in the line before being sent as complete American units.

Several hundred of them were with the 10th Lancashire Fusiliers for a couple of weeks. On the first occasion they experienced enemy shell fire, some got mad and shouted "Say, Tommy, let's go and deal with the b—s who are shelling us." They had little idea of the real situation; that between them and the German guns there were the lines of German infantry and machine-guns that would have mown them down.

Another memory of the Yanks is collecting their mail for despatch. As they handed over their letters to me I was fascinated by the addresses; many were to places named in the popular song hits of those days. We all used to sing about my old Kentucky home and way back in Tennessee and about Dixie and Georgia, Alabama and Mississippi, Maryland or Carolina and Virginia. Now I realised that these places really existed!

My education was being progressively extended. As an eighteen-year-old, who had spent all his life in a Midland town of 100,000 people, I had now become closely acquainted with Lancashire men of a very different background and character. Now I was talking to Americans, another type of man and answering their questions. Later I was to go into action with the ANZACS, the shortened name given to the Australian and New Zealand Army Corps. In the area behind the Battle Front, I had seen Chinese coolies working by the roadside and bivouacked near to proud Sikhs and watched them grooming their horses and cleaning their transport wagons. I had also been in brief contact with Portuguese troops, but strangely, I thought, I had seen no French poilus. They were south of us on the Western Front and apparently keeping a low profile after their enormous casualties in the Battle of the Marne in 1914, and later at Verdun. We never saw one of them or heard anything about their activities.

THE Vth CORPS GAS SCHOOL

Next day I boarded the train of cattle trucks which came up daily from Abbeville, and for some hours we jogged our way back there. In my truck was a red-haired Welshman named Pinkerton, a lance-corporal of the Royal Welsh Fusiliers. He too had just come out of the line, not far from where the 10th Lancashire Fusiliers were when I left them. Among other things he asked me if the LFs had had a go at Aveluy Wood yet, and told me about the RWF's unsuccessful attempt to drive Jerry out of it. "No," I said, "but the rumours are that we are to have shot as it soon, and if we do, it will be my first time 'over the top' in a big show."

At Abbeville we had a laughable experience when we changed trains, or rather, thought we had. We loaded ourselves with all our kit and set out through the streets to another railway station, where, after some time, our train come rumbling in, and we got back into the same cattle truck! Some men, more experienced, had not left the cattle truck at the first station.

About tea-time, we arrived at Cramont, where the Vth Corps Gas School was located. There was a windmill, some bell-tents and a large marquee tent where we had meals. In the marquee were trestle tables and wooden forms, and here good plain food was plentiful compared with our trench rations.

At night I slept in one of the bell-tents with seven or eight artillery NCOs, most of whom were Scots who had been in action during the great retreat... sorry, retirement.

I listened to them discussing their experiences; how they had continually to shorten the range of their shells, and then finally to fire at targets on their flanks as the Germans broke through. Some of them had even fired shells point blank at the masses of advancing German infantry before blowing up their guns by various ingenious methods. A few of them had saved their guns, bringing up their horses at the last minute and driving off while some machine-gunners held up Jerry a little longer.

Next morning Pinkerton and I reported to the school's RSM, another Scotsman, who looked us over and said to me "I see you've just come out of the line, laddie." He told us that we were too late to join this week's course, but could start next week with the next intake. In the meantime he gave us a light fatigue, clearing out rubbish in the windmill, which did not take much time. So Pinkerton and I walked down to the village and made friends with a French ex-soldier with one leg who invited us into his cottage for coffee. Henri was pleased to be finished with the war, and was farming again with the help of his wife, and an ancient man with no teeth.

During the remainder of the week Pinkerton and I explored the countryside, drank coffee, talked with the locals and enjoyed our break from the war, which grumbled and rumbled in the far distance.

I thoroughly enjoyed the gas course, which I found a mental stimulus after the months of physical activity. I took full notes at the lectures, and enjoyed the various stunts when we fired gas cylinders, exploded gas shells and wore our gas masks during a mock attack.

The course ended with a written examination on the Saturday, and on the Sunday morning after breakfast, one of the instructors told me that the school commandant, a colonel, wanted to see me in his office. I was escorted there by the school's RSM and stood before the colonel, who congratulated me and said that I had come out first in the exam.

The colonel said he would like to keep me as an instructor at the school, and asked how long I had been in France. He also asked me if I had been wounded yet, and noted that I was not yet nineteen. Finally, he said that in view of my short service in France he thought he ought to give the job to a man who had done longer service in the line.

BACK TO THE FRONT

So, on 15th June, I travelled back to the front from Cramont via Abbeville in the usual cattle trucks, and eventually arrived at battalion horse lines at Acheux. I had left on 30th May, and as we had then been in the line ten days, I expected to find the battalion out of the line. They were, however, still in the trenches at Auchonvillers; so that night I went up with the rations, and reported back to an officer who was new to me. He asked me who I was and where I had come from, and I said "57043, Private Hodges, No. 2 Platoon, reporting back from a gas course."

He stared for a moment and then he said "You will have to join No. 4 Platoon; your old platoon, No. 2, has been wiped out while you have been away on the gas course." All this meant that I had to find No. 4 Platoon, in the dark, and claim my rations without delay or I should get none. It also meant that I had a new platoon officer, a new platoon sergeant, a new section leader and few men that I knew. They told me that Jerry had made a vicious trench raid during my absence, and by questioning them I gradually found out what had happened.

The German gunners had put down a very heavy box barrage, which had completely isolated the section of trench occupied by No. 2 Platoon, preventing any reinforcement. It was all over in a few minutes. Picked German troops had entered our front line, probably through the old 1916 trenches which I had helped to block with barbed wire gooseberries.

Everyone in my old platoon had been killed, wounded or taken prisoner. Those down in the sap were trapped and either killed or severely wounded. The German troops had evidently known about the sap and threw down some of our own Mills bombs which were conveniently stacked in wooden boxes nearby.

Among those taken prisoner were the officer on duty, (not 2nd Lieut. Stott), Corporal Croot, the young soldier who took charge of us on our journey from Calais to the Battalion, Lance-Corporal Singleton, my section leader, and about a dozen others whom I knew well. Sergeant Mercer, my platoon sergeant, had both legs shattered by a Mills bomb, and many others had been badly wounded too.

My first hand account eventually came when young Wenderleish, with whom I had been ever since we came to France, returned from hospital some weeks later. He had been wounded in the upper arm, a flesh wound, during the preliminary shelling, which he described as terrific. He saw the German troops, all big chaps, leap into our front line, and while some used our Mills bombs, others grabbed the officer, Corporal Croot, Lance-Corporal Singleton and others. He said they lifted them up out of the trench to other German troops who hustled them across no man's land to the German front line.

Wenderleish saw all this happen, fascinated by the precision and the speed of this trench raid, "All over in no time" he said. Then, clutching his wound with his other hand to try to stop the bleeding, he bolted down the communication trench and reached the battalion first aid post.

Many years later, I had the opportunity to read the official account of this big German raid of the 4th June 1918.

> At 2.30 a.m., the Germans commenced a furious bombardment with guns and trench mortars against the front held by the 10th Battalion of the Lancashire Fusiliers. At 2.40 a.m., they lifted the barrage to the support line and continued to bombard it and the flanks, thus creating a box barrage.
>
> As the barrage lifted from the front line to the support line, parties of well-armed Germans, who had used the old trenches crossing the new No Man's Land, broke into the battalion's trenches on a frontage of several hundred yards, overcoming the garrison on the left flank. On the right they were met with vigorous Lewis Gun fire, and Lance-Corporal H. J. Colley with two men bombed along the trench and succeeded in ejecting the intruders.
>
> Many casualties were inflicted on the Germans, but the Lancashire Fusiliers lost one officer and twelve other ranks killed, twenty-one men wounded and two officers and thirteen other ranks taken prisoner. Lance-Corporal Colley was awarded the Military Medal for clearing the trench with Mills bombs.

Later, on 24th August, during our attacks on Martinpuich, Colley, who had been promoted to sergeant, again recaptured a section of trench, this time at the cost of his life. He was awarded a posthumous Victoria Cross for his courage and his tenacity.

In the reorganisation that followed the wiping out of No. 2 Platoon, its Platoon Officer 2nd Lieut. Stott, was transferred to take charge of the Stokes trench mortar section, and I had no further close contact with him.

I was sorry to lose Lieut. Stott as my platoon officer, and I also had every reason to be grateful that he chose me to go on the gas course. I was also sorry to lose my platoon sergeant, a key figure in any platoon. Sergeant Mercer was a man who had inspired confidence and trust and a very ready obedience from the boys. He was older and more experienced than we were and we had always had a very good relationship with him. I don't know whether he recovered from his grievous wounds, but one wounded survivor of that savage raid told me that as he lay bleeding in the bottom of the trench he said to the boys, "You can't do anything, lads. Put up your hands and cry Kamerad." They had no other choice in those bitter circumstances, cut off from all help and further leadership.

I also missed Corporal Croot, who was exceptionally mature for his nineteen years — but still a boy at heart. He was an extrovert with a great sense of humour, and being our own age and having trained with us we both liked and respected him.

Among the severely wounded in that raid was a Lancashire lad whose personality had greatly impressed us; he had been like an uncle. He was a very strong short sturdy man; a miner in civil life, and his happy character and friendliness had been very much admired and appreciated by the boys. When I asked how he had taken the raid and his wounds, I was told "Just as you would expect." No greater tribute could have been made and there was no need to ask more.

I did not remain in No. 4 Platoon long enough to feel at home as I had been in No. 2, and I have no lasting memories of the various personalities with whom I spent the next few weeks.

TOUTENCOURT AGAIN

It was not until Sunday, 23rd June, that the Lancashire Fusiliers were relieved and marched out of the line to Toutencourt via Forceville, having been in the trenches for five weeks; a longer period than usual.

Coming out was always a wearisome business, handing over and briefing the relieving troops; struggling past hundreds of men in the narrow communication trenches; everyone heavily loaded with full kit.

On this occasion I was fitter than most, having had rest and good food at the gas course, but many of the boys were exhausted. We looked forward to emerging at last from the congested trenches to a sunken road or a field track where we could form up and march in column of four. This was not the enjoyable, almost exhilarating experience of our training route marches in England, with the band playing in front. Then we had felt so strong and fit; I had always enjoyed the sound and the rhythm of marching boots; the marching songs; the quips and the jokes and the ten minutes' rest every hour.

It is a very different experience when one is cold and weary after a long period in the line. Then, one stumbles along, head down, watching the feet of the man in front, dreaming of warmth and sleep. One even has thoughts of hot food and hot baths — but these are idle dreams since at best; a cold barn awaited us, with some dirty straw and perhaps a billycan of hot tea. However, there are great compensations. We were alive. We had survived another spell in the line! So we plodded along the seemingly endless communication trenches, waited for shell fire to cease, and then came to a fork in a communication trench.

Here, a staff officer stood with a shielded torch and a list of regimental numbers and names. "Give your number, name and initials to the officer as you come to him," said a sergeant. Some were directed to the left fork; some to the right; "and never the twain shall meet again". I was sent to the left and most of the surviving boys that I knew went to the right, and just disappeared into the darkness. Of the Northampton boys, only Jim May, Reg Thompson, Whitehead and Wally Beale remained with the 10th Battalion; those who had been directed to the right fork were on their way to join the 17th Battalion, Lancashire Fusiliers. I never saw any of them again, except a few survivors whom I met in Northampton after demobilisation.

Eventually, we were slogging across the downs towards Forceville with the straps of our equipment cutting into our shoulders and our water bottles and entrenching tools swinging against our thighs. The worst was over and our spirits rose, though our shoulders ached under heavy loads, and our feet were sore because we had not taken our boots off, and our socks were nearly worn out. Most of us had been without sleep, except for "cat naps" between sentry duty and working parties, and we limped along, dead tired but not dejected.

At such times of elemental need, one adjusts one's priorities; I have seen men discard treasured personal items of kit, anything which would lighten the load. When the chill air of the hour before dawn begins to exert its depression, all conversation and even thought ceases. One feels utterly weary, clammy and cold as one thrusts a foot forward into the space occupied a second before by the foot of the man in front. I remember an occasion when we were led along the wrong field track and were hopelessly lost; a "hopeless dawn" was breaking and lighting the sky as we struggled on; some men were sullen and others savage in their wrath and condemnation of our officers for their apparent inability to read a map. At last, as dawn lit the sky, we reached the village where we were to rest, and we stumbled into some barns, utterly exhausted, and slept and slept.

This time we were bound for Toutencourt Wood, now quite a familiar place, where we knew there were some bell-tents. Perhaps tomorrow we might even get a hot meal of fresh meat instead of the usual stewed Chicago Bully, and I was looking forward to another trip to the army bath house and a change of underclothes. What one really longed for was a real bath, in hot water, with plenty of soap, and then, oh then, a change into lice-free underclothes, followed by a meal sitting at a table with food on a plate. These were but idle dreams that could never come true until the war was won. After so long a spell in the line, we also hoped for a few days' rest; an opportunity to beat the mud out of our puttees after hanging them to dry from the trees in Toutencourt Wood.

A FALSE ALARM

On arrival at Toutencourt Wood we had hot tea and berghu (porridge) and then quickly bedded down in the tents for a good sleep. We knew from experience that it would not be long before the RSM laid on a training programme, which he called smartening us up to look like soldiers, but was more realistically to get us fit and trained for the next trip up the line. On this occasion we had not been in the tents for more than an hour or two when we were awakened by loud shouts "Fall in! Out of it! Get moving!" Hurriedly though sleepily, we put on our equipment, grabbed our rifles and formed up outside; marched through the trees and down to the road and were soon slogging along — back to the front!

Amid the groans and curses the rumours multiplied; the enemy had broken through; we were going to counter-attack; we were only going up as a reserve in case Jerry was renewing his big offensive. Backwards and forwards the rumours passed up and down the column as we marched. In front the sky was lit up with the flashes of our guns and the noise of shell fire grew louder. Ammunition limbers thundered past us and we were choked with dust until we left the road and took to field tracks, and then we began to see shrapnel bursts in the lightening sky.

Eventually, we stopped at an empty trench, a quarter of a mile I judged, behind the front, and here waited for further orders as daylight increased. Time elapsed, nothing happened, and we began to get restless and hungry too. Men smoked or dozed as the sun grew warmer; it was going to be a hot day. Were we going forward? A runner arrives with a message; he is directed to the colonel, who speaks briefly with the adjutant. We watch and wait, and then we see the company commanders with the adjutant. The front is quieter now; seems to have settled down for the day to the usual routine of occasional shell fire and stuttering of machine-guns, but the rumours begin to circulate again.

At last our company commander, Captain Sankey, returns and calls for the platoon officers; now we shall soon know. "Fall in," says our officer, "and move quietly after me, we are going back to Toutencourt Wood, the flap is all over."

With a mixture of relief and exasperation, we followed him down the trench to a sunken road and then round the edge of a wood to another road where we formed up and commenced the march back. As soon as we arrived at the tents again, we were lined up and inspected by an officer I did not know, and our platoon sergeant was told to take the name of every man who did not have a full water-bottle, iron rations and gas mask. It had been noticed in our hurried departure from Toutencourt, that some men had failed to take their gas masks, and then at the inspection after our return, it was discovered that some had eaten part of their iron rations, and some had taken a few swigs at the water-bottles. All these were heinous crimes on active service, and those guilty received the appropriate punishment, probably fourteen days Field Punishment.

We boys were beginning to realise that war is a ruthless and exacting taskmaster, demanding not only courage in the exciting hours of trench warfare, but endurance during long periods of danger and discomfort. This war had been going on so long, and so many millions of men had been, and were still involved, that it dwarfed not only the individual, but even the battalion by its sheer size and relentless demands on them.

There we were, in June 1918, just a small part of a huge impersonal machine that swallowed up men; every day the dead are buried; the wounded limp or are carried out of the line; new drafts arrive to fill the gaps; new officers come up with the rations and are apportioned to a platoon, soon to disappear and again to be replaced.

However, we were young and we soon recovered our strength and our usual high spirits. I sat one afternoon under the trees listening to the conversation among the boys as they sat and laughed and talked. Some were shaving; some were beating the dried mud and chalk out of their puttees and trousers and a few were writing letters. They were sunburned, tousle-headed, full of life; I thought they looked like lively young cockerels moving about in the dappled sunshine of Toutencourt Wood.

BATTLE TRAINING FOR AVELUY WOOD

Toutencourt was no longer the relatively quiet place in which we had spent four days in April. It was now a regular target for enemy bombing planes, and so we moved to some tents in a field nearby, and began a training programme for the capture of Aveluy Wood. During those beautiful summer days in late June and early July, we were practising for our rumoured attack on Aveluy Wood. It had been in German hands since the March retirement and our generals seemed determined to take it whatever the cost.

How beautiful were those early hours before the heat of the day; how strong and fit we were; how full of life. Reveille at 5 a.m., breakfast at 5.30 a.m.; and it was a good breakfast, berghu and then bacon; with the bacon fat as a dip for our bread. Fall-in at 6 a.m., and then we marched to the woods, where wild strawberries grew thickly in large brambly clumps between the rides which dissected the wood. Our senior officers, the colonel, major and adjutant, mounted on their well-groomed chargers, rode up and down the grassy rides directing operations. We advanced this way and that in short rushes as per the Infantry Field Manual, led by our platoon officers and NCOs.

It was quite good fun; we privates thought it was a bit of a mike. It certainly did little to prepare us for the capture of the blasted, leafless area which had once been Aveluy Wood, which, as we had seen on our night patrols from the trenches was a foul ruin of shattered tree stumps and stinking shell holes. Here, at Toutencourt Wood, the trees were alive and leafy; and as we lay in the rides and among the tangled undergrowth waiting for the next order, we could eat the wild strawberries. In the late afternoon we returned to our tents and were given a good meal; stew or possibly roast meat, followed by duff with jam and a billycan of tea. Lights out was at 9 p.m., and we were up early again next morning for another day of exercises in the woods; this was not soldiering as we had known it; it was more like an Annual Camp of Territorials; it couldn't last.

SPECIAL TRAINING FOR THE LEWIS GUNNERS

During this period of battle training the Lewis gunners were given special training by the battalion machine-gun officer. They fired at targets, and also practised moving forward and taking up strategic positions to give covering fire when their platoon was advancing.

Every platoon of infantry had a Lewis gun section of six to eight men in the charge of a corporal or a lance-corporal armed with a Colt or a Webley revolver. The men in a Lewis gun section did not have rifles, but they had to carry between them a Lewis gun weighing about 30 lbs., various spare parts and the heavy canvas panniers full of ammunition.

The No. 1 on the gun, who was the most experienced Lewis gunner, carried the heavy gun on his shoulder and he fired it. The No. 2 carried the spare parts and when in action he loaded the magazines. The others carried the heavy canvas panniers of ammunition slung in pairs over the shoulder, one in front and one behind.

The Lewis gun fired forty-seven rounds from a circular pan in 3 seconds, but it was usually fired in short bursts to avoid overheating. It could jam if the bullets were not very carefully loaded into the circular pan, as a friend of mine discovered when he was an Observer in the Royal Air Force and had a jammed gun at a critical moment and was forced down and captured.

During the battle training all the Lewis gun teams practised taking their gun to pieces on a blanket and reassembling it quickly. They also were given instruction on the very careful loading of the bullets into the magazines.

When a battalion marched up the line to relieve another battalion in the trenches, the heavy Lewis guns, spare parts and panniers loaded with full pans, altogether a considerable weight, were transported in a horse drawn limber as far forward as possible.

On one occasion, when we were relieving one of the Royal Naval Division battalions, the limber got lost on the way up the line, and could not be found. Eventually, when the relief took place and the RND men came out of the trenches, they had to leave their Lewis guns in situ, much to the chagrin of our officers and the Lewis gun teams.

THE BOMBING SCHOOL

The second-in-command of A Company was still Lieut. Drummond; his tent was pitched on the other side of the field; we used to watch him washing himself all over with water in a green canvas bucket with rope handles. He always ended this public performance by having his batman pour the bucketful of water over him as a shower bath to the accompaniment of our cheers. He took some of us several times to a bombing school in that area, where we were introduced to the Egg bomb. We learned to use it by striking the percussion lug at one end of the bomb on our boot heel; then count three and throw. How I distrusted them; I much preferred the good old Mills with its cast iron serrated case and its safe split pin with a ring to pull it out. The new Egg bombs had a much lighter case which I thought compared unfavourably with the Mills, and I certainly could not have carried them as casually as I later carried a Mills bomb in each breast pocket when we were going over the top.

Having had good food and regular sleep during this period of so-called battle training in perfect summer weather, we felt strong and very fit. As I looked at my sunburned companions I could not help thinking how sad it was that such strong happy healthy youngsters were training for battle, for wounds and death. Of course, I kept these thoughts to myself, and joined in the laughter and jokes as we stood in line in the hot sunshine waiting for our turn to use the new Egg bombs. There was to me a deep poignancy about this happy scene — a group of lively youngsters, having a break from war, yet training for war.

The weather was perfect, and we were almost in holiday mood, free momentarily to enjoy our young lives as we laughed and joked with Lieutenant Drummond. Although I too was enjoying this rare break from discomfort and danger, I also felt a deep sadness about the tragic waste of so many young lives. A sadness which I still feel after many years.

BOUZINCOURT

The period of battle training came to an end on 9th July, and during the night of 9th-10th, we went back in the line in the Bouzincourt area, not far from Mesnil. This area bore the marks of the concentrated trench warfare of 1916. The support trench that we occupied for the first three days ran right through the ruins of the village of Bouzincourt, now a grass grown area full of heaps of rubble. Company HQ was in a cellar that was only half blown in and had been strengthened with sand bags. Not very far away was our front line, which was not a continuous trench and was sited in a very dangerous position; at one end we could be enfiladed from higher ground in enemy hands. Once the sentries were posted and the Lewis gun positions manned, those of us who were free for the time being began to explore our territory, made improvements where possible and explored the trench system, such as it was, to get the feel of our own section and its relation to our flanks. I still remembered the sap.

A WORKING PARTY IN NO MAN'S LAND

During the night of 11th-12th July, about thirty of us were led by Lieutenant Drummond, second-in-command of A Company, to a position beyond our own front line; such as it was. We scrambled out of the trench and followed him quietly in a half left direction, and eventually came to a partly dug trench in no man's land which had evidently been started by previous working parties. The trench varied in depth from three feet to six feet, and Lieut. Drummond told us to start digging with as little noise as possible. I was working in a shallow part with two older men named Carpenter and Fisher; both were miners who made my efforts look puny by comparison.

We were quite close to the outskirts of the town of Albert, which was in German hands, and their flares probably revealed us to them. Very little progress had been made when we came under fierce shell fire. I crouched in this shallow trench, holding my spade close to my face for protection, from shell splinters. We joked about the lucky ones who had spades and the unlucky ones who had only a pickaxe for protection. We just had to stick it out until the shelling ceased, and then we were told by our sergeant to move along to a deeper part of the trench for greater safety. We had to step over two or three of our dead lying in the bottom of the deeper part of the trench.

A little further on we found some wounded, including Lieut. Drummond, who was standing on the top, looking down into the trench and calmly directing those wounded men who could walk. He helped several to climb out and sent them back to our front line. Very little was accomplished by the working party, but while a stretcher-bearer bandaged his bleeding wrist, he stood and joked with us and then led us back to our own line. We never saw him again after that night, and many of us greatly missed him. He had the gift of leadership in a very special way, inspiring us by his courage and a real personal interest in us. Especially was this so when we boys had just arrived at the front.

I still remember the time we first experienced intense shell fire. Lieutenant Drummond told us to crouch on the fire-step with our backs to the trench wall, drawing up our knees to our chins and covering our faces with our arms. "Now," he said, "you have covered your vital parts and there is nothing else to be done but to stick it out until Jerry stops shelling, and", he said, "if any of you do stop one, well, what better way to die than in the front line for your King and Country." That was a spirit which appealed very strongly to the men of eighteen in those critical days in the spring of 1918. We were fortunate in having such good officers; Lieut. Drummond, the second-in-command of A Company and 2nd. Lieut. Stott, my first platoon officer, were two of the best of the many officers I served under on the Western Front.

The spirit of those far off days now seems rather quaint to some. Two world wars have receded into the past. New generations have been born who know nothing of war. No longer does Remembrance Sunday touch chords of personal experience, except to the dwindling number of people who can remember those times. In its earlier form as Armistice Day, the whole population shared haunting memories and emotions in a nationwide two minute silence, in which the nation renewed communication with its past, remembering not only its dead, but their finest hours as a nation, and gave thanks to God. No doubt the loss of our great empire has been traumatic in its effects, but occasionally a violent reaction against the old traditions occurs. Incredibly some who strive for peace refer to War Veterans as War Mongers!

A DANGEROUS GRANDSTAND

On 13th July, my platoon was moved into a section of the front line where immediately in front of our parapet the ground fell away quite steeply, so that one had the feeling of being in a grandstand overlooking no man's land. It was a very unusual situation. During daylight we could not move many yards to our right because the trench petered out to a depth of only eighteen inches to two feet.

During the night, the two sentries on duty kept in contact with the company on our right about one hundred yards away. We did this by a regular patrol. One of us would go quietly along the shallow trench, feeling very exposed, especially when the German flares went up. Then about twenty minutes later one of the sentries from the other company would pay us a visit. We also visited one another when we were without a light for a cigarette.

TRENCH MORTAR FIRE

One day I crawled out of the back of our trench and explored an old unused trench in which were several dug-outs which had been blown in during fighting two years earlier. There were many interesting relics of that period, and I discovered that it led diagonally from our short, rather isolated stretch of front line, to another old 1916 trench from which our own Stokes trench mortars fired over our heads at the German positions.

We had been warned by the troops we relieved to watch out for a German sniper who, they said, sometimes occupied a little ditch near a tree stump out in no man's land. There was little we could do except keep our heads down, since to try to see him would be to become his target. One day our own toc emmas started firing over our heads in an attempt to deal with him once and for all. That is what they said, but we had mixed feelings about their efforts when pieces of metal came whirring back to us, threatening to decapitate the sentries.

The British Stokes mortar was a simple weapon; it consisted of a metal base plate and a 3 inch tube about four feet in length. The mortar had a 12-bore cartridge in its base which was detonated by a pin in the bottom of the tube when the 20 lb. bomb was dropped into it. "Elementary, my dear Watson." The Stokes mortar was very mobile, and a team could quickly set it up, fire fifty or even a hundred in a few minutes, with three or four in the air at once. The range was 200-500 yards. Naturally, this usually attracted some retaliation from the Germans, either by shell fire or by their trench mortars. Their big one, the Minnenwerfer, was a terrifying weapon; it fired a bomb up to four feet long, weighing 150 pounds.

This enormous bomb had a deadly blast; the three boys, Fox, Willard and Waite, who were killed during our first night in the trenches near Mesnil, were killed by the TM blast. The crater was enormous too, as big as a house, we used to say. We felt absolutely helpless if we saw one coming. At night, the glowing fuse could be seen moving across the dark sky, and in daylight a small black dot in the sky very quickly became larger. A high explosive shell has a trajectory and can be heard coming, but a

Minnie just sailed through the air, turning over and over with a "swish-swish-swish" and then came down almost vertically.

OFT IN DANGER, OFT AT WORK

This could have been our hymn in this very dangerous trench, for every evening without fail, as at Auchonvillers, Jerry plastered us with his HE. Some men moved along to the left; others remained where they were. A common remark was "If your number is on it, you'll get it wherever you are." To some this seemed to be a comforting, almost fatalistic attitude during this period of shelling, which occurred with teutonic regularity. We knew it would continue until the prescribed number of salvos had been fired, but sometimes one of our humourists would say "Now then, Jerry, that will do! You'll only hurt someone if you keep on."

When, after about twenty minutes, the evening hymn of hate ceased, we would stroll along the trench to see what damage had been done and find if anyone had been hit. Gunga Dean, our sanitary man, would check the latrine situated just behind the trench, and grumble if it had been damaged. While in this trench, we had very little sleep, being either on sentry on the fire-step or working on necessary trench repairs. At night some of us were sent back about a quarter of a mile through winding trenches to a sunken lane, where the horse transports unloaded fresh supplies of trench mortars. Others would fetch rations from the sunken lane and also carry up sandbags, reels of barbed wire, screw pickets, and boxes of Mills bombs.

There was always something to be done. One evening we had a direct hit by a German 5.9 inch shell and three dead had to be buried and some wounded who could not walk had to be carried by stretcher, which was a difficult job for the stretcher-bearers in narrow winding trenches.

Any spare time could always be filled with the never-ending work of repairing and strengthening our parapets with sandbags filled with soil from the rear of the trench, always keeping a very wary eye open for the persistent sniper.

Recalling those dangerous and very strenuous days and nights in the battered trenches near Bouzincourt the spirit was marvellous. We worked almost unceasingly to maintain our positions. We had very little rest, and sleep was impossible. Yet we lived in top gear, youth, humour and comradeship triumphing over the appalling conditions.

OBSERVATION BALLOONS

Life in the grandstand at Bouzincourt was dangerous, but never dull. One sunny evening, a really beautiful summer evening, the front was unusually quiet. Behind us, hanging in a long line across the summer sky, was a string of British captive balloons. They were tethered behind a wood and hung lazily and motionless in a row. Suddenly there was machine-gun fire, and a German plane swept on the balloons. As we watched we saw the crews, two men in each basket, jump out and fall. We saw their parachutes open while the balloons burned and crumpled slowly to the ground. When the German pilot had set fire to the last of the balloons with incendiary bullets, he turned and swooped and fired at the men descending by their parachutes. Then diving to within a few feet of the ground, he came roaring towards us, actually passing right over me.

We all fired our rifles; every man within range had a go, but apparently we did no damage to him and he actually had the nerve to fire his machine-gun at us as he roared over us. There were black crosses on the wings of the plane and I could see his goggled face as he streaked across no man's land and disappeared from sight.

RATIONS UP!

This was the welcome cry along the trench when the ration party arrived. Our rations were adequate, provided they reached us. There was bread, cheese, jam, margarine, tea, bully beef in tins and sometimes Machonichies, a meat and vegetable ration we called M and V. Water, which was carried up in two gallon petrol cans, was usually flavoured with petrol and sometimes also with chloride of lime, presumably when the source of supply was suspect.

The bread ration varied; four or five men to a loaf when we had recently received a new draft to replace casualties, or three to a loaf when we had recently suffered casualties but still received their rations. As the ration party came in sight, the first question we asked was "How many to a bun?" and the next question was "What are the cigs? any Woodies?" Woodbines were always prized above other brands because the tobacco was mature, whereas White Cloud and other unknown brands were hated because of the acrid taste of green tobacco which we suspected had been foisted on the government by fat profiteers who smoked cigars themselves.

The issue of a tin of Fray Bentos bully beef was always greeted with great delight because it was the best brand, and also because bully beef was usually put directly into a stew with dried vegetables. The latter were quite a novelty; I had never seen them before and wondered what was in two heavy sandbags I carried up one night slung across my shoulder. They were full of varicoloured, small, hard pieces that swelled into larger pieces of vegetables when soaked by the cook.

We liked our tea strong, sergeant-majors, we called it, especially with condensed milk, also out of tins. Sometimes we had porridge, always known as berghu which was one of the

Indian names we picked up from the old soldiers who had served in India in the days when, as they so often said, soldiering WAS soldiering! Other Indian names also used were pozzi for jam, rooti for bread, char for tea and bundook for rifle.

If the company cook had found a sheltered spot, a cellar or a church crypt, he was able to get a good fire going, and sometimes he even produced a roast and veg, and very occasionally we had fried bacon. Then the cry was always "Any dip?" During our three months on active service we had adapted to the new way of life and were remarkably happy and cheerful considering the strange conditions. Life was sweet and we felt very alive; physically we were very fit and a few hours sleep (when possible) was enough. We no longer looked nor felt like the inexperienced boys we had been on arrival in this strange new world. It does not take long to mature in the trenches!

HYGIENE IN THE TRENCHES

We cleaned our knives and forks after use, by pushing them in and out of the earth, and wiping them on our puttees. Our sanitary man, always known as Gonga or Gunga, was Private W. D. Dean; his nickname was a pun on his surname, Dean, from Gunga Djinn and was typical of Lancashire wit. This special job of sanitary man was usually given to an old sweat who would dig a latrine behind the trench, usually enlarging or deepening a shell hole.

We had no water to wash with — none whatsoever! Sometimes we saved a little of our tea to shave, and there was often water in nearby shell holes, but this was not safe to use. There was a risk of mustard gas contamination, causing deep blisters. An old schoolfriend of mine, not in my battalion, was in hospital for months after washing his hands in a contaminated shell hole, and he bore the scars on the back of his hands for life. When very thirsty, I have drunk water from a clean puddle of rainwater, and then used some to shave. Water to drink in the trenches was always in very short supply and sometimes we were very thirsty indeed. If we were in a reserve trench we could sometimes get water from a village well. On one occasion I drank the water from a dead man's water-bottle. We were, however, strictly forbidden to drink the water in our own water-bottle. This was regarded as part of our iron rations, which included a tin of bully beef and some army biscuits. Our iron rations could be used only by permission of an officer.

Life in these primitive conditions had a peculiar quality; we were free of many things which affect life in the civilian world. Our world was stripped of unessentials; each man was complete in himself, his equipment, weapons and food were his responsibility. We could move at a moment's notice; everything was concentrated on the present moment; our past life was another world, our future could not be planned or foreseen. Small pleasures gave great satisfaction; a hot drink, a clean pair of socks or some clean rags in a parcel from home.

HUMOUR IN THE TRENCHES

"Hi! Gonga," someone would say. "Where have you dug it today?" or, if enemy shell fire made the place too dangerous to visit, "Gonga, can't you find a better hole?" Gonga had dark eyes in a pale thin face, a black Charles Chaplin moustache, and a natural gift for telling a good tale.

"Wai, lads, talking about a better 'ole, did I tell yer 'ow me and Algy took cover one day in the same shell 'ole?" (Algy, a bugler, and Gonga were mates.) "It wus a luvly shell 'ole, only jus' bin made by a German 'owitzer'. Algy, 'e wants, us to

144

move to 'nuther 'ole, and I said no, stop 'ere, it's a big 'ole, on'y jus' bin made, so what more d'ya want? Wa'l lads, jus' then, a shell thumped inter the side of our luvly 'ole....!" Gonga paused dramatically, and rolled his dark eyes at us... "it wus a DUD! Ther y'arr, I ses to Algy, NOW can yer find a better 'ole?"

On another occasion Gonga told us how... "I nearly got a 'blighty'.

"We wus advancing up this 'ere slope, and we comes under shell fire. The 'orficer, he ses — take cover, men! Ther waddn't nowhere to take cover. So,... what did I do, lads?" Gonga holds the suspense and rolls his dark eyes "Wai, I cuddent see no cover ... So, what did I do, fellers?" More eye rolling. "I jumped in among two or three other blokes for a bit of cover like... and then... Whang!... a bit of shrapnel 'it me in the arse, an' I made orf for the aid post."

Gonga was wounded several times and survived the war still telling his stories. He was a most unsoldierly figure; not the type one would pick for a ceremonial guard, but always reliable.

Two men who were inseparable were Carpenter and Fisher; the first time we boys went into the trenches, near Mesnil, Fisher was a prisoner. He had been sentenced to twenty-eight days field punishment — what the offence was I never knew — but his twenty-eight days FP did not preclude him being in the line with all of us. As soon as we were out of the line, Fisher was in custody again, serving his sentence. In July, Carpenter and Fisher were with me when we were digging a trench in no man's land near Albert; when we came under heavy shell fire they were quite unperturbed. In August, I found them fighting in the front line — this was very shortly after I had been appointed Battalion Gas NCO, and was inspecting gas masks.

"What on earth are you two doing?" I said. "Haven't we got enough fighting with Jerry only one hundred yards away? And anyway, I thought you two were buddies." Carpenter looked at me, blood streaming from his nose as he stood embracing Fisher, who had just butted him with his head as they clutched one another for a little friendly shin bashing. Mopping his bleeding nose, Carpenter said, "Nay, Corporal, we was only butting and shin paring for a bit of fun!" They both survived and after the Armistice I came across them again when I was going round the billets in Vergies one evening with the Orderly Officer. They were both very respectable then, having scrounged new uniforms and were in a posh billet; both being then officers' servants.

WAR SONGS

Some of the songs we sang when on the march to the trenches gave vent to our private feelings, so we always laughed as we sang one old favourite "I want to go Home. I want to go HOME! Don't want to go in the trenches no more, where there are whizzbangs and shrapnel galore. Take me over the sea, where the Allemande can't get at me! Oh my! I don't want to DIE. I wa'ant to go HOME!" Nostalgia or homesickness was expressed in many popular sentimental songs of that period. "The roses round the door make me love Mother more. I see my sister Flo, and folks I used to know."

Another favourite was "Roses of Picardy" with its sad haunting tune. Also "There's a long trail a'winding to the place of my dreams." And "Keep the home fires burning, where the hearts are yearning. Turn the dark clouds inside out, till we all come home."

Then our thoughts of the home which many of us would never see again were expressed in "When you're a long long way from home."

Another, sung to the hymn tune "What a Friend we have in Jesus," was "When this blinkin' War is OVER, OH! how HAPPY I shall be. When I get my 'civvy' clothes on THAT will be joy for me."

There were also songs that were semi-humorous and semi-bitter, such as — "We'd be far better off in a Home, we'd be far better off in a Home. We'd be far better off, far better off, far better off, in a HOME!" This we sang to the tune of a well-known hymn.

Then there was the bitter song which expressed our exasperation at any inexplicable military delay — sung to the tune of Old Lang Syne. "We're here because we're HERE, because we're here, because we're HERE." This went on ad infinitum, or until someone started another song which expressed the awful futility and hopelessness of this long drawn out war "If you want to find the Captain, I know where he IS, I know where he IS, I know where he IS. If you want to find the Captain, I know where he IS. He's hanging on the front line wire!" (or alternatively, on the old barbed wire!) "I know cause I've SEEN him, hanging on the old barbed wire." "I've SEEN him, he's hanging on the old barbed wire."

This song had many verses, we often sang it when we were marching. The verse about the Captain was followed by one about the SERGEANT, then the CORPORAL, then the PRIVATE, and even about the SANITARY MAN! (The one about dear old "Gonga" always made us laugh uproarously.)

Then there was a very witty song which we sang mournfully to the tune of "Nellie Deane."

147

"If the SERGEANT steals your RUM never
MIND!
"If the CORPORAL steals your FAGS, never
MIND!
"If the LANCE-JACK takes your JAM,
"He can't take your EGGS AND HAM!
"So be HAPPY once again, NEVER MIND!"

The very thought of the Lance-Jack stealing our EGGS
AND HAM, always sent us into fits of laughter at the very
IDEA of US ever HAVING eggs and ham which COULD be
stolen.

So we often followed this song with —

"Oh My! ain't it a lovely WAR!
We have plum and apple JAM!
Never BACON and EGGS or HAM!
Form fours! Right turn!
Think of all the money you earn!
Oh My! Ain't it a lovely WAR!"

RELIGION ON THE WESTERN FRONT

The compulsory church parades, which were a regular feature
of army life in England, could not take place on the Western
Front. Even in England, they were mainly of a military nature.
This involved lots of spit and polish, disciplined marching and
getting into position in a hollow square with the regimental
drums forming a central feature from which the service was
conducted.

I remember an occasion when thousands of us were
correctly paraded in the open air near the East Coast, and just
as the service commenced, several squadrons of "Gothas"
arrived overhead. These German planes regularly flew in from

the sea and dropped bombs on coastal towns. The noise of their engines drowned the voice of the chaplain, and the service was interrupted, while we all stood still in our ranks, dropping our heads down to our chests to reduce the chance of being spotted by the German planes.

On the Western Front, formal religion was in the hands of army chaplains, who wore officers' uniforms with a dog-collar. There were several varieties to suit the main British denominations. Most of us were Church of England and wore an identity disc on a string around the neck which gave our name, initials and C of E. Others were Baptists, Methodists or Congregationalists, or some other less numerous denomination. There were also some Roman Catholics.

Occasionally, the Church of England chaplain found an opportunity to conduct a Holy Communion service, and on one occasion I heard that there was to be one in a field behind the reserve line.

I was given permission to attend this service by my platoon officer, but only about a dozen men were interested enough to attend.

The subject of religion rarely cropped up in the trenches, but the ever-present nearness of death occasionally raised the question of what happens afterwards. We were so familiar with sudden death and so disciplined and hardened to it, that the usual philosophy prevailed. This was expressed by "If your number is on it you'll get it, and if it isn't, you won't."

As for the army chaplains, there was only one who visited us in the trenches. He was the Roman Catholic chaplain. He seemed to have genuine concern and interest, but as he passed along the trench he would ask "Are you one of mine?" The rest of us he passed by. I admired his courage and his devotion to his job in coming into the front line, for none of the others ever did. I would have welcomed a chat with him, and I suspect that I was not the only one who wondered if there was anything in religion.

What was the truth and how could one find it? Religion seemed to be basically real from what I remembered of what I had heard in church in dear old England, but it was obscured by forms and ceremonies, and I had never heard anyone speak plainly and convincingly about it. Here on the Western Front, the subject was evaded by our army chaplains who joked with us and sometimes passed round a packet of cigarettes. Here were thousands of men, living on the edge of sudden death, our perceptions very sharp, experiencing life and death in stark reality. Largely untaught in religious matters, we were unable to even define let alone express our secret longings.

The scenes of war, then so familiar to us, were very real in one sense, but I also felt that they were artificial. I was conscious that Nature was basically unaffected by the war, though violently disturbed by it for four long years. Despite the man-made desolation, crimson poppies still grew in vivid clumps on trench sides and parapets; wild flowers persisted in shattered woods; larks still soared and sang high in a blue sky, and beautiful white clouds floated majestically over the battle front.

It sometimes seemed as if "life was merely a play", as Shakespeare said — "each man in his time, playing many parts." All of us had already played a part in several normal scenes of life; first, our childhood, now a memory; then adolescence, growing up in wartime Britain. A few had played a short part in Scene 3, a wife and kids, but NOW we ALL had to play our part in THIS GREAT SCENE, which could have appropriately been "billed" as ....

WAR ON THE WESTERN FRONT, now in its 4th YEAR.

What would be the NEXT scene? As one brave wag said, when his battalion went over the top... "THIS way, chaps,... to ETERNITY."

What a setting for religious revival there was in the First World War! If the TRUTH had been told by our army chaplains, they might have reaped a great harvest from the ploughed soil of our abnormal lives on the Western Front, while our perception of life and death was so keen, and our need to know and our hunger for the TRUTH was so URGENT.

Twenty-five years passed before I heard and believed the TRUTH about Jesus Christ... about the real meaning of the Cross... about sin and about salvation by repentance towards God and faith in the Lord Jesus Christ, and received Him as my own personal Saviour and Lord.

Now, in spite of the passage of more than seventy years, I still have many enduring memories of the Western Front, its muddy trenches, twisting and turning endlessly; the millions of sandbags, many rotting with age, some new; the slippery duckboards and the damp dug-outs; the barbed wire in no man's land.

These memories of days and nights on the Western Front are still fresh, and sometimes vivid scenes and sounds flash through the mind like a kaleidoscope. Stand-to at dawn, how cold it was; is there going to be a rum ration? Cleaning my rifle for a platoon officer's inspection; will it pass?

A sudden rush of whizz-bangs, cordite fumes stinging the eyes and throat. Blimey! THEY were a bit close! Anybody hit? Then a cry for stretcher-bearers... Two dead and three wounded...who are they?

When I am alone, perhaps shaving or waiting for a kettle to boil, other haunting memories come unbidden, and suddenly I think of names and faces of boys long dead, and sometimes I think sadly about the vital matter of Religion on the Western Front.

SHRAPNEL

On 16th July, we were moved to a reserve trench near to Senlis, and employed on the improvement of some old unused trenches which had obviously not been occupied for some considerable time. The weather was sunny and very warm and we worked in our shirt-sleeves as we deepened the old shallow grass grown trenches. We seemed to be in a position where the enemy could not observe our every movement, which was a pleasant change.

However, one afternoon we came under fire in a way which was unusual, at any rate, to the boys. The lazy summer silence was suddenly broken by explosions high in the sky above us.

Looking up, we saw groups of black dots which looked quite harmless as they expanded into dirty-green and white spirals of smoke. It was quite fascinating to watch these coiling clouds of green and white smoke high in the sky above us, but it quickly became apparent that WE were the target. We took what cover there was as pieces of jagged, hot metal darted and hissed through the air and then thumped into the ground. As someone said when it was all over "Well, it makes a CHANGE, after whizz-bangs, Five-point-nines and Jerry's Trench Mortars!"

LABOURING FOR THE REs

On 18th July, my nineteenth birthday, "A" Company was moved again, this time to some bivouacs dug into a bank along the road just outside Englebelmer. Here we were employed as labourers to a number of Royal Engineers who were digging deep into the chalk of a hill and constructing a strong point overlooking the Ancre valley. The company was divided into three shifts, each working 8 hours (from 6 a.m. to 2 p.m., 2 p.m. to 10 p.m. and 10 p.m. to 6 a.m.). I was on the afternoon shift, 2 p.m. to 10 p.m. Our task was to work in the shafts and tunnels, filling sandbags with the chalk which the engineers hewed out with their miners' picks, and to fetch and carry the sawn timber which they fitted into place as the work proceeded. The RE workings and the track leading to them were periodically shelled by large calibre howitzer batteries directed by the German artillery observers in their captive balloons. There were three or four entrances to this strong point, one of which was a vertical shaft intended for machine-guns on a lift! During the week I was working there, several of the entrances had near misses, and one was blown in by a direct hit.

This area had been well behind the front until the German spring offensive, and the fields had been tilled and sown and the corn was standing high. The enemy was able to observe some parts of this area and so the engineers had hung large camouflage nets on the trees and on tall poles along the Englebelmer-Martinsart road near our bivouacs. After our experiences in the trenches in front of Mesnil and Auchonvillers and Bouzincourt, we found life comparatively pleasant here with eight hours work, eight hours sleep, a luxury indeed; and eight hours free, except for the usual fatigues of fetching water and our rations.

A FALSE SENSE OF SECURITY

On our way from the bivouacs to the RE workings we walked along the road, where we were hidden from enemy observation by the brown-green camouflage netting. Then we dropped into a trench for about 150 yards, and then crossed several fields which were not under enemy observation, being in "dead" ground.

Several times as I crossed these fields to commence an afternoon shift, I was deceived by the apparent innocence of the summer scene. One afternoon I was on my way, alone, to start work; I was thoroughly enjoying this break from the trenches; having regular food, and sleep in the bivouacs near to Englebelmer. The day was hot, the grass knee-high along the track across the fields to the RE workings. The sun was shining and the bees were humming as they dawdled among the red poppies and other wild flowers along this grassy path. Like the larks singing high in the blue sky, I thought, they are not affected by the war, so they hum and dawdle among the wild flowers.

This vivid experience of nature in its simple summer beauty was like a sudden glimpse of my childhood in my parents' garden; it was a swift moment of vision, of normality seen retrospectively through the ugliness of war all around me. I was lulled into a false sense of security, and tempted to loiter along this pleasant grassy path, until, I came to four huge howitzer craters, freshly made, and got a whiff of lyddite on the summer air — it was the familiar smell of death, and I hurried on and was soon humping chalk into sandbags. The German observation balloons were not up there in the summer sky for nothing.

PROMOTION

On 24th July, I was told by my new platoon officer, 2nd Lieut. Robinson, whom I scarcely knew, to report to battalion headquarters. This was in the opposite direction to the route to the engineer workings. I reached it by climbing up a steep bank opposite our bivouacs on to a field which was bearing a good crop of wheat, following a path along the side of the field which led to another wheat field which sloped downhill to the Bouzincourt-Hedauville road not far from Senlis. BHQ occupied a long row of dug-outs along the bank which I descended from the second wheat field.

I reported to the regimental sergeant-major and he took me to the adjutant's office in one of the dug-outs where the battalion orderly room sergeant worked at his papers on a large packing case. The adjutant, Captain Milne, told me that the Vth Corps Gas School's report on me was by far the best of any others who had attended the Gas Course. He therefore proposed to make me up to full corporal and to appoint me battalion gas NCO. "By the way," he said, "are you nineteen yet?"

"Yes, sir," I replied, "I was nineteen last week."

I returned to my bivouac and told Second Lieut. Robinson of my appointment, and then collected my kit. I had no special friends in the platoon, having been in it for only a short time following my return from the Gas Course, and finding that my old platoon had been virtually wiped out during my absence. In any case one third of the platoon was asleep after a night shift, and another third was at work at the RE workings, so I left with few goodbyes.

On my return to BHQ, I was closely questioned by the RSM as to my military history, qualifications and aptitudes. He then told me to get the sergeant tailor to sew on my corporal's stripes, and the following day Lieut. Smith, MC, the intelligence officer, gave me a pair of green and black epaulettes to put on my shoulder straps, signifying that I was the battalion gas NCO.

Other specialists at BHQ, also wore coloured epaulettes; Sergeant Webb and his team of signallers wore blue epaulettes; Sergeant Swift and about half a dozen men who were observers, wore green epaulettes, and Corporal Butler and about a dozen runners wore red epaulettes.

My promotion and appointment was almost a surprise. The weeks since I returned to the front from the Gas Course had been so full of incident that I had forgotten the promise of a good report from the Colonel at the Gas School. Possibly no action had been taken about my promotion until I had become nineteen.

NEW FRIENDS

During service in the armed forces in wartime, one is inevitably a mere cypher; a pawn that can be moved at any time by the powers that be; powers that are usually quite impersonal.

During my service I seemed to be doomed to a constant and progressive isolation from my friends and the various companions with whom I served. First, I had planned to join the Army with two friends of my own age, Bumper Wells and Bert Chapman, who both became eighteen years of age in June 1917. As I was to be eighteen on 18th July, I had anticipated my call-up and reported with them, but this little plan to be the Three Musketeers was soon spoiled. At the end of all the form filling and the signing, we were separated; Chapman being drafted to a training camp at Luton, and Bumper and I to one at Dovercourt on the east coast. We did not see Chapman again until the war was over. Then, after some months of general training, Bumper and I were separated; I was posted to a divisional signal school to train as a signaller, and Bumper was sent on a physical training course, and eventually became a lance-corporal with the battalion PT instructors.

I was sent out to the Western Front during the German spring offensive, and Bumper remained in England until August and soon returned to England with a bullet in his thigh. When I arrived at the base camp at Calais with about a thousand other boys, we were arbitrarily split up into groups of 200-300, or whatever number was required to fill the gaps in various battalions.

Later, there was another split of those of us who were drafted into the Lancashire Fusiliers, some of the 10th Battalion being suddenly sent to the 17th Battalion.

Then I was sent out of the line to a Gas Course and while I was away my No. 2 Platoon was virtually wiped out. On my return I was put into No. 4 Platoon. Now I was suddenly an NCO at BHQ where everything and everyone was new to me. I soon found, however, that there was a very good spirit among the NCOs at BHQ principally because we were all specialists in our own line, and were trusted by our officers to carry out various duties without supervision.

I quickly found new friends among these NCOs, especially Corporal Wilkinson and Corporal Thomas, both of whom had been in France for several years. Corporal Wilkinson was the NCO in charge of the linesmen signallers, and was responsible for keeping the telephone wires intact to the four companies and to brigade HQ. He risked his life many times when repairing the broken wires under shell fire in the open, and was killed at Neuvilly in October. Corporal Thomas, the pioneer corporal, was many years older than me, but we always shared rations and usually shared the same dug-out or bivouac. He won the DCM a few weeks later. Corporal Thomas, who had taken part in the fighting withdrawal from Havrincourt — 21st March until 2nd April — always insisted on having at least one day's rations in hand, and these he kept in a clean sandbag. He used to say "Never take it for granted that the rations will reach us now that the front is on the move." When I was with him during our advance from August 8th to November 11th, he always remembered the old trenches, dug-outs, etc., and where possible we used them.

Other new friends were Sergeant Swift, the observer sergeant, from whom I soon took over the extra duties of orderly sergeant, and Sergeant Parr and Corporal Butler. These had also been on active service for several years, and had survived many battles. Sergeant Parr, a very good soldier and an attractive personality, was in charge of the machine-guns at this time, and was killed soon after his promotion to company sergeant-major of B Company.

Corporal Butler, who was in charge of the BHQ runners, often accompanied one of them, they always worked in pairs, when they were taking messages to the companies. He was badly wounded in the arm a few weeks later, and went down the line, so I did not get to know him very well.

As the battalion gas NCO, I had no men permanently under my orders, and when I posted gas sentries or required men to carry out other duties given to me, I borrowed men from the other NCOs. Sergeant Webb lent me signallers, Corporal Thomas, pioneers, Sergeant Parr, machine-gunners and Sergeant Grendon, the provost sergeant, lent me regimental police.

The regimental police were all experienced soldiers; some wore several wound stripes and three or four blue chevrons on the cuff of their sleeve, indicating various periods of active service. I found it convenient to use them as gas sentries, mainly because they were often free from other duties.

I quickly adapted to my various duties and responsibilities, but nevertheless when I made my first tour round the four companies to examine the gas masks of all the officers, NCOs and men, I could not help thinking "Can this really be me?" Sergeant Brown, MM, who had been posted to Brigade HQ as brigade gas NCO, and whose job at battalion HQ I had just taken over, came with me on my first inspection of the battalion's gas masks. He told me always to ask the permission of the company commander, and to ask him for one of the junior officers to accompany me on the inspection.

I took my responsibilities very seriously, but I also enjoyed my new freedom. As a private in a platoon one is under constant supervision and closely defined orders. In the trenches the routine is two hours on the fire-step as sentry, four hours on other duties, and so on through the days and nights until moved to another sector. When one moved through trenches and along tracks, it was always under the command of an NCO or an officer. Now, in my new job, my duties extended along the whole of the battalion front. I was responsible as battalion gas NCO only to the brigade gas NCO and also occasionally to the divisional gas officer.

The day after I was appointed, the Germans shelled BHQ for about half an hour with gas shells. I shouted to the gas sentry to sound the gas alarm, which consisted of beating an old brass shellcase hanging for this purpose. During this attack, many shells burst on or near the long bank of earth in which the HQ dug-outs were situated, and I heard one in particular thud into the bank close to me. It did not explode, and when the bombardment ceased and we were able to take off our masks, I searched for this dud shell. I found a round hole about four to five inches in diameter in the earth roof of my dug-out, marked it, and later in the day when Sergeant Brown came to BHQ I showed it to him and suggested that we dig it out for identification of the type of gas the Germans were now using. He was impressed by my keenness and congratulated me on my observation and sent a report of my suggestion to the divisional gas officer.

THE STROMBUS HORN

As far as I know, no action was taken about my suggestion, but not long afterwards the divisional gas officer came up to battalion HQ perhaps he wanted to see his new gas NCO. He brought me a strombus horn and a cylinder of compressed air and told me to have them placed in Bracken Trench at a certain map reference, and to give the troops there instructions for its use. He also gave me a trench map of the battalion front, from which I was very surprised to see that divisional HQ had our trenches, and all those known to be occupied by the enemy, marked on maps! I knew, in theory, that the generals must have such maps, but I never thought that I would see one, and still less, that I would be given one.

The strombus horn and cylinder with red rubber tubing were in a heavy wooden box with rope handles through which was inserted a very stout pole. It was a clumsy apparatus about one foot square at the top and three feet from top to bottom. I detailed two of the regimental police, Braithwaite and Whittle, to lift the pole on their shoulders with the heavy box hanging between them, and I led the way, with my map, to Bracken Trench — or so I thought! The DGO had clearly pointed out the trench to me — on the map, but unfortunately no one in the trenches had ever heard of Bracken Trench!

Both my men were old soldiers and they sweated and swore as they plodded along the narrow winding trenches, and suggested more than once that we dump the —— thing and give up looking for Bracken Trench. Eventually, after a very unpleasant few minutes under fire from whizz-bangs, I agreed with them. In our search for Bracken Trench we were evidently spotted by the German artillery observers as we moved along a trench on higher ground and became visible for a few moments through their field-glasses.

Whizz-bangs, the German high velocity shells have an instantaneous fuse, and they always seem to arrive, as someone wittily remarked, before they get here! Whizz-whizz-whizz-bang-bang-bang, as they explode in a close pattern of three or four at a time, repeated very quickly. Whizz-whizz-whizz-whizz-bang-bang-bang-bang, as the howl of the shells coincided with the whizz of the flying pieces of hot metal. One has less warning than when one is sitting in an express train and another suddenly flashes past in the opposite direction. By the time the noisy crash and clatter is heard, it is too late to take cover or even think of doing so. One is either already a casualty, or once again has miraculously escaped death or injury, as on this occasion.

So we hurriedly retreated from the high ground to a Lewis gun post, where we left the clumsy contraption with Lance-Corporal Unsworth, an old A Company friend, who said "Thou canst leave it theere on't fire-step, if tha minds, Corporal." I gave him the same instructions I had received about its use, and I very gladly "left it there", and I never heard of it or Bracken Trench again.

Incidentally, I had been taught at the Vth Corps Gas School that the strombus horn was to be used only for a cloud gas attack, and that this form of gas attack had long since been replaced by gas shells.

As I led my little party back to BHQ, we passed through some trenches where other sections of A Company were occupying some dug-outs. Recognising some boys who had been with me in our training days in England, I stayed for a few minutes talking and exchanging news of who had been killed, or who had "got a Blighty". To my great surprise, one section told me that their section leader was Lance-Corporal (Basher) Gordon. I asked how they fared with him, and learned that he was still the same old Basher, but now unfortunately for them, he was using his authority to pinch their rations! I reflected that the old saying is very true "The leopard cannot change his spots".

FURTHER RESPONSIBILITIES

A week after my promotion to "full corporal" and appointment to battalion gas NCO, I was told to take over from Sergeant Swift the duties of Orderly Sergeant of the Headquarter Company. These were duties performed in every company by a sergeant or a full corporal. Lieutenant Smith gave me an army notebook and a pencil, and every week I had to hand in a statement of trench strength at the battalion orderly room. This meant counting heads and stating on a form how many signallers, runners, observers, machine-gunners, pioneers, regimental police, clerks, cobblers and tailors, officers' servants, cooks and others there were.

Orderly sergeants always wore their "belt and bayonet" when on duty, and I found it to be such a bother to be constantly detaching one's belt and bayonet from the remainder of one's equipment that I took the first opportunity to acquire another belt and bayonet from one of the casualties.

I quickly got to know everyone in the headquarter's company because I was constantly warning men for various duties, either as the battalion gas NCO, or as the orderly sergeant. I had to arrange a rota of gas sentries day and night, detail men for ration parties, and once, while we were occupying these dug-outs, I had to march some men to a bath house. I began to wonder as time went on if there was any limit to my many duties since the adjutant, the intelligence officer, the RSM, and even the transport officer on one occasion, gave me jobs to do. However, all this was valuable experience and training for me in readiness for the big British Offensive which began a few weeks later.

PREPARATIONS TO RELIEVE THE RND

On 29th July, Lieut. Smith took me with him to make arrangements for the 10th (Service) Battalion, Lancashire Fusiliers to take over a section of the front from the Hood Battalion of the RND (Royal Naval Division). We went to a part of the front I had not seen before, on the left of the positions we had occupied in front of Mesnil.

On my first tour of the line in April near Mesnil, the trenches had been poor, with no communication trenches and the front had little depth. Now, at Hamel, from where in a few weeks we were to go over the top at the start of the "Big Push", the trench system was much greater in depth and well constructed.

Lieut. Smith led the way as we entered trenches a long way from the front line, and we made our way tortuously through communication trenches to some very deep dug-outs or saps near the Albert-Arras railway line.

We descended into one of these saps and explored it by the light of an electric torch, which was quite a novelty in those days. Like the sap that the Germans raided in May at Auchonvillers, it was damp, very cold and inhospitable. I think Lieut. Smith was looking for suitable dug-outs for the HQ staff, such as the colonel, adjutant, signals, runners, etc., but these deep cold dug-outs were unsuitable We went through more trenches, and while Lieut. Smith went into HQ dug-out of the Hood Battalion, I found the battalion gas NCO. He was very friendly, brewed up some tea and promised to leave his small stock of anti-gas material for me.

We could never have a large stock of anti-gas material, but I found that if after the shelling ceased we were troubled by gas because some of the gas shell holes needed treatment, I could sometimes get chloride of lime from our horse lines. These were usually several miles behind the front. On one occasion I borrowed an army bicycle from the signallers; it was a very heavy machine, painted green and with very strong broad tyres. I cycled back to our horse lines in daylight, on rough tracks to the wood where the wagons and horses were.

Part of the way was hidden from enemy observation by trees and camouflage netting, and where there was no cover I peddled as fast as the heavy machine would permit. I returned with half a sackful of chloride of lime and taking with me a man with a shovel, I treated three or four shell holes and he covered them with soil. However, there were many occasions when it was impossible to leave the trenches and cycle back to the horse lines; it would have been here at Hamel owing to the depth of the front.

Lieut. Smith and I returned to BHQ and preparations began for our next move, which involved me in many duties as orderly sergeant. However, I was enjoying my responsibilities and the friendly relationship with Lieut. Smith, who often described me as "my corporal". He took me with him on many other occasions and I learned a great deal through carrying out his orders. On one occasion when we were visiting another battalion's HQ he came out of the HQ dug-out and told me that they had been having a pretty thin time here. "So" he said, "if Jerry tries to get rough with us, we must be ready for him!" We had seen some boxes of Mills bombs in a dump at the far end of a sunken lane we had come through, and he told me to get them distributed. He said, "As soon as we have taken over these trenches tomorrow night, you will collect a party of men and fetch enough of these boxes of Mills bombs to supply every section."

NAVAL CONDITIONS

In the dusk of the next evening the relief began during heavy rain. There had been several heavy storms during the previous week, and some of the forward trenches were two feet deep in water; even deeper where the ground dipped down the Ancre valley. As the relief proceeded, Lancashire Fusiliers met Royal Naval Division men in a long communication trench that was more than knee-deep in muddy water which was becoming quite "soupy" as more soil was brushed off the trench sides by so many men passing each other.

One of the RND officers, a sub-lieutenant, called out to his men — "Pass the word back for Petty Officer Jones to come forward." Immediately, one of our Lancashire wits said "E'eh, la'ads, if THIS is sta'ate of yon trenches we're meking for, WE could do wi'some BOS'NS". Someone else said — "And we could mik use of a bluddy 'arbour master." These remarks, of course, caused roars of laughter, and as we swished our way past one another, one of the RND ratings capped everything by saying — "It's enough to make YOU lads wish you hadn't volunteered to go to SEA."

Whenever we met the Royal Naval Division I was always impressed by their discipline and high morale and interested too in these sailor-soldiers who retained naval ranks and customs. Their six battalions had fought in the March battles during the retirement and when they were cut off from all communication with their divisional HQ, they had fought their way back.

THE ORIGIN OF THE ROYAL NAVAL DIVISION

The origin and the formation of the RND is very interesting, and also its long connection with the XXth The Lancashire Fusiliers.

At the outbreak of war in 1914, the British fleet was already mobilised and at sea on manoeuvres, but there was a vast surplus of naval reservists which could not immediately be used at sea. Also Kitchener's call for recruits for the Army resulted in many more men volunteering than could be used immediately in military units.

To use this great surplus of naval reservists and the recruits who had volunteered to join Kitchener's New Army, the Royal Naval Division came into being with battalions named after famous admirals of the past — ANSON, BENBOW, COLLINGWOOD, DRAKE, HAWKE, HOOD, HOWE, and NELSON.

A depot was formed at the Crystal Palace, where the young volunteers were trained, and soon attracted tens of thousands of men. A number of my schoolfriends joined the RND at Crystal Palace, where naval parlance was used on every possible occasion.

The white ensign flew, bells recorded the passage of time, men requested leave to go ashore and when they returned, they came aboard, and if they did not return on time, they were reported not as missing but adrift. Young men from civil life, many of whom had never been to sea, quickly adopted all these naval terms and ceremonies, and the great traditions of the Royal Navy became the mainspring of their exceptionally high standards.

When in 1916, the Royal Naval Division went to the Western Front, the battalion names were retained, as were the naval ranks and customs. All ranks wore khaki, but Royal Navy badges were worn on the caps of the officers and chief petty officers, and khaki naval rings of rank, with the curl, were worn on the sleeve.

Platoons were commanded by sub-lieutenants and companies by lieutenant-commanders, and the non-commissioned officers held the rank of petty officer or chief petty officer. Ratings wore gaiters, not puttees, a black naval ribbon on the cap, inscribed in gold Royal Naval Division.

The link between the Royal Navy and the XXth of Foot, The Lancashire Fusiliers, is reforged every year at the Gallipoli Celebrations which commemorate the anniversary of the Lancashire Landings at Gallipoli in 1915. Two midshipmen of the Royal Navy commanded the pinnaces from the cruiser *Euryalus* which led the landing craft which took the Lancashire Fusiliers to the beach at Cape Helles on 25th April 1915.

The Lancashire Fusiliers won six VCs that day before breakfast and the two young midshipmen won the Distinguished Service Cross.

The Royal Naval Division also fought in the Dardanelles Campaign with great valour and suffered great losses. From 1916 onwards the RND fought on the Western Front, and now in 1918, the 52nd Brigade, of which the 10th Battalion of the Lancashire Fusiliers formed a part with the 12th Battalion of the Manchesters and the 9th Battalion of the Duke of Wellingtons, regularly relieved the battalions of a brigade of the Royal Naval Division on the Somme.

RAIN AND STILL MORE RAIN

On this occasion, when we relieved the Hood Battalion at Hamel, some of the BHQ staff occupied some very aged dug-outs in the bank of the Albert-Arras railway embankment.

These dug-outs were preferable to the waterlogged trenches where the four companies were. I shared a very small hole dug into the earth of the embankment with a regimental policeman named Widdowson; he was about thirty-five years of age, which I thought was old!

We squatted in the hole, staring out at the rain-drenched landscape; a typical wet day in late July with no hope of any change. About five feet from us, and a foot or two below us, there was an old cart track filled with muddy rainwater. Beyond there was a group of 1916 graves among the shell holes, old and new. Was it possible, I thought, that we were fighting in the same war in which they had died? As for 1914, when the war had commenced, that seemed an age ago, for then I was at school, aged fifteen. Now, only four years later, I felt ten years older.

FIVE POINT NINES

As I sat musing, a 5.9 shell roared down very close to us, and burst with a loud crash just beyond the graves on the other side of the field track. Widdowson, who had been in France for over three years, was quite unconcerned. He had survived several wounds and many battles, including the appalling winter conditions at Ypres and Passchendaele. He regarded a tour on the Somme battlefront as greatly preferable, despite its grim record of unceasing casualties since 1st July 1916.

By this stage of the war, the Line had acquired its own history, and the small minority of men in the battalion who had fought in some of the great battles of 1915, 1916 and 1917 spoke of those days AS history. "When we were in the old front line", they would say, meaning before our big Somme Offensive in 1916. Or, they would say, "Oh that was before Jerry pulled back to the Hindenburg Line in March, 1917" or,

"When we came back the first time from Ypres to the Somme."

To us, the young soldiers of 1918, whose task it was to finish the war, those old days were indeed simply history. I had read the newspaper accounts of these old battles; I was familiar with all the famous place names, and now here I was on the very spot where some of those old battles had taken place.

Now, they told us, WE were going to finish it. The thinly held Line of General Gough's 5th Army of 21st March was now heavily reinforced. We had held and contained that great attack, despite our heavy losses, and NOW, the tide was about to turn.

Widdowson was sitting behind me in our cramped quarters, and he casually said "Better pull your legs in, Corporal, you might need 'em yet."

German 5.9s are noisy brutes, but usually they can be heard coming with an ever increasing roar which reaches a crescendo that hurts the ear drums. Then they explode with an earthquaking stunning thump. For about ten minutes they continued to whine and growl over us before bursting with violent crashes in the sodden field. Those which were very close to us like the first one, roared down with a terrifying crescendo of noise and thumped into the ground with tremendous force, scattering deadly pieces of jagged metal.

Despite their destructive power, most of us preferred them to the German 77mm Whizz-bang, which arrived, three or four at a time, with no warning except the final rush, and then exploded like giant firecrackers into slivers of steel which sighed and screamed through the air. Sometimes the nosecap would buzz past like an angry bee. When the shelling ceased, Widdowson brewed up some tea on a Tommy Cooker, a very primitive heater consisting of a small tin, about the size of a

Nestles milk tin, full of solidified fat from the cookhouse. When the fat eventually ignited, it would, after an age, boil some water in a billy can, and then tea and sugar was thrown in.

SUMP HOLES

Before going on my rounds of the waterlogged trenches to warn men for duty as gas sentries, I wrapped strips of an old groundsheet round my legs from boot to thigh in a rather vain attempt to keep dry.

The Royal Naval Division had made valiant efforts to drain away the rainwater by digging sump holes in the sides of the trench bottoms, into which one's leg sometimes slid when wading along the trenches.

I eventually despaired of keeping my legs dry, and concentrated on holding up my tunic pockets where the water was deeper. After returning to the railway embankment I stripped off the strips of groundsheet, removed my puttees and squeezed the water from my trousers.

AN AERIAL DOGFIGHT

On 4th August, the fourth anniversary of the outbreak of war, the weather changed, and we were pleased to be able to sit outside our primitive dug-outs, and dry in the warm sunshine. A British reconnaissance plane flew overhead returning from a trip over enemy lines. As it droned over us, we suddenly heard machine-gun fire, and saw a German fighter plane circling, diving and firing at the British plane.

The German plane was more manoeuvrable than the slower British plane, which clumsily dived and attempted to loop in its efforts to escape the machine-gun bullets. In two or three minutes it was all over; the British plane crashed about one hundred yards from us. Half a dozen men ran out to it, hoping to find the pilot and/or the observer alive, but they returned shaking their heads. Later, an RAF lorry arrived for the bodies.

A SURPRISE RELIEF

We were very surprised to be relieved during the night of August 4th-5th, and pulled back to Forceville. Obviously, something unusual was in the wind, since we had been in the line only a week. We were pleased to get back to dry land again, after our experience of "naval" conditions.

OPEN WARFARE, AUGUST TO NOVEMBER 1918

(The Final British Offensive)

ADVANCE PARTY

During the afternoon of August 5th, I was detailed for an advance party, consisting of one officer and five NCOs, one from each of the four companies, A, B, C and D, and myself from the battalion HQ company. When we had all assembled at BHQ and the officer had been briefed by the adjutant, the little party of six set off, marching along various field tracks behind the front.

We marched about twenty-five miles south, from Forceville to Fouilly near Villers-Bretonneux. (Villers-Bretonneux had been recaptured on 24th April in a night counter-attack by Australian and British troops during the big German Offensive, thus saving Amiens only ten miles to the west.)

We did not know where we were going, or why. Actually we were on our way to take part in the Battle of Amiens, which was to be *the turning point* in this long war.

Neither did we know that this great battle was to begin on August 8th, a day which the German General Ludendorff called the Black Day of the German Army. Secretly, the British 4th Army of 100,000 men and 534 new Mark V Tanks, under General Sir Henry Rawlinson, had been preparing since June.

Now, with the Australian Corps of 5 Divisions and the Canadian Corps of 4 Divisions, this powerful force was poised for an attack on a forty mile front. This great British advance, which came to be known as The Big Push, was finally to defeat the German Army and to end the war in three months! Little dreaming that this was possible, we slogged along in the summer heat, and as we marched, men in dugouts and bivouacs along our route were very curious. They wanted to know where this little party of one Lancashire Fusilier officer and five NCOs was bound.

Anything out of the ordinary always attracted attention, and rumours quickly grew and spread if there was an inkling of what was on. We could tell them nothing; no one knew anything yet about the coming British offensive. Our sense grew that something big was about to happen because there was evidence of strict security. The mounted military police were much in evidence on the 6th and 7th. I remembered Pearson's warning "Never get mixed up with them blokes, keep well clear of them." When we came to Heilly there was an Expeditionary Force Canteen with a crowd of men round it. When we tried to approach we were stopped by the MMPs and prevented from even speaking to the New Zealanders crowding round it.

This was the first time I had seen the New Zealand men, and I was surprised that some were black, and learned they were Maoris. Others were very darked skinned — half Maori; in fact I don't remember seeing a New Zealand soldier with fair hair.

The Anzacs (Australian and New Zealand Army Corps), had been secretly moved south for their historic attack on August 8th, and we were being moved south to mop up.

Mopping up is necessary to prevent the enemy emerging from dugouts behind our advancing troops and attacking them from the rear. There was also a need to ensure that enemy wounded were disarmed, cases having occurred when they too fired on troops who had passed by them. There was one tough and very experienced officer of whom it was said that he never left any wounded enemy soldiers behind him.

During this long march we passed through Senlis, Henecourt, Heilly, Bonnay and Corbie to Fouilly, and en route it was our job to find billets for the rest of the battalion, which was on the march in columns of four, three or four hours behind us. This was the first of my many experiences as a member of an advance party. On such occasions one is sometimes able to lead one's company to barns or deserted factories, but more often we had nothing to offer but a stubble field or a wood.

FIGHTING ORDER

By this stage of the war, the infantry had been relieved of their heavy packs, and had adopted fighting order or battledress. This was a skeleton order equipment; belt and braces with haversack on the back in place of the valise or pack; rolled groundsheet, entrenching tool, water-bottle; gas mask worn on the chest in the alert position; steel helmet, rifle and bayonet; 120 rounds of SA ammunition; Mills bomb in each breast pocket, and more in a spare haversack if desired.

The haversack held a mess tin, towel and shaving kit, extra socks, iron rations (tin of bully beef and army biscuits) and any personal items. Other odds and ends such as picks and shovels, flares, SOS rockets, two gallon petrol tins filled with water, emergency rations (not to be touched until authorized by an officer), were frequently distributed among a platoon of men.

Assigning these extra items was one of the more unpopular jobs, which as an NCO, I had to do. Stretcher-bearers carried a rolled stretcher in lieu of a rifle and wore an armlet marked SB. Signallers carried heavy signalling equipment, reels of telephone wire, buzzers, carrier pigeons in a basket and aircraft signals (strips of coloured cloth which could be laid out on the ground for various reasons). Lewis gun teams carried their gun and many heavy panniers full of ammo. We had now been stripped to the bare essentials of an infantryman on the move and ready for action. We remained so until the end of the war.

CAPTURED GERMAN POSITIONS

Still in ignorance of what was to happen, we saw ourselves as a Flying Column soon to be thrust into action. We certainly had no idea of the impending big British offensive, nor that it would change the whole character of the war as the infantryman had known it for four long years of trench warfare.

On August 9th we followed the Aussies, mopping up over the ground they had just captured. We were amazed and thrilled at the depth of the penetration, five miles deep in the German line. This had previously been unheard of. When eventually we came to some German field guns, we swarmed round them, laughing and talking excitedly to one another. Scrawled on them in white chalk were the words "Captured by the 1st AIF" (Australian Imperial Force). We were delighted and said "Good old Aussies!"

Further on we came to an area which had obviously been well in the rear of the German front line before the attack. We came to a German position where there were well-equipped dug-outs which had been hastily abandoned. Corporal Thomas and I made the mistake of sleeping part of a night in one which smelt of cigar smoke. There were jokes about millionaire's battalions, in which everyone smoked cigars, but after using the blankets and gray overcoats they had left behind, Thomas and I fervently wished we had slept elsewhere — we were lousy!

When Corporal Wilkinson heard of our state, with his irrepressible wit, he said that, being German lice they had probably been specially trained to bite the British. This was typical of his Lancashire wit.

Following up the Australian advance, and seeing many German dead, we came to Morcourt, where there was a large railway depot. Here, in the long sidings, the retreating Germans had set fire to a huge dump of coal. This was an immediate challenge to about a dozen of our older men who had been coal miners in civil life. They set to work enthusiastically, without orders, to try to dig through this very long bank of precious coal, and prevent the fire from consuming it all.

They worked very hard and shifted a large quantity, but the task proved too big. When Jerry started shelling the sidings with Blue Cross gas, I ordered everyone to wear their gas masks. As usual, this was not popular, but those who ignored the order were soon coughing and sneezing and some were retching with streaming eyes.

After the attack, I examined the masks of some of the men and found several that were defective because of a torn rubber face piece or a rusting canister. I wrote "Condemned" on the label in the satchel, signed it and told them to obtain a new gas mask at the very first opportunity.

The next day, some of us had a swim, naked, in the Somme at Mericourt-sur-Somme. Later, at Chuignolles, we crossed another railway line from which the Germans had shelled Paris with their long-range Big Bertha gun, which was mounted on a very strong platform on wheels, which ran along the railway line.

After this we met face to face a battalion of Australian troops coming out of the line as British troops took over the advance. I saw that some of them had German spiked helmets (Pickel-Haubes) slung on their arms.

Meeting these tough mature men, their tanned leathery faces grinning as they exchanged jokes with us in passing, made the Byng Boys realise that we were still comparatively young and inexperienced. However, we were very soon to have the experience of going over the top time and time again and becoming mature. There were other occasions when we young British boys came into contact, briefly with the Australians and realized that they were from a very different mould than the average British Tommy. They were all volunteers, proud, independent, very outspoken, physically strong and tough, and very aggressive in battle.

By our British conventions, they were totally uninhibited, having grown up in a society unhampered by a class system. Army regulations, and especially saluting officers were irksome to them, and they often expressed contempt for the British Tommy's rigid respect for officers. "None of your 'Tommy' officers for us, they boasted, we pick our own — the best soldiers from the ranks."

I sat near a noisy group of Aussies one day listening to their backchat with one another; they were always cracking jokes and laughing; they were very witty. I was surprised to see that their colonel was one of them, in all but rank; they chatted and laughed with him quite informally, calling him Dick. One of them in reply to his remark, said, "OK Digger, you win!" As the group of men broke up, still cracking jokes, their colonel, a lean tanned tough looking man over six feet tall, strolled away laughing with no salutes exchanged, just a friendly wave of the hand.

The Aussies couldn't be regimented; they were individualists and their independent spirit was very effective in attack because they acted without waiting for orders during the ever changing circumstances of battle, and were quick to seize the initiative in a crisis. This independent proud spirit, which was so effective in battle, so much admired in attack, never submitted to the rigid military discipline of long standing British Army traditions. Consequently, they were sometimes a headache to the British generals, who nevertheless knew their value and always used them for tough assignments. British troops had a good relationship with them and envied their high pay; an Australian private was paid as much as a British subaltern.

A LONG MARCH BACK TO BEAUQUESNE

On 16th August, just as we were expecting to make physical contact with the enemy, we were suddenly and inexplicably withdrawn from the advance, and commenced a long march back through Heilly and Herrisart and on, and on and on, endlessly it seemed, to Beauquesne, a distance of well over thirty miles.

During our training in England, we did progressively longer and stiffer route marches; at first only a few miles in skeleton order, which is belt and braces without packs, but with haversacks, water-bottles and entrenching tools. By the time we came to France we had marched twelve to fifteen miles in full marching order. I always enjoyed these training route marches; the rhythm of our marching feet, the feeling of well being, the songs we sang. No one enjoyed that exhausting march in the heat of August to Beauquesne.

It was a forced march, much of it along roads filled with army transport of every description on its way to the front we were leaving. The summer air was filled with dust and there was very little singing; even "Wilky" was subdued. We all longed for a drink, but no one dare drink from their water-bottle without permission. March discipline was strict; ten minutes rest after fifty minutes marching, and the predominant thought in our minds was — how ever much further is it to Beauquesne?

A man in B Company stumbles and falls out of the marching column of men, and as we pass we see his company commander, Captain Armstrong a very tough officer who had risen from the ranks, standing over him. He was shouting — "Get up man, get up … you are not done… get up!" As the man staggered to his feet, "Now then, you are ON your feet… you CAN stand, and if you can stand, then you can MARCH … so march!"

Once again we realized that there is literally no limit to what is expected and can be demanded from a soldier on active service.

BEAUQUESNE AT LAST

Beauquesne, well behind the front had been little damaged by the war. On arrival we were given hot tea and "berghu", an Indian name for oatmeal porridge. After seeing to various duties, I got myself a billet which had a wooden floor, but I could not sleep, partly because I was lying on a hard surface, but mainly because I was lousy, and the lice both British and German, became so active when I got warm. Although tired after the long march, I tossed and turned all night.

Next morning, the RSM appeared, a resplendent figure in highly-polished Sam Browne belt, buttons all agleam, and not least, a fierce gleam in his eye. We had a strange love-hate relationship with our RSM. Everyone respected him as a highly-trained and experienced professional soldier, who had won the Military Cross for his leadership during the March retirement.

Now, however, he laid on a stiff training programme, to smarten us up, he said, and make us LOOK like soldiers! It reminded me of Bruce Bairnsfather's cartoon which showed two British Tommies just back from the front. They were passing the gates of Buckingham Palace where the sentries stood, looking very smart. One of the muddy unkempt Tommies said to his mate, "Look, Bill, soldiers!"

Our RSM once told some of us NCOs of the HQ Company, that he had demeaned himself at the outbreak of war in 1914 by offering to take down his crown and put up three stripes because he was so keen to join this 10th Battalion of the Lancashire Fusiliers, which was raised in Bury on 6th September 1914.

Some of the survivors of the March retirement told how he had led a group of men out of a German encirclement, being quite ruthless in using our own dead as shelter when trapped in a trench with no cover from German troops on higher ground. Then, using Mills bombs very effectively, he enabled the survivors to break through the encirclement and escape in the dusk to safety.

After the training programme was over the majority of the men spent the evening in the well-stocked estaminets, many of them happily getting drunk on vin blanc and cognac.

BACK TO THE FRONT!

About 9p.m. that evening, 19th August, there was a bugle call from the guardroom for orderly sergeant. I reported and found the adjutant, Captain Milne and the intelligence officer, Lieut. Smith, both there and in a flap. They said, "Get all the men on parade, Corporal, at once, in full marching order, we are going back to the Line IMMEDIATELY!"

I rushed round the village, shouting the order to get dressed in full marching order and fall in at once in the main street. Unfortunately, quite a number of the NCOs were also drunk, and as I went from place to place, exhorting other NCOs to get their men on parade, some gave little response. I heard my officer, Lieut. Smith, say to Capt. Milne, "This is terrible, sir, Corporal Hodges appears to be the only sober NCO we have." This was an exaggeration, but looking back, I wonder where the RSM was, since I don't remember seeing or hearing him.

Eventually, we got everyone formed up in the main street and started the long march through the night, back to the front only three days after we had been withdrawn from it. Some of the men were in no condition to march, but they had to! What a night it was! The next day, the offending sergeants and corporals were reduced to the ranks, and new NCOs were appointed on the spot. Among those disgraced was Corporal Butler in charge of the HQ runners, whom I never saw again, as he was badly wounded a few days later. Also reduced to the ranks were the sergeant cook, an old soldier in every sense, and, of all people, the provost sergeant, in charge of the regimental police, Sergeant Grendon. Grendon, a born soldier regained his stripes, but he was never again given charge of the regimental police. This job was given to me by Lieut. Smith until an older and more experienced NCO arrived and took over from me. So at the age of nineteen years and one month, and with experience as an NCO of less than four weeks, I was thrown in at the deep end. However, I had already established a good relationship with these experienced soldiers — Brandon, Braithwaite, Corbishley, Hayley, Raynor, Tydesley, Watson, Whittle and Widdowson, as reliable gas sentries.

Talking over so many responsibilities at my age was abnormal, but so were the times. So many experienced NCOs, mature men, had been killed, wounded, gassed, or taken prisoner in the German spring offensive, that responsibilities far beyond our years or experience, were suddenly thrust on us. Another nineteen-year-old was promoted to corporal and put in charge of the battalion's machine-gunners.

Training for responsibility is usual and very desirable, but in such an emergency, with no more mature soldiers available, we boys had to take responsibilities in the heat of battle. In these circumstances, it didn't take long for the boy soldiers to mature, since so much was expected of us.

When I look back to these momentous days in the spring and summer of 1918, I now realise how much was expected. At battalion HQ I was never free with so many and varied duties; many of which were unfamiliar to me. I also now realise how lonely I was. At the time I was fully occupied with my duties as battalion gas NCO, for which I had a mere week's training at the 5th Corps Gas School, and also with the duties of orderly sergeant, which were quite new to me and more complicated in a HQ company which had so many differing functions than a company of four platoons.

Still more responsibilities and duties were mine now that I was put in charge of the regimental police, but on the other hand, this was an advantage because I could now officially use them regularly as gas sentries.

I was a novice in war experiences compared with these experienced soldiers. They realised this too, but gave me full support both as reliable gas sentries and when I led them into action on Thiepval Ridge a few days later.

It had been impressed upon me at the Gas School that the duties and responsibilities of a gas NCO were very important. After my appointment I realised how extensive they were too. I could easily have occupied all my time visiting the other four companies, examining gas masks for faults, treating obnoxious gas shell craters, and instructing gas sentries in their duties.

By now I had lost touch with my old friends, the young companions of our training days at Dovercourt, Clipstone Camp, Colchester and Norwich. Only occasionally did I come into brief contact with them, usually while checking their gas masks.

One day young Whitehead, who had joined the army with me, stopped to chat for a few minutes as he passed by battalion HQ on some errand. He brought me up to date as to who had been killed and wounded lately. He told me that Crouch, one of the boys who had joined the army with us, had been severely wounded in the leg and was almost certain to lose it. We also talked about George Dunmore's death; and that his friend, Fred Ablethorpe, had written to George's parents in Northampton to break the sad news, hoping to ease the sudden shock of an official telegram.

As Whitehead was speaking about this, I had a strange feeling — a premonition that I would not see him again. He may have had a similar feeling for we were loath to part. The next time I visited "A" Company, I was told that he had just been killed.

THE BYNG BOYS PREPARE FOR GENERAL BYNG'S ATTACK

During the night of August 19th-20th we arrived at the rear of the battle area. It was obvious that the big British offensive had begun here too. The battalion HQ staff were drastically thinned out; various trades such as the tailors, the boot repairers and clerks being kept in the rear with the transport at "B" echelon, now at Acheux.

All the others were organized into a HQ company under the command of Lieutenant Duckworth. I heard the adjutant say, "Now then, Algy, YOU are now in charge of the HQ company, and for goodness sake, smarten some of them up a bit."

This, Algy proceeded to do, telling Corporal Thomas, the pioneer corporal, to make his men stow away the saws and hammers, bags of nails and axes less conspicuously. Until then, one of Thomas's men, Bob, had always had a handsaw tied to his rifle with a bit of string! This, of course, offended military discipline and smartness, but as Thomas said to me "One of my first duties when we stop anywhere for the night is to fix up an officers' latrine, and then I've got to 'mackle up' some sort of shelter for the CO, and I can't do very much without a few tools." We boys thought that Colonel Cotton, our CO was quite elderly and had to be looked after, I realize now that he was probably only about forty.

EMPTY TRENCHES

As we moved forward from Acheux over familiar field tracks, with the well-known village of Mailly-Maillet on our left, and Englebelmer on our right, we came to our old reserve line and found it empty. We thought it very strange to go on from there to our old front line trenches in daylight, and to find them empty too. In the past we had always scuttled through Mailly-Maillet or Mesnil in the dark and often under enemy fire. Evidently the troops who relieved us when we marched south to support the Aussies had commenced the attack and we were now supporting them.

We crossed the railway line not far from our old close support trench, between Auchonvillers and Mesnil, with Aveluy Wood on our right. At last, the Germans had been driven out of it after holding it against many attacks ever since they captured it on 27th March.

Then another strange thing happened. Our rations were brought up to us instead of us having to go back from the trenches to fetch them. To our further amazement, they included a large juicy joint of raw meat. A joint of meat was very unusual at any time, and in the present state of affairs very inappropriate because we were going into action, and there would be no opportunity for the company cook to do anything with it.

As if I hadn't enough duties as the battalion gas NCO, the orderly sergeant, and temporary charge of the regimental police, I had recently acquired another. My predecessor as battalion gas NCO, Sergeant Brown, used to distribute the rations to the various sections — signallers, runners, police, observers and machine-gunners, etc. Corporal Wilkinson had acquired the job temporarily when Sergeant Brown went to brigade HQ, but now it was mine! I asked Wilky what I should do with the joint of lovely meat. He said "You'll have to dump it, we can't use it. It's a bloody shame, but what else can you do?"

I distributed the rest of the rations to the various sections during a short halt in a trench, and when we moved on, I left the lovely joint of meat there! This incident, and our long march from the sector where the Anzacs had successfully broken through, right back to the rear at Beauquesne and then the sudden recall to our old familiar front, illustrates how little was known by anyone at a battalion level. I can only conclude that when we marched all those miles south from Forceville to support the Aussies, we were a flying column to be used as circumstances required. Why we were sent all those weary miles to the back area at Beauquesne and then so quickly and suddenly recalled to our former front, we never knew. Truly it was "not ours to reason why, but only to do or die".

WE CROSS THE ANCRE

However, here we were, poised for our part in General Byng's big attack with the 3rd Army. During the 20th August, we passed beyond our old front line between Mesnil and Hamel, going downhill to the River Ancre and wading through lagoons of water, reeds and rushes.

During our descent to the river, we were fired on from behind; rifle bullets whipped and whined past us. Presumably they were fired by our supporting troops, who from a distance mistook us for retreating Jerries! Corporal Wilkinson ordered one of his signallers to flash LF-LF-LF-LF in morse code with the lamp; and then the firing ceased.

We came to a small stone bridge and some army pontoons over the river, and crossed to Authuilie (the site of it), where the German front line that we had known, was now deserted.

At Ovillers, we took our first prisoner; a very poor specimen, who, to us boys, was an old man. He was small, bearded and very docile. We found him lurking in a dug-out, one of a long row dug into an earth bank. I was really fascinated to see these enemy dug-outs in the German front line, which we had been near but had never seen, in our night patrols from Mesnil.

Ovillers! I thought of an old school friend who was killed here. W. J. P. Woods and I were fullbacks together in one of the house elevens four years earlier. He was two years older than me, and had come out here as a young officer in 1916 to take part in the first Battle of the Somme, and was killed in action here in July, 1916. Other school friends had also been killed in this area, W. L. McColl, a school prefect, was killed while serving as a 2nd Lieut, in the 6th Northants in this Ancre

Valley in February 1917. Ernest Mace, who used to be with me in the school orchestra, was killed at Thiepval in 1917 while serving as a 2nd Lieut, in the 6th Northants. A. E. Owen, also with me in the school orchestra, was killed while a 2nd Lieut, in the 7th Northants. H. W. Hayward, another school prefect, was killed at Thiepval in 1916 while serving as a 2nd Lieut, in the 6th Northamptonshire Regiment. Norman Beale, a special friend was killed at Guillemont in 1916 while serving as a 2nd Lieut, in the 7th Northants.

WE ATTACK ACROSS THE OLD 1916 BATTLEFIELD

Leaving Ovillers, we commenced the long ascent, out of the river valley to the high ground from which the Germans had dominated the British positions on the other side of the Ancre Valley ever since their March offensive had been halted. On our left we could see the blackened stumps of Thiepval Wood on the high eastern bank of the River Ancre, where, in 1916 the Germans had again held the high ground overlooking the British positions.

Then, the villages of Thiepval and Pozieres, standing on high ground, had been turned into fortresses, with the famous Mouquet Farm and the Liepsig Redoubt between them. Now, we saw only the remnants of those strong positions, just the remains of many belts of barbed wire on rusted iron pickets, the shattered concrete emplacements and possibly the ruins of Mouquet Farm. As we advanced up the great Thiepval Ridge, passing these remnants of the formidable German defences of 1916, from which they had inflicted such grievous casualties on the British 4th Army, mostly Kitchener's volunteers, we could imagine how strong these positions must have been then on 1st July 1916.

In 1916, the Germans held a very strong entrenched position on the two spurs of ground which extend in front of Ovillers and La Boselle. The British attacked up two valleys which they had named Sausage and Mash, and were caught in a deadly cross-fire from the German machine-guns entrenched on the spurs. Within ten minutes of zero hour, 80 per cent of the leading battalions were casualties; very few reached the German trenches. Examples of some of the recorded losses were —

2nd Battalion Middlesex Regiment, 22 officers and 592 other ranks.

8th Battalion Yorks and Lancasters, 23 officers and 613 other ranks.

9th Battalion Yorks and Lancasters, 23 officers and 517 other ranks.

In two hours the 8th Division lost 218 out of 300 officers, and 5,274 out of 8,500 other ranks.

The Ulster Division had over 9,000 casualties.

Despite these enormous losses, Haig told Rawlinson, the Commander of the 4th Army, that he wanted the attack continued the next day, and at 10p.m. the 4th Army issued an order to all corps to continue the attack. British troops continued to swarm up this death strewn slope from the Ancre Valley.

On 26th September 1916, the 6th (Service) Battalion of the Northamptonshire Regiment lost 128 killed and 345 wounded, including the colonel, the adjutant, 3 captains and 9 lieutenants.

Similar losses were sustained by many other regiments as the 1st Battle of the Somme continued to drain the life-blood of our nation until the middle of November, when "General" winter brought it to an end.

It has been said that the Somme battles of 1916 became the graveyard of Kitchener's new army. 84 battalions of men, who had volunteered, who were certainly Britain's best, left their trenches at 7.30 a.m. on a beautiful summer day. By 8.30 a.m., 10,000 lay dead, and the attack continued until, at the end of the first day, July 1st, 21,392 had been killed, 35,493 wounded, and 585 were taken prisoner; a total of 57,470 casualties in one day. Battalions who had trained together for nearly two years were virtually wiped out, and local newspapers feared to publish the news, but eventually there was page after page of casualties.

Never before, or since, have so many British soldiers died in such a short space of time, nor has such a desolation of shattered villages, shell-torn fields and splintered trees been made in such a relatively small area. Here, by the River Somme and its small tributary, the River Ancre, between July 1st and November 18th 1916, when winter rains and sleet came, so many of the generation that had responded to Kitchener's call, died.

They were in many ways the elite of our nation, the crème de la crème. The tragic contract between their high spirits and high hopes and the reality proved that their enthusiasm and superb courage were not a viable substitute for proper military training and sound strategy. They were brave amateurs fighting well-trained professionals. The disaster of 1st July 1916, was the worst day in the entire history of the British Army. So many casualties with nothing achieved.

By the time the offensive had wallowed to a halt in the November mud, the British, French and German casualties had risen to over a million. A once beautiful countryside had become a sodden sterile wilderness. The area chosen for this combined British and French offensive stretched from

Gommecourt in the north to Fricourt in the south, an area of open rolling chalk based country.

The Germans were well prepared in defensive positions. Villages had been heavily fortified, there were vast belts of barbed wire; well-sited machine-gun positions, and deep shelters in a complex network of trenches and strong points. At Fricourt, the 21st Division and the 17th Division, both New Army Divisions, had many casualties; the West Yorks (50th Brigade of the 17th Division) were virtually annihilated — 710 casualties, including twenty-two officers — the highest battalion loss. One company of Green Howards was wiped out within a few yards of its jumping off point. At La Boselle, the 34th Division, one of Kitchener's New Army Divisions, lost more heavily than any of the fourteen Divisions engaged on 1st July. The Tyneside Scottish and The Tyneside Irish were badly hit; 80 per cent of the men in the leading battalions becoming casualties. From the high ground of Thiepval Ridge, the Germans had clear views of the whole area chosen for attack by Kitchener's New Army. Especially was this so around Albert, where they could see every movement of the British troops.

Now, in August 1918, another New Army composed mainly of boys of eighteen and nineteen, the Byng Boys under the command of General Sir Julian Byng, were attacking up the same slopes of the Ancre Valley. This area had been, before the war, a countryside of singular rural beauty, not unlike parts of England's Hampshire, with rich cornfields, productive orchards and marshy meadows. Through it flowed the River Somme, one of the minor waterways of northern France, and its tributary the River Ancre, which flows westwards from Bapaume and then southwards to Albert.

Across this area the Route Nationale, an old Roman road lined with tall sentinel like poplars, ran from Bapaume to Albert and Amiens. A network of rural lanes linked the many villages nestling in the folds of the undulating slopes, and from the uplands, which are almost solid chalk like the English downs, views extend to up to three miles. On some of the slopes there were thick woods, the names of which had now become very familiar to a generation of British young men.

For the first two years of the war, there had been no great battle in the Somme area. It was known as a quiet sector of the long Western Front which extended from the beach near Ostend to the Swiss frontier near Belfort. When the initial war of movement gave place to static trench warfare in the autumn of 1914, the Germans had advanced, and in so doing had created a large salient, an enormous bulge into Northern France known as the Noyon Salient. The Front, before the 1st Battle of the Somme, had remained basically the same since 1914, and had become known to the British troops as "Our Old Front Line".

Here the Germans occupied the long ridge of high ground on the eastern side of the River Ancre where it flows south to Albert. They held very strongly entrenched positions which overlooked the Ancre and the British trenches, having dug deep shelters in the chalk and constructed fortifications for their machine-guns on spurs which extended from the ridge, thus enabling their machine-gunners to give covering and cross-fire to adjacent areas.

Two miles behind the British trenches was the beleaguered town of Albert, where windows gaped in the battered houses and the few remaining civilians lived in the cellars. Four roads led from Albert until they petered out into trenches with names like Centre Way, Peel Trench, Dead Mule Corner and the Bowery. One of them, the State Highway, led towards Bapaume behind the German lines and this road was the main avenue of battle along which hundreds of thousands of British troops marched on their way to death or wounds.

1st July 1916, was an exceptionally beautiful summer morning with not a cloud to be seen. At 7.30 a.m. it was quite hot already as the fourteen Divisions of British troops left their trenches to attack on an eighteen mile front. The majority of them were Kitchener's volunteers, a New Army of untried civilians who less than two years before had been clerks, crofters, miners, shoemakers, solicitors and shopkeepers.

This New Army had received little training of value; their instructors being quite ignorant of modern trench warfare. Their training consisted mainly of drilling, marching, PT, musketry and advancing in artillery formation according to the Manual of Military Training of the Boer War. They received no instruction or training in raiding enemy trenches, or bombing with the Mills bomb to clear enemy trenches. They had never been trained to dig trenches or to drain them, or to put up barbed wire defences or help sappers to construct strong points or shelters.

This untried and partly trained New Army of men, in superb physical condition, was thrown into the attack against the German Army which in 1916 still contained a majority of professional soldiers who were entrenched on a long crest from Gommecourt in the north to Fricourt in the south. These hard facts, the brutal realities of war, were not faced or taken into account by our generals, and the flower of British manhood was sent into the attack as if taking part in a great military exercise.

Whole battalions advanced, strung out in long lines, each man an arm's length from his neighbour; and so they fell.

The British Official History of the 1st Battle of the Somme is as follows —

> The position was, in fact, that of storming a fortress, in which according to precedent, there should be a main assault on the weakest spot, several other subsidiary ones on other possible weak spots, strong enough to be converted into main assaults and carried through, and also false assaults.
>
> Instead, the distribution of force was as uniform as the methods of attack were stereotyped. Men advanced at a walking pace and were mown down by the German machine-gunners, strewing their bodies in no man's land.
>
> Battalions attacked in waves, one hundred yards apart in symmetrical lines, upright at a walking pace, rifles and bayonets held aslant in front of them. Men were cut down like corn as they advanced wave after wave, they were easy targets. German snipers picked off the officers by their dress, Sam Browne belts and collar and tie in the first few yards, while overhead the larks were singing.

The 1st Battle of the Somme officially ended on 18th November 1916, in snow and blizzard on the Ancre.

Total casualties in 1916 were given at British GHQ as 607,784.

The official Allied figures for the Somme were British 419,654, French 204,253.

The British dead and severely wounded in the 1st Battle of the Somme swallowed up the heart of a whole generation. Nowhere was the advance more than eight miles. The objectives laid down in Field Marshall Haig's orders for the first day were still unattained when winter closed in.

The only gain was a narrow strip of blood-soaked ground, which the Germans so easily took back again in their 21st

March 1918 offensive. A glorious victory had been expected — a horrible bloodbath had occurred. A most unsuitable place had been chosen for the attack; throughout the battle the British had the enemy above them in deep shelters, with machine-gun emplacements and excellent observation posts.

Haig and his chief of staff, who drew up the plans for this great offensive, never made any contact with the fighting men apart from motoring about behind the front from one Corps HQ to another.

CHURCHILL ON FRENCH AND HAIG

"French was a natural soldier. Although he had not the intellectual capacity of Haig, he had a deeper military insight."

"He had more imagination than Haig, and he would never have run the British Army into the same long drawn out slaughters."

"A sincere desire to engage the enemy! That was Haig. That was his message. That was the impulse which he imparted to his troops throughout his command until the last minute before 11 a.m. on 11th November 1918."

"Like a great surgeon before the days of anaesthetics, sure of himself, steady of poise, knife in hand, intent upon the operation, entirely removed in his professional capacity from the agony of the patient, or the anguish of relations or of new learning, he would operate."

"A sincere desire to engage the enemy. Woe betide any officer — Colonel, or Brigadier or General who failed in that. Experienced, resolute men, with courage proved in battle, were sent home at an hour's notice for refusing to order — not to lead, for that would have been easier — their troops to certain destruction."

"Fight and kill and be killed, but obey orders, even when it was clear that the Higher Command had not foreseen the conditions, or — go, and go at once, to the rear, to England, or to the devil."

"That was the high tension current which flowed ceaselessly from the Commander-in-Chief, through more than forty months of carnage.

"All along the chain of responsibility from Army HQ to Corps HQ from Corps HQ to Divisional HQ from Divisional HQ to Brigade HQ, and from Brigade HQ to Battalion, this ruthless, and often inevitably blind force was continually applied."

THE END OF THE CHAIN OF COMMAND — THE PBI

No wonder the infantry were known as the Poor Bloody Infantry by the other branches of the British Army; it was a title which we accepted and were in some sense proud of. The PBI always carried the can. They had to because as the orders were passed down from GHQ to Army HQ and thence to Corps HQ and on to Divisional HQ, to be then passed down to Brigade HQ and then Battalion HQ the ultimate carrying out of those orders was the sole responsibility of the officers, NCOs and men of the infantry battalions. We were at the END of the long chain of command. As President Truman once said in a different sense when he had the responsibility of making the final decisions, "the buck stops here".

There was no one to whom the infantry could pass on the orders; we had to carry them out; we were the front line troops who were in physical contact with the enemy, in battles and in raids on one another's trenches. Even in relatively quiet periods, we were separated from the enemy only by no man's land, that area between our front line and Jerry's which was always and inevitably an unknown area. No man's land was always a place of tension and fear, even to troops who had had much experience of it. When we were out there on a wiring party, we felt completely exposed when the German flares shot up into the dark sky. We stopped mending the barbed wire and stood quite still, with our faces down on the chest, lest they should be seen by a German sentry or machine-gunner.

When the machine-guns periodically traversed our front, it was even more difficult to stand motionless, but after some experience one got to know the difference between the sound of the bullets that were harmless to one and the sound of the ones which came with a vicious crack-crack-crack.

When we stood on sentry in the front line at night, or in a slit trench out in no man's land, watching and listening, there was always tension because of the possibility of being taken prisoner in a sudden attack by a German raiding party.

THE BYNG BOYS ATTACK THIEPVAL RIDGE

Now, in 1918, we were advancing, in the open, across the 1916 battlefields. In our advance we passed the remains of woods with well-known names, now only shattered tree stumps. We crossed old grass grown trenches which had been blown in and smashed by the 1916 shell fire; we saw the rotting remains of old sandbagged parapets, belts of machine-gun ammunition, rusty bayonets, cartridge clips, and, among the flourishing weeds, groups of old graves.

It was a desolate scene; lifeless, a place of death and decay and neglect, with a history which seemed far more remote than two or three years. Was it possible, I thought, that it is only two years since my old school friends had fallen on these slopes?

The names of these villages and woods were familiar to the Byng Boys, they were a part of British history, and now we were fighting for them again. I remember passing Pozieres. I would not have known that it was the famous Pozieres where thousands of British troops had died in 1916, but for a rough notice scrawled on a piece of wood near some grass covered ruins. They were foundations of houses with cellars choked with weeds in full flower. Nature unaffected by the war.

These famous names and battles stirred the Byng Boys. On our right was Delville Wood, once an area of 150 acres of oak and birch, with dense hazel thickets, now blackened and shattered tree stumps. In 1916, the South African Infantry Brigade was ordered to take it at all costs, and what a cost it was.

Of the 121 officers and 3,032 men who went into the attack on 14th July, only three officers and 140 men came out alive when they were relieved on the 20th July. Others, from hospitals and prisoner of war camps, were later found to have survived.

As we continued our assault of Ovillers Ridge, away on our left was the site of the village of Thiepval. Before the war it was surrounded by apple orchards, and there were great trees in the beautiful park surrounding a lovely chateau in which the seigneur and his family lived. All we could see of this once lovely scene, where the chateau once stood, was a large reddish mound of brick rubble amid the desolation of war.

I quote from an official account of this 2nd Battle for Thiepval Ridge which, written many years after, gives a much larger view than we had as infantrymen taking part in it.

"BYNG'S THRUST TOWARDS BAPAUME"
"On 23rd August 1918, General Byng's 3rd Army attacked

north of Albert through the early morning mist. Byng's infantry were mainly boys hastily rushed out to France before their training had been completed. When the mist lifted, the attack was held up while the British field artillery moved up to new positions. During the lull, the German commander discovered, by raids, that more than 50 per cent of Byng's infantry were mere boys.

Encouraged by his discovery, the German general brought up reserves and counter-attacked on a fifteen mile front. The attack was met by almost point blank fire from the newly arrived British Field Artillery, and the "Boys" having been now "blooded" fought like veterans.

"Attack and counter-attack raged along a fifteen mile front north of Albert. By the 24th August, the front ran along the edge of an old 1916 Somme battlefield upon which the brothers, fathers and uncles of the boys had fallen. Now the boys were to attack across this old battlefield to capture again the places whose names had become a part of British history in 1916.

"At 4.45 a.m. on 23rd August, the Byng Boys attacked an opposition less strong than that which had shot down 60,000 of their predecessors in one day on 1st July 1916. All day long the pressure was kept up, and by evening the 12 Divisions of Byng's Army had advanced as much as three miles in some places, taking 5,000 prisoners. All day long the boys edged inexorably forward, cleverly finding the weak spots between the strong points held by the German machine-gunners. The German line did not break, and once they were well within the network of the old battlefield trenches, their veteran infantry, stiffened as usual by their machine-gunners, fought with determination and skill.

"However, the young British infantry quickly learned methods of outflanking enemy posts or threaded their way between the strong points. By 26th August, the attack reached the Siegfried Position, a deep system of fortifications over fifty miles long, stretching from Bapaume, past the Flesquieres Salient to St. Quentin. During the last week of August pressure was maintained, heavy and unrelenting, and by 29th August, Byng's Army was past Bapaume in the north, and Rawlinson's Australians had reached the Somme south of Peronne.

"On 30th August, massed artillery pounded the thick belts of barbed wire and the infantry moved up for another assault.

"It began on 2nd September, led by fifty tanks (almost the remaining strength of the Tank Corps). The tanks trundled massively forward through the wire, the infantry following close behind and then taking the trench in storming rushes. By evening Ludendorff realised he had to cut his losses. He ordered his troops retreating from Byng's 3rd Army at Bapaume and Rawlinson's 4th Army at Peronne to withdraw right back to the Old British Defence Line from which Byng's 3rd and Gough's 5th Armies had faced the great German onslaught of 21st March. There the German troops prepared to stand."

When I read, many years later, the above official account of this great battle, I was even more puzzled than I was at the time. The 10th Battalion Lancashire Fusiliers was a part of the Vth Corps of General Byng's 3rd Army, and as such was obviously destined to take part in "Byng's thrust towards Bapaume" on 23rd August. Why then were we suddenly withdrawn from trenches on the Vth Corps front near Aveluy Wood on 4th August, and sent south to mop up for the Australians who were to be the "Spearhead" of General Rawlinson's 4th Army attack towards Peronne on August 8th?

One can only conclude that someone on the staff made a bloomer. If they did it certainly wasn't the first time!

THE BATTLE FOR THIEPVAL RIDGE AS WE SAW IT

The actual line of attack taken by the 10th (Service) Battalion Lancashire Fusiliers from 23rd August onwards, was from Authuille and Ovillers and up the Ovillers Ridge towards Pozieres, Martinpuich and Courcelette. During our advance up the slopes of Thiepval Ridge, Corporal Wilkinson kept the HQ company in touch with the four other companies of the battalion by using the signal lamp.

From now on signal wires were used only when we were not on the move, and this meant that the burden of very dangerous work which Corporal Wilkinson and his linesmen had constantly borne when we were in fixed positions in trenches, was eased.

At one stage of the advance the HQ company halted briefly near an old rusty British tank, one of the many relics of previous assaults up this great ridge. Corporal Wilkinson told one of the signallers, a youngster named John Grace, to take the lamp up on to the top of the tank, where he would have a good view, and to keep watching for signals from the flanking companies.

Grace, an eighteen-year-old who had only just come out to the Western Front, was inattentive to his duty, and was sharply rebuked when Wilky noticed a distant lamp flashing the call sign of the HQ company.

"Watch for the lamps, lad, ALL THE TIME, both sides, that's what I've put you up there for. Answer that call, and take a message if they send one and KEEP AWAKE, you can't daydream when you are on duty OUT HERE, lad." This youngster was killed the next day while under my command.

Later that day we prepared to capture Martinpuich, which process developed into a long night of moving here and there in the dark until the staff had got the many battalions taking part in the dawn attack in their correct positions.

The great Thiepval Ridge in front of us was dissected by the main Albert-Bapaume Road, with Guillemont, Delville Wood and High Wood on our right front, Martinpuich ahead of us in the centre, and Courcelette and Thiepval Wood on our left front.

A few hours later, in the dawn attack, I crossed this Albert-Bapaume main road as I advanced with the regimental police from Pozieres to the crest of the great ridge between Martinpuich and Courcelette.

Both these villages had been destroyed, like Pozieres, in the 1916 battles and now consisted of broken beams and brick rubble. A large mound of stone dust was all that remained of Martinpuich church which had been pulverised literally to white stone dust two years earlier. The same formidable task that had faced our predecessors in 1916, now faced us. As before, the Germans held the high ground, the crest of Thiepval Ridge.

During that night the countryside was alive with thousands of troops, all on the move; we were either passing other battalions or being passed while waiting for fresh orders. That night was cold and there was some mist; at one stage we were told to sit down, and then about a hundred guardsmen came past us. Someone remarked that about every fourth man was carrying a two gallon petrol can full of water in his left hand. Some of us looked at these cans of water rather enviously. We were always short of water, but Corporal Wilkinson, famed for his humorous remarks, said, "E'eh la'ads, tha knows why they've got all that water? It's because they are guardsmen; they'll all have to wash and shave before going into the attack." Roars of laughter greeted this interpretation of the reason for all that water. Actually, they were a guards' machine-gun company, and the water was for their machine-guns.

THE DAWN ATTACK

Shortly after this incident, we moved again and then waited for dawn and the order to move forward into the attack. Eventually, we began to advance in line through thick mist; long lines of men all moving forward; whole battalions in line. At this stage there was no sound of war; it was just like a huge military exercise.

It was so strange; the silence and the long lines of men; only their heads and shoulders could be seen, moving in line above the thick white ground mist. Then the eerie silence was broken; ahead of us in the mist, a German machine-gun began to stutter. An officer of another company loomed up close to me in the thick mist and briefly walked with me. "What do you think, Corporal, is he firing into the blue?" "I think so," I replied, "but this mist won't cover us much longer, it's getting thinner."

More machine-guns began to fire ahead of us, but no one near me was hit. We wondered why there was no enemy shell fire, and concluded that Jerry was withdrawing his guns. Our guns were silent too, as they were moving up to new positions.

At this stage of the battle it was so quiet that it was uncanny. Then, as the mist began to clear, we came to the main road from Albert to Bapaume. I crossed it at an angle, leading about a dozen men, mostly regimental police, going down a steep bank on to the road.

Machine-gun fire from the left came in bursts as we quickly crossed the road and entered a large empty gun-pit which had been dug into the bank on the other side of the road.

Wounded men who could walk, who were officially known as Walking Wounded, were coming back down the road; some had head wounds; some a bleeding arm or shoulder. One man hobbled into the gun-pit with a large bloody field dressing on his leg above the knee; his trousers had been slit open and were flapping round his leg above the knee. Tommy Braithwaite, one of the regimental police, told him to wait in the gun-pit until the machine-gun fire out on the road ceased.

None of us went back to the road, but scrambled up and out of the gun-pit on the field side, where we joined other Lancashire Fusiliers who were moving towards Martinpuich. As we advanced up the long grassy slope, the German guns suddenly opened up on us and shells began to burst just ahead of us.

At this stage I saw no officer near us, but everyone seemed to know what to do. The NCOs led their sections; short rushes forward and then down flat for a minute or two, just as we had been trained to do.

A Lewis gun team of five or six men ran past us as we lay, and I saw them fling themselves into a large newly-made shell hole about sixty yards ahead of us. Only a few moments later, as I with about eight regimental police ran past them in our next rush forward, I was amazed to see the whole team lying dead in the positions they had just taken up. The "Number One on the gun" lay with his Lewis gun in position on the forward lip of the shell hole; his back split open from the shoulder to the waist. I was shocked, and at the same time fascinated, as I sped past by the resemblance to a carcase in a butcher's shop.

I led several more short rushes forward and then we came to and crossed an old 1916 trench where many others had just been killed by shell bursts. We who still lived looked at them as we passed with a strange detachment; this unexpected capacity to endure the sight of shattered bodies, headless trunks and detached limbs still makes me wonder, when I think back to that day and others like it.

We were young; we were very fit; we had been trained and now we were quite acclimatised in spirit to a war in which death was a general expectation and the loss of a limb was counted a lucky escape. In fact, a wound that would take one back to dear old Blighty was always an occasion for congratulations from one's comrades.

Although for seven months I was a part of this bizarre scene, I now look back and marvel at the courage and the confidence of that generation of men who, for four long years, held the Western Front; they not only fought in the many battles, they HELD that gigantic system of trenches and strong points which stretched right across Belgium and Northern France, which the millions of men of a whole generation — British, Belgian, French and German — had dug and lived in and died in.

OVER THE CREST OF THIEPVAL RIDGE

When eventually, the enemy shelling ceased, we began to wonder if Jerry was again withdrawing his field guns. His machine-gunners still held the top of the great ridge, and word was passed to us by our officers to wait where we were while the East Yorks had a go and tried to outflank them.

After a time we began to advance again by short rushes; I and some of the regimental police got to within about one hundred yards of the skyline of the ridge. Just ahead on the right, I saw some German prisoners being led away, and then in our next rush forward we ran fast to the top of the slope. As I breasted the crest and saw the reverse slope before me, bullets cracked and whined past me. Some were so close that I instinctively flinched, tucking my chin into my left shoulder as I ran even faster down the long slope before me ... to get it over quickly.

There was no cover here, and no one stopped except those who were hit. We all ran to gain some cover in a large stone quarry that we could see at the bottom of the long downhill slope before us.

Breathless but unhurt, I reached its shelter and sat down for a moment to get back my breath. Looking back up the long slope down which we had run, I could see the dead lying, and some walking wounded, still coming down.

Private Neate, one of the HQ runners, showed me his steel helmet. In the front of it, dead centre, was a round bullet hole, and in the back there was a jagged hole as big as a golf ball where the bullet had emerged. It was quite pretty! Later, when the RSM saw Neate wearing it, he told him off for not getting himself another one from a dead man.

I helped some wounded to the Battalion First Aid Post which had opened up for business in the shelter of the quarry. Then some German prisoners came along from the other end of the quarry, carrying some of our wounded on stretchers. I particularly noticed a young German lad, about my age, who was holding his left arm, which was soaked with his blood. He was very pale and he looked appealingly at me, so I took him to the First Aid Post and spoke to a corporal about his condition, but he said "Those b—s must wait till we've seen to our own men."

SPECIAL ORDERS

As I turned away, the Adjutant spotted me and called me to him. He said "You can read a map, Corporal Hodges, now look here." He then spread out his map on a large rock and showed me a place where, he said, I was to take half a dozen men, and establish a post. The place was near to Martinpuich, which was still the battalion's objective. I have often wondered what I was supposed to do. He said, "We shan't be long following you." It was almost like being sent in advance billeting! I would have asked for more detailed instructions, but at that moment the Brigadier General arrived and the Adjutant left me abruptly to talk with him and the Colonel.

Before I was out of earshot, I heard the Brigadier say, "The Lancashire Fusiliers will attack again at 11.20 'Ack emma', with the Manchesters in support." This made Captain Milne's order still more incomprehensible to me, but since orders are orders, I looked round for my regimental police. Some of them were dealing with German prisoners, but I collected two or three of them, a couple of Wilky's signallers and one of Corporal Thomas's pioneers.

I led them up among the rocks and along and up a narrow grassy path to a grassy bank above the rocks. Suddenly, without any warning, a salvo of large howitzer shells came down, it seemed almost vertically. There was no whine, just the final rush and tremendous roar as they burst on the bank and in the quarry below us. The explosions were so violent and so sudden that I literally hardly knew if I were still alive. We were all enveloped in thick browny-black cordite smoke which made our eyes and throat smart.

As it began to clear, Private Fiske, one of the signallers, saw me, and he said "Oh, Corporal, I thought THAT was you," as he pointed to the body of one of the regimental police who lay on the grassy bank, dead, horribly mutilated, in a pool of blood.

"No," I said. "Where are the others?" We found Signaller Grace, a boy of eighteen who had just come out to France; he was conscious, but both his legs were bleeding badly, and he was very pale.

I ran back along the grassy path by the bank and scrambled down into the quarry to the First Aid Post, while Fiske and the other policeman carried him down. I insisted that the medical orderlies give him priority. I spoke to Sergeant Pearson, who was in charge, but later I heard that he had soon died. The pioneer had a small flesh wound in his right hand, which incidentally, was already minus two fingers which he had lost earlier in the war.

The RSM saw me return with the wounded and I asked him what I should do now. He replied, "You've had your orders, Corporal, get some more men and try again."

SECOND ATTEMPT

So I started out again with six men and led them up the steep slope out of the quarry to a deserted road which we followed for about one hundred yards or so.

A platoon of another company of Lancashire Fusiliers came along the road, and the young officer leading them asked where I was going. When I told him what my orders were, he got out his map and we studied it together. Eventually, he said "Look, Corporal, NOBODY knows who or what is in front of us, we'll all spread out and cross this field together."

We left the road and advanced in a long line, about ten to fifteen yards apart. About half-way across this large field, I came to a very large deep shell crater, probably made by a German howitzer shell. It had burst in soft soil, which was heaped round the hole, and in it were about half a dozen German soldiers; some dead, some wounded. Two or three of them put up their hands and looked apprehensively up at me. One of them looked as if he hadn't had a shave for a week, but the others were scared-looking boys younger than me.

I beckoned them to come up out of the shell hole, and making sure that they took no weapons with them, I just pointed back the way we had come. I watched them start and then hurried on to catch up the line of men.

They would probably have preferred to be taken back, as I took a much larger number back to the POW cage in October, but on this occasion I had other orders to carry out and I left them to find their own way to captivity.

Continuing a cautious advance across this large field, we came to an old grassy trench, probably one of the 1916 trenches. We dropped into it and walked along it, coming to several British wounded and a young British officer covered by a groundsheet. He lay on the fire-step, all alone. As I passed I lifted the end of the groundsheet to see if I knew him, and I thought sadly of his parents.

The young 2nd Lieutenant then sent two men out of the trench to reconnoitre, and they went cautiously up the slope to the skyline. When they returned he decided we should stay where we were and wait for further orders. Daylight was fading and after sentries were posted we sat down to rest; it had been a long day. We had been on the go since the previous evening without rest or food, having received no rations.

I eventually fell asleep for a time, despite a light summer rain, sitting in the trench with my back to a grassy wall and with my steel helmet rammed into the soil to shelter my head from the rain. The map reference which the adjutant had given me, where I had been ordered to establish a post, was still ahead, probably still in enemy hands.

My recollection of what happened during the next few hours is blank. We had had no food since the attack had started from Pozieres. I had mixed feelings about my unsuccessful attempt to carry out the orders given to me by Captain Milne. What had I been ordered to do? It was obviously impossible to do more while the battle front was so confused and Martinpuich was still in enemy hands. I had not slept since the attack on Thiepval Ridge began, yet I felt "guilty" about sleeping. I was not under the command of the young officer and felt responsible for my six men. Two men had been killed in my first attempt to carry out the vague orders I had received. Suppose I was found asleep while officially on duty in the front line!

Many confusing thoughts and emotions were present as well as hunger and exhaustion. All I remember is that the night passed and nothing more happened. Exactly when I and my companions became connected again with the rest of the HQ company I have no memory.

Looking back on these events after nearly seventy years, I realise that no one was interested in me and my six men. The fighting had ceased for the night and was resumed the next day on a bigger scale. Now I realise that it had been good experience for me, and only one of many similar experiences still to come.

ATTACK AND COUNTER-ATTACK AT MARTINPUICH

Next day the attack on Martinpuich was resumed, with A company and C company in the lead and B and D companies in support. There was strong resistance from well-placed

German machine-guns and considerable enemy shelling. Late in the afternoon of this warm sunny day, I believed it was Sunday and thought briefly of the quiet scene back home where people would be going to church, the HQ company was moving forward on the left of B company.

There had been a lull in the shell fire immediately in front of us. Suddenly shells began to burst all along the crest of the slope up which we were advancing. An officer of B company who was well in front of his company, turned back from the crest and began to come back, waving and pointing to us to go to the left. Later I heard that he had seen a large body of Germans advancing to counter-attack.

The HQ company quickly trotted about eighty yards to our left and a little to the rear, and took up position in an old 1916 trench. It was badly damaged, grass grown and shallow. We manned those parts of it which gave us most cover, and waited to see what would happen next. Soon the enemy shell fire ceased, and shortly after that several grey clad figures appeared momentarily on the skyline. Then they rapidly scuttled back over the crest and out of sight.

"They were Jerries!" someone shouted, and then we saw further movements as another small group of Germans ran along the skyline carrying a heavy machine-gun. The German heavy machine-gun was mounted on a sledge and could be mistaken for a stretcher; at first that is what I thought it was. By this time everyone was trying to get a shot at them and several were seen to fall.

Then there occurred a very tragic incident. An officer of the machine-gun corps came up from the rear, calmly crossed our battered trench and walked diagonally across our front to the right towards B company's front. When he was about half-way to the skyline and about fifty yards to our right, a burst of machine-gun fire came from the Germans immediately in front of us. The officer appeared to spin round, and then he fell dead in full view of us all.

Then a sergeant of the MGC led two gun teams into our trench from the rear, and they quickly set up their machine-guns. The sergeant said to us — "If those Jerry bastards come... LEAVE THEM TO US!"

Our own officers were consulting with the company commander of B company, Captain Armstrong, whose men were about one hundred yards away on our right in another old trench, a little in advance of ours. It was decided to attack at 6 o'clock, and B company were to give us covering fire. As soon as this was known, some of the men discarded their tunics and rolled up their shirt sleeves ready for the rush up the slope. I collected together the regimental police to form a section. The officers' servants and the runners made up another section. It had every appearance of being another costly frontal attack. Surely, I thought, there could be better ideas after four years of war!

I was standing near Lieutenant Duckworth, who was rolling up his shirt sleeves, when Corporal Thomas came up. He had been exploring the possibilities on our left front, and said "Let me have a go, Sir, there's an old grassy communication trench which runs right up to the crest; we can enfilade them from there instead of making a frontal attack."

Algy gave him permission to try, and Thomas, an experienced soldier, older than most of us, grinned and said to Private Corless, one of the signallers, "Come on Dick, let's have a go at the bastards — follow me." He hurried off down the trench to the left, followed by Dick Corless, and we saw glimpses of them as they moved crouching up the old shallow grass grown trench leading towards the skyline. We heard several rifle shots and then there was a pause; then more rifle shots and after another pause, Corporal Thomas stood up on the skyline and waved to us. Dick Corless could also be seen and then, over the skyline, came about half a dozen German machine-gunners with their hands up.

The German NCO followed them down to us, swearing furiously at them for surrendering, while Corporal Thomas brought up the rear. When they reached us the regimental police took charge of them, and Thomas said to the German NCO who appeared to be a Bavarian and had a short stubby black beard, "YOU had better shut up, or YOU won't see the Fatherland again!"

One of my regimental police said "He'll be lucky to reach the cage alive if he doesn't shut up," and another man said to him "Give me that Iron Cross, you bloody Boche!" This was life and death "War in the Raw".

For his part in this incident, Corporal Thomas was awarded the DCM and Private Corless was mentioned in despatches. Dick told us that he and Thomas reached a position from which they could see the German machine-gunners, and that Thomas then proceeded to pick them off one by one until the survivors had had enough and began to cry "Kamerad". It was very unusual for German machine-gunners to surrender. They were often killed at their guns rather than surrender, but in this incident some of them survived, and undoubtedly many British lives were saved by Corporal Thomas's ruthless skill. Also, two German machine-guns were captured.

Meanwhile, on our right, the German counter-attack was developing very fast. The Germans pressed forward with great determination, inflicting heavy casualties on B company. Some of them actually captured part of the advanced trench that B company had hastily occupied, when we were alerted to the fact that a large body of Germans, estimated at about three companies, were advancing down the forward slope of the next ridge.

Sergeant Colley, MM, on his own initiative, rushed forward to the survivors in the advanced trench and formed a defensive flank. Eventually, after more fighting, the Germans were driven out and the counter-attack was held. Sergeant Colley was very badly wounded and died that night. For his courage and tenacity he was awarded a posthumous Victoria Cross.

After it was dark, the German counter-attack petered out and they withdrew. About 1 a.m. the 9th Battalion of the Duke of Wellingtons came up from behind, and the Lancashire Fusiliers were relieved. Next day the Duke of Wellingtons continued the attack in the direction of Flers, a village which became the scene of very violent attack and counter-attack. This village changed hands several times.

INTENSIVE ENEMY SHELLING

For several days the 10th Battalion Lancashire Fusiliers was out of touch with the enemy physically, but not out of touch with his shell fire. Once again, as we were advancing towards a typical ridge of this rolling Somme countryside, 5.9 shells began to burst just ahead of us. It was evident that this was no casual shelling and there was no cover for us on this slope. On our left, there was a cemetery at the edge of a ruined village. We ran to it and lay among the graves.

I lay down between two graves, their low mounds of earth were my only cover. At times like this, one wishes that one's gas mask in its satchel on the chest was not there, so that one could press oneself down a bit lower.

The shelling continued for ten to fifteen minutes and was so intense that death or injury seemed inevitable. After a short period of fear, I became strangely calm and unafraid, accepting the fact that we will all return to the earth some day.

Later, we went on over the ridge and into the next valley, where we had another very unpleasant experience of enemy shell fire, this time with many casualties. This valley ran roughly north and south, parallel with the front. A narrow country road or field track ran down the centre of it, and on either side on the gentle slopes of the valley, the Germans had made, with their customary thoroughness, a large number of bivouacs of corrugated iron sheets on timber frames.

It was decided to spend the rest of the night here, and the men were pleased to occupy these bivouacs for a few hours. Although not shell proof or even shell splinter proof, they were weatherproof and soon became warm with the heat of our bodies. I posted a gas sentry and warned two other men to be ready to take a turn during the night.

GAS SHELLS

Maintaining a gas sentry rota was one of my duties. Sometimes I could get another NCO to be responsible for a night and he would post sentries from his section of machine-gunners, or from his pioneers; but more often than not I posted the regimental police, and lost a lot of sleep changing sentries.

However, on this occasion, nobody had any sleep, because less than an hour after we arrived, the Germans started shelling the valley. Once again we had evidently been spotted from their observation balloons. At first they were gas shells, blue cross variety, which, while not lethal, are a very clever tactical weapon. I knew from past experience that the men were inclined to ignore this type of gas shell, and I made myself very unpopular as I went from bivouac to bivouac telling everyone to wear their gas masks. Most of the types of gas shells used by the Germans came over with a wobbly whistling sound and burst with a harmless sounding plop. They wobbled in the air as they arrived by the dozen and burst plop-plop-plop-plop giving off a small cloud of smoke which thinned as it dispersed.

So a gas shell seemed innocuous compared with high explosive shells, which arrive with a roar and burst with a crash, scattering fragments. The blue cross shells now being used were Jerry's latest tactical weapon, and were often mistaken for HE because there was no wobbling noise as they came over. The danger was that some men were unwilling to wear their gas masks, and then, if Jerry switches to a lethal type of gas such as phosgene, this can irreparably damage the lungs or kill outright. I constantly warned men of this danger, telling them that the irritation of the nose and throat, which many of them did not think was a sufficient reason for wearing their respirators, was only the first stage. Pain in the stomach and severe vomiting could follow, plus numbness of the limbs. They would then be sitting ducks for Jerry's lethal green cross gasses.

I had learned at the gas course at the Vth Corps Gas School that most of the types of gas shells used by the Germans contained a liquid, which became a gas on exposure to the air. Thus it required only sufficient explosive to crack the shell case although it sounds relatively harmless.

When I became Battalion Gas NCO, one of my responsibilities was to ensure that men realize the danger from a quiet gas shell, and to urge them as well as order them to wear their gas masks. Sometimes when we were sitting waiting for orders to move on, I would give a short informal talk about the various gasses and their awful effects when one is exposed to them without a gas mask. My constant warning about the deadly effects of the various German gas shells was confirmed later in civil life when I knew of men who died prematurely after years of ill health coughing their lungs away.

At the bivouac site, I reported the situation to the officers, and then set off on another round of visits, going from bivouac to bivouac, often stumbling because it is difficult to see when the gas mask eyepieces are misted with breath. At each bivouac, I lifted the side of my respirator to shout into the doorway. By this time, as I had expected and feared, despite my many warnings, some of the men were coughing, sneezing, and some were retching. They were in just the right condition to be lethally gassed by phosgene or any combination of Jerry's green cross gasses if he chose to switch to them.

I reported again to Captain Milne on the condition of some of the men. I told him that the valley was filling with gas and, as there was no wind, the concentration of gas would increase. I was given the order to get the men out on the road with their equipment on, and ready to march.

JERRY SWITCHES, NOT TO PHOSGENE BUT TO HE

Two groups had moved off and others were preparing to follow when suddenly Jerry switched his shelling, not to phosgene as I had expected, but to HE. These shells were the deadly 5.9s, and at first they burst along the rear crest of the valley, but then they shortened the range and shells began to burst on and near the road. Soon there were shouts for stretcher-bearers, and wounded men were collected and carried to an emergency first aid post, where the MO and Sergeant Pearson and their staff began to attend to them.

By this time nearly all had taken off their gas masks and were trying to take cover wherever possible. Then a salvo of 5.9s burst with a roar near to the first aid post killing several stretcher-bearers and wounded men waiting for attention. The MO was wounded, but continued to attend others. As one of the wounded stretcher-bearers was being carried past me, he continually cried out "Put me down... put me down... let me die on the ground." I watched him go past, carried shoulder-high by four men, as they stumbled along the now shell-pitted track.

Jerry had got the range exactly now, and a 5.9 burst very close to them. They were all killed instantly. I went with another stretcher-bearer to see if anyone was alive, but they lay as they had fallen, with the stretcher shattered to pieces.

About a month later, there was a similar incident, when one of a succession of officers who in turn commanded A company, was killed in the same way. He had been company commander of A company before I joined it and had been wounded. Shortly after his return, he was wounded again, this time seriously, and while being carried by our stretcher-bearers, they and he were all killed by shell fire.

Eventually, the shell fire ceased, and after some delay, we marched off in the first light of dawn. At the end of the valley the track joined a road which turned uphill towards the front. As we reached a crest, we could see in the distance, as daylight increased, the last of the enemy flares which every night went up into the sky, hung for a time and went out and fell. Another NIGHT on the Western Front was ending; another DAY was about to begin.

Marching along this road, we passed through a cutting with an embankment of earth on either side, into which the Germans had dug deeply and constructed the largest dug-out I had seen. Into this we all crowded, hardly believing our good fortune as we came to wire netting beds in tiers, and charcoal burners in the aisles between the long rows of bunks. All this provision for his troops was a further evidence of our enemy's skill and thoroughness in all that he did.

Here there was opportunity to sort ourselves out, find out who had survived, record casualties and reorganise duties. Eventually we all had a welcome drink of hot tea. We spent all the daylight hours in and around this huge dug-out, and then at dusk our transport wagons found us, and I once more did the job of counting heads and dividing and distributing the rations.

As soon as it was dark, we were on the march again, on our way to the front.

ATTACK AND COUNTER-ATTACK AT FLERS

Continuing in the wake of the now ever-moving front, we came, in the middle of a very dark night, to a place near Flers, where there were some ex-German dug-outs which Jerry had dug into a long earth bank. We moved into them, and after posting a gas sentry, I fell asleep in one of them for a few hours. At daybreak we began to stir, and when we emerged from the dug-outs, we discovered that the field adjoining the dug-outs was literally littered with dead bodies. We realised that we had arrived during the night at yesterday's battle area, and, what a battle it had evidently been. Hundreds of dead, both British and German, still lay just as they had fallen.

It was obvious that the British artillery barrage had caused many of the German casualties; legs in top boots and other parts of men in German uniform were strewn about. Others had been killed in a British bayonet charge. One German and one British soldier had actually succeeded in bayonetting each other. Many walked across the field to see this strange sight, which, battle hardened as we were, deeply impressed us.

This area, near Flers, had been the scene of several British attacks and German counter-attacks. The HQ company had not taken any part in these attacks, but I was given a first-hand account of one German counter-attack when I was checking gas masks of A company later. They had advanced up a slope, led by Captain Sankey, my first company commander, and as they reached the skyline, they met the German counter-attack head on. One man told me how Captain Sankey was killed with many others, and how the survivors were driven back by this strong attack. He said "When I saw those Jerry bastards in field grey coming up the reverse slope, I looked at their bayonets and big field boots and I was quite willing to retire when the sergeant gave the order."

The Germans were always referred to by us as "Jerry bastards" but we all respected their courage, professional skill and their determination. Their NCOs, and some of their private soldiers, displayed great initiative; more, I sometimes thought, than we did when not led by a determined officer.

This may be one of the reasons why the British toll of young officers was so high. In the seven months from April to November, my company, A company, had no less than five company commanders. The first was captain Sankey, a hard and very determined officer; he was wounded and was replaced by Captain Jowett, a very much loved officer who was killed while attempting to help a wounded man who was lying out in the open between us and the Germans. Sankey returned to the battalion and was killed at Flers, and his successor was not with us long enough for me even to get to know his name. He was the one who was wounded and then killed with stretcher-bearers. The next was Captain Hamilton, a natural leader, who was mortally wounded in the attack at Gouzeaucourt in September. The one who replaced him was Captain Wareham. He was wounded in our attack on Neuvilly on 12th October.

When the Lancashire Fusiliers finally held and occupied Flers, I saw some of A company's dead still lying there, but minus their boots, which Jerry had taken.

The faces of some of them had turned black in the warm sunshine, but I recognised Private White, Pearson's buddy. He was one of those whose boots Jerry had taken. In the centre of the village I came to a large grave in what had probably once been the village green. In this soft soil a temporary grave had been hastily dug for a dozen or more Lancashire Fusiliers. Their names were written on a piece of wood nailed to a stake. I was sorry to see that Sergeant Hastings was one of them. He was the sergeant who led a party of men out of the line to go on various courses. I had just been called out of no man's land to go on a course at the Vth Corps Gas School near Abbeville. How long ago that seemed now!

The names of some of the boys who had trained with me in England were also scrawled on the wood. Two I remember particularly because they were close friends; one a tall thin youth with light sandy hair, his friend a short stocky boy. They were an odd couple when seen together as they usually were. Now their lives had ended together.

ANOTHER INCIDENT IN THE WAR GAME

Shortly after this, I was sent by Lieutenant Smith to take a special rifle to one of the companies. It had telescopic sights attached, which made it very clumsy to carry. I was told to deliver it to the officer in command of the two forward platoons. I set off with my own rifle slung on my left shoulder and the heavier telescopic rifle on my right shoulder. This made it impossible to swing my arms.

I was accompanied by a battalion runner, who told me that it was very tricky going up the line here in daylight. He said we would certainly be shelled. The reason for this "comforting" information was that there was, of course, no safe communication trench leading to the forward troops who had gone up to the front in the dark and dug themselves in. The only way to reach them was along a field track which the German artillery observers kept under constant observation.

One could imagine them passing the news back to their guns, "Here are two more to have a shot at." They were already shelling two men who were dodging on and off the track about one hundred yards ahead of us as the enemy shells burst.

I decided that it was sheer suicide to follow them along the track, remembering also how two battalion runners had been killed in similar circumstances a few days earlier. We had watched as they crossed open ground and saw how the enemy shells eventually bracketed them as they ran for cover. Finally a shell burst near to them and Greenoff was killed outright and his young companion mortally wounded.

They were buried, and two other men were appointed as replacements. One of these was an older man, about thirty-five, who had been a London bus driver; I found his cockney accent quite refreshing amongst the Lancashire dialect. He asked me what sort of job this was as a battalion runner, and I told him he would be more independent than in a platoon, but no safer. Indeed, that same night two more battalion runners were hit by a shell burst. One returned in a great state of shock, and when two more runners went out and found his companion's body, it was still warm.

Battalion runners had to be self-reliant and knowledgeable; some had long service on the Western Front and most of them had been wounded. They always worked in pairs on a rota drawn up by their corporal, and were constantly exposed to danger as they carried messages, as were signaller linesmen who were sent out in pairs to repair telephone wires broken by shell fire. Despite experience and skill in moving across exposed areas, they often suffered heavy casualties.

So on this trip with the telescopic rifle I decided to leave the track and led the way to the left, but still going forward. This move was evidently noticed and the German gunners continued sniping at us, much to our indignation. As the runner said, "We expect to be sniped with a rifle, but it's a bit thick when Jerry uses his artillery to do it; they must want something to do!" We came to a recently ploughed field, and here the enemy shells seemed to be less dangerous, as they burst deep in the soft soil, throwing up huge sprays of soil.

Still going forward but bearing half left across the ploughed field, we staggered along with pounds of soil on each boot. At the edge of the large field, to our delight, we discovered a railway cutting. We hurriedly slid down a steep bank to the track and started to trot forward for about 200 yards. In this deserted railway cutting, we felt secure and even stopped to enter a small railwayman's hut by the side of the line. Here we found a sack of potatoes which we were tempted to pilfer, but refrained. Further on we climbed up the embankment and cautiously emerged into a field which we soon discovered was in dead ground, and thus out of sight of the keen and competent German artillery observers. I commented to the runner "Well, you know which way to go in future when they send you up to the front line here."

Looking back after many years, I am amazed how we youngsters treated all these incidents as a game with a sporting chance. It was the same when I watched Sergeant Swift observing the German front line with his field glasses. He would carefully choose a suitable spot where it was difficult for him to be observed by the enemy, and then pass back information to our trench mortars.

After delivering the precious telescopic rifle to a rather unenthusiastic officer, we stood chatting to the troops and exchanging news of what had happened to whom. Our front line here was a field ditch behind a hedge; the ditch had been deepened in some places to as much as four or five feet, but we moved along the top, feeling reasonably safe behind the hedge, until Jerry started shelling. Then we hurriedly departed, feeling that we had had enough shelling for one day, and returned to BHQ in the dusk, along the track, now comparatively safe.

SALVAGE PARTY

There seemed no limit to the variety of odd jobs which various officers gave me to do. One day even the lieutenant quartermaster, who spent most of his time at the wagon lines at B echelon, gave me one.

This is how he put it to me, "Ah, Corporal, I want you to muster a dozen men and collect some picks and shovels for me. Just follow up the tracks of B company and recover as many picks and shovels as possible. I've got no more to issue until I get some back."

He made it seem a harmless enough exercise, but after searching a wood in which B company had spent the previous night before moving on, we were soon in trouble. Nothing escapes the attention of the opposition in daylight in a forward area, and doubtless we were seen from one of the observation balloons strung out across the sky behind the enemy line. We had loaded ourselves with a wonderful variety of picks and shovels, both British and German, which we had laboriously collected in and near the wood. We had left the shelter of the wood and were about to enter some deserted trenches, when Jerry started shelling us seriously.

I called the dozen or more men to follow me and started walking along a trench hoping to find another way back to BHQ. Soon I lost my way and even my bearings in a maze of old deserted trenches, and began to wonder which way to go next. As it now seemed we were caught between two lots of shell fire, I decided to call a halt and wait on events. After about a quarter of an hour the shelling ceased since Jerry could no longer see us moving, and I led the way in the direction in which I hoped BHQ was. It was no joke bending low in some of the shell-battered trenches to escape further observation, while carrying half a dozen picks and shovels each, and our rifles.

The quartermaster had the grace to thank me. "A good effort, Corporal," he said when we finally handed over our haul.

DIVISIONAL OBJECTIVE

We had been told that the divisional objective, a new expression to me, of the 17th Division was Le Transloy. This was on the Bapaume-Peronne road, and we were told that when this line had been secured, we should be withdrawn for rest, reinforcement and a refit. It didn't happen; we continued to advance. Actually after a few more miles to Rocquigny, we stopped for a few days while the tide of battle went on without us. At Rocquigny there was a soda-water factory where we found thousands of bottles of soda-water packed in straw in light wooden crates. We gleefully drank it generously; we even shaved in it because of the usual shortage of water; and the news of this find spread far and near; men and horse drawn limbers came from every unit in the vicinity.

THE MAINTENANCE OF DISCIPLINE AND MORALE

One day I was very pleased to see Tim Costello again. He had been wounded and had that day returned to his company from hospital. I told him how the whole character and style of the war had changed since we were together in the trenches at Mesnil, Bouzincourt and Auchonvillers.

"Yes", he said, "I can see it has; do you remember Death Valley? What a place that was!" Then he said, "What I want to know is, whatever has happened to my old platoon sergeant? I've been told he's now a company cook!"

The sergeant in question had been a first-class platoon sergeant of No. 1 platoon when I used to be in No. 2 platoon. I used to admire the way he handled his platoon, but now something had happened. Had his nerve cracked? Some said that he tried, or threatened to put his foot under a passing transport wagon. Although no one really knew what had happened, I like to think of him as the efficient platoon sergeant I knew in those summer days when we practised in Toutencourt Wood for an attack on Aveluy Wood.

During my service in France, I saw only two cases of shell-shock; the first was young Harvey, who collapsed at the first enemy shelling. The other was an older man named Locke, who returned to the company after recovering from a wound. He told us as soon as he arrived that he would not be able to stand shell fire again. Sure enough, as soon as we came under shell fire he was grovelling in the bottom of the trench, screaming and filling his mouth with soil.

I only heard of one case of cowardice; this was a sergeant in another company whom I did not know; and I never heard any particulars of this case. The RSM nipped in the bud all discussion. "Never!" he said, "never talk about any case of cowardice you may hear of. You NCOs must at all times uphold the honour of the regiment."

Pride of regiment was continually instilled into the NCOs by our RSM. Minden Day was celebrated while we were in the trenches by an issue of wine, and the exploits of the 1st Battalion (that incomparable battalion!) at Gallipoli in 1915 (six VCs before breakfast!) was never allowed to be forgotten by the RSM and one or two other old soldiers. Just as the traditions of the Royal Navy became the standard for young men in the Royal Naval Division, so the traditions of our regiment were constantly set before us.

The Battle of Minden was ancient history to the Byng Boys; it took place during the Seven Years War, 1756 to 1763, when England was allied with Prussia against the French. Six British infantry regiments took part in the battle, the Hampshires; the Suffolks; the Lancashire Fusiliers; the Royal Welsh Fusiliers; the Kings Own Scottish Borderers, and the Kings Own Yorkshire Light Infantry. The British were given the order "Advance with drums beating at the proper time." Without waiting they advanced with drums beating, not to receive the French cavalry, but to attack them, with the support of the Royal Artillery. They won the day. During their advance the British infantry picked roses and put them in their head-dresses, and the Battle of Minden is remembered by the Lancashire Fusiliers on 1st August each year, when the regimental colours and drums are ceremonially paraded with roses which are worn by the officers and men in memory of Minden Day. By such means are regimental traditions preserved.

The Lancashire landing on W beach at Gallipoli was more recent to us; it took place at 6 a.m. on 25th April 1915, when the 1st Battalion XX The Lancashire Fusiliers stormed the beach defences, which were so strong that the Turks considered them impregnable. The Lancashire Fusiliers were landed in pinnaces and ships' lifeboats towed from HMS *Euryalus* and HMS *Implacable* in line abreast to the quarter mile long strip of powdery sand between two headlands on the Gallipoli Peninsula. Many Lancashire Fusiliers were killed by Turkish fire in the sea; many who reached the beach were mown down, but some landed on rocks at the north end of the beach. They managed to get on to the cliff above the beach and outflanked the Turks. At the end of the day, only sixteen of twenty-five officers and 300 of 932 men, were left and sixty-three out of the eighty naval ratings who manned the boats were killed or wounded.

Six VCs were awarded and "Six VCs before breakfast" has been the regiment's proud boast ever since. Commander-in-Chief, General Sir Ian Hamilton, in his Despatches said, "No finer feat of arms has ever been achieved by the British soldier than the storming of the Turkish trenches on the morning of 25 April 1915." Vice-Admiral de Robeck, in his Despatch said "The dash and gallantry displayed was superb." The motto of the regiment is *Omnia Audax* — daring in all things.

FORTITUDE UNDER FIRE

Although death or wounds were an ever present threat in the forward area, there was, with very few exceptions, an outward attitude of unconcern.

When we were in the trenches at Mesnil in April, or at Auchonvillers in May, or at Bouzincourt in July, with HE shells exploding great spouts of soil and stones all around us, or if there were shrapnel bursts of black and greenish yellow in the sky above us, usually someone would shout, "Go it, Jerry! Send em over", thus refusing to show any fear.

After I was promoted, and then had special duties to perform, I found that the necessity to carry them out, even under shell fire, made an attitude of unconcern easier, especially if I was leading a party of men. In the big attacks, from August to November, when thousands of men were all moving forward, as we were at Thiepval Ridge in August, and enemy shells were bursting just ahead of us, we still kept going forward, almost mechanically.

Emotion was numbed; we ignored the dead as machine-gun bullets hissed and cracked past us, some cutting into the ground in straight lines. Although I saw men fall right and left of me, and passed by some horrible sights, I had no thought of death for myself. No one stopped to help wounded men who groaned as we passed; the one overmastering impulse of all who still lived was to keep going forward. We youngsters had, in a few short months, become quite acclimatised to the facts of life and death on the Western Front.

We accepted the fact that it was a very dangerous place; that death or wounds were its natural, constant and its inevitable state, and, that we were all, officers, NCOs and men in it together. Individually, everyone was afraid sometimes; but morale was always maintained by firm leadership. Even when nerves are frayed, a good leader can overlay men's fears with his own determination and quick positive orders. These, and example, always produce instant action by trained soldiers.

Personally, I am neither by temperament, nor upbringing, the tough physically courageous type; but in dangerous situations I often experienced exhilaration instead of fear.

I faced the facts of life and death, on the Western Front, and they are, that the moment the fear of death made a man try to avoid it, he ceased to be a soldier. The answer to fear is discipline, to be ready to die any day, at any time, but to fight to live. A disciplined soldier can learn by experience how to live and fight another day.

FINS WOOD

After a few days at Rocquigny, we moved forward in the wake of the now continuing advance, and spent a night in Fins Wood. Hundreds of transport horses and mules were tethered in a long line under the trees quite close to us. When enemy shells burst in their vicinity; they were terrified, rearing and kicking and making loud shrill screaming noises.

I received and dished out the rations to the various sections, posted gas sentries and then attempted to get a few hours' sleep. I lay on the leafy ground under a tree, having my groundsheet/cape under me and another one which I had scrounged, over me, including my face.

I soon went to sleep, but I was up again soon after dawn, telling everyone to wear their gas masks. Jerry was literally drenching the area with gas. The gas shells came over continuously, bursting with their innocuous plop-plop-plop and releasing the liquid which gave off gas.

As usual, the foolish attitude of some of the men was "Oh they are only gas shells, and anyway most of them are bursting outside Fins Wood." I could see that the continuous rain of hundreds of gas shells into the shallow valley outside the wood was creating a thick cloud of gas which could be very dangerous. Fortunately for us the wind was not blowing in our direction, but when the shelling ceased, Captain Milne sent for me and we discussed the possibility and effects of a change of wind on such a high concentration. Eventually he told me to go to the two forward companies, A and B, and warn the company commanders of the possibility of a change of wind causing this heavy concentration of gas in the valley near the HQ Company to drift in their direction and catch them unawares.

I had no idea where exactly the two forward companies were, but one of our HQ runners had already been to them and so he accompanied me. Just as we were emerging from Fins Wood we met several wounded men; one of them was being carried by two of our stretcher-bearers. As we passed, I saw that the man on the stretcher was a corporal; he was unconscious and his face and the gas mask on his chest were red with his blood.

The runner and I came out of the wood and crossed a road on which enemy HE shells were bursting intermittently as we ran across. We struck off down a field track where there was little cover for us. As the German observation balloons were up, we hurried across open ground to another small wood. Here we lingered for a few minutes to read the names on a large group of wooden crosses which bore the names and rank of guardsmen who had fallen in the capture of Fins. Leaving the wood we hurried across more open ground and came to a trench which overlooked another wood with very tall trees. Thankfully we dropped into it and further along came to a lone machine-gunner of the Machine-Gun Corps. We talked to him for a few minutes while behind us a battery of our Heavy Artillery pounded the wood and the area beyond it. Huge explosions erupted black smoke and soil high above the tall trees as the shells roared down.

The machine-gunner said that they were armour piercing shells. We all wondered what the target behind the trees down the slope could possibly be. When at last the shelling ceased, the runner and I went forward towards the wood and before we reached it came to another trench. Here we found some Lancashire Fusiliers who directed us to company headquarters — a dug-out with a heavily sandbagged entrance, where I asked for the company commander.

Captain Hamilton, A Company, and Lieut. Gibbs, B Company, both came out to the entrance to talk to me; they were evidently sharing a joint company HQ. I told them about the drenching we had had early that morning, and gave Captain Milne's warning of the possibility of gas drifting down to them unexpectedly by a change of wind, and I advised that all gas sentries should be warned.

Before I returned to the HQ Company with the runner, I spent some time talking to old friends in A Company. They all spoke highly of their new company commander; one man told me how he had been out with him during the night, crawling about near the enemy positions. "He likes to know the lie of the land before he leads us into an attack," he said. I too was very impressed by him; he was a born leader of men and because he personally led his men, he could always draw the best out of them. Unfortunately, such men do not last long on the Western Front.

I had already met him briefly at a pay parade since HQ personnel always received their pay from their old company. He sat at a table with the company quartermaster, who called out the names in alphabetical order.

During the long wait I talked to Corporal Collins, MM, always known as "Lottie". (Miss Lottie Collins was a Gaiety Girl who sang the popular song Ta-ra-ra-Boom-di-ay.)

During our conversation, Corporal Collins showed me a newspaper cutting from his home town about himself, and also a photograph which astonished me. It was a print of an X-ray negative which clearly showed that Lottie had a bullet, in his heart! He told me that the surgeons had told him that it was too dangerous to attempt to remove it. So, he had been sent back to the front, and was an NCO in A Company.

When eventually it was my turn to receive my pay, I saluted Captain Hamilton at the pay table. He said "I haven't seen you before Corporal."

"No sir, I have been with Captain Milne since July as Battalion gas NCO."

He looked at me and smiled, and then said, "Well Corporal, if you ever want to come back to A Company, I will give you sergeant's stripes." When I did eventually return to A Company after the war had ended, Captain Hamilton had been dead three months.

The HQ runner and I returned to Fins Wood, and I reported to Captain Milne, and then went to join Corporal Thomas. As I passed the battalion first aid post, Sergeant Pearson beckoned to me. I went to him and he said "Come and look here." He led me to the body of a corporal whose face was covered with dried blood. It was the corporal I had seen earlier being carried on a stretcher. Sergeant Pearson seemed quite upset as he lifted the blanket off his face. He said, "I thought it was you when they carried him in, as he's your build; but then I saw that he was not wearing your black and green tabs."

A few days later I visited A Company trenches again. One man looked very surprised and said, "We heard that you had been killed." Another man said, "Yes, that's right. Someone told us that the big corporal was dead."

LEAVE FROM THE FRONT

All leave from the Western Front had been stopped when the German Spring Offensive broke though the British defences in March, 1918.

The Byng Boys, who had joined the Army in the Summer of 1917, had six days leave at the end of November, but when we were transferred to the Lancashire Fusiliers in early April, we were told our entitlement to our next leave would date from our arrival in France and not from our last leave in England. Leave from the front did not recommence until August, and was then running at seventeen months instead of the usual twelve months.

The man whose name was at the top of the battalion list for leave was a company signaller, and he was killed by shell fire while mending a break in the line to BHQ. Corporal Wilkinson and the HQ linesmen brought him in, and they wrapped him in a groundsheet. He was a tall youngster and they buried him in a shell hole which they enlarged. One of the signallers read a scripture from his pocket testament and committed him to God. No officer was present. After this incident, there was some criticism about this very sad death of a man who was waiting for his leave chit to come through.

Corporal Wilkinson spoke to the signals officer, who promised that he would make representations to the colonel. After this the man who was next due for leave did not go up the line, but stayed down at the horse lines, until he went on leave. None of the Byng Boys had a leave from the front since our active service was insufficient, only seven months, 6th April 1918 to 11th November 1918.

It must have been a very strange experience to return home on leave from the Western Front; one of the older men described it on his return to the battalion as a short visit to another planet where he found it impossible to communicate with the natives!

Sometimes the conversation in a dug-out or a barn turned back to civvy street, to places and events that now belonged to a past that was a closed book. We accepted this philosophically and quite cheerfully; we knew that many of us would never experience life there again.

That is why, I suppose, we made such a fuss of a man who got a Blighty; a wound that would take him to England and not merely to a Base Hospital. A Blighty was regarded as a prize which only the lucky few would receive. As for leave from the front, well, who was going to last seventeen months? One man did; an observer named Green, I hardly recognised him when he gleefully departed dressed in a new tunic with his buttons all clean!

Some of us suffered another kind of deprivation; we had nothing to read; nothing to feed the mind in the limited world of active service. Men would read the letters they received over and over again; would even read them out for comment or discussion. No detail was too small or insignificant to be of interest or to stimulate a conversation about that other world. When Lance-Corporal Avery came back from his leave, we pumped him dry for scraps of information about the world we had left and might never see again. Unfortunately for me, most of his reminiscences were of the numerous visits he had made to various pubs and the glorious booze-ups in which he had played a prominent part.

A WORLD WITHIN A WORLD

The Western Front of the Great War was another world. A world within a world. Not, however, in the sense that many normal phases of life are lived in one world.

Here on the Western Front all life was completely different. In the open fields of France there were no streets, no houses, no shops, offices or factories; no regular place of work; no regular food or sleep. One's life was not one's own; instead there were onerous duties, strict discipline, a chain of command and instant obedience to orders. There was comradeship and battalion pride; everything was shared, whether rations, duties, discomforts or dangers. Death was always hovering, but trench life was not lived in tension or fear; it was lived in top gear. Physical health was excellent, and the high spirits and humour which are normal in young men were always evident.

The infantry of 1918 was young, fresh and strong; inexperienced, but quick to learn and act in changing circumstances. There was a strange enthusiasm in being an infantryman, with everything you possessed attached to you; one was always ready to move at a moment's notice. Life was uncomplicated, and the nearness of death sharpened one's awareness of life; there is exhilaration in danger, and courage is contagious. There is what G. K. Chesterton called a contradiction in terms, a strong determination to live which takes the form of a readiness to die.

In this strange world, "Civvy Street", the front line soldier's name for the civilised world which he may never see again, became the unreal world. It was the world where he once lived in a house, sat at a table, slept in a bed and went to work. Now he lived in a real world, close to nature; his past life is irrelevant, his future is uncertain, and the present moment is his life. Small pleasures please; they give a satisfaction out of all proportion to their old values; a hot drink of tea or a clean pair of socks; regular rations or a rest from duty; a letter from home, or even an opportunity to wash and shave.

THE HINDENBURG LINE

By the end of August, the Germans had been pushed back to their Siegfried Line, a massive system of fortifications over fifty miles long, which stretched from Bapaume, past the Flesquieres Salient to St. Quentin.

This line was always known to the British as the Hindenburg Line. It had been to this previously prepared position that the Germans carried out their strategic withdrawal on 16th March 1917. The Hindenburg Line was four to seven miles deep, with two sets of trenches which were about three miles apart. Each set had two trenches about half a mile apart. In addition, there were exceptionally wide and deep trenches to impede our tanks. By this withdrawal from their old and indented front, they had been able to conserve and reorganise manpower.

The construction of the Siegfried Line had been ordered by Hindenburg and Ludendorff, who realised that although they had inflicted grievous losses on the British New Army during the Somme battles from 1st July, to the middle of November 1916, their defences were being badly disorganised and their reserves of men were being used up. At that stage of the war they had still been fighting on two fronts; the Russians did not surrender until 1917.

They also knew that this Somme type of fighting would be renewed in the Spring of 1917, and so in September 1916, they began to build this great and formidable system of rear defences to which they secretly retired in March 1917, on the eve of the British Spring Offensive.

The Hindenburg Line was cleverly sited so that the ground over which the British troops must approach it had very little dead ground. Tens of thousands of British prisoners of war were employed on its construction, receiving only the barest rations; many were permanently ruined in health by their privations. On my return home after the war, I met and talked with men whose physique had been ruined; one man I worked with had such poor health that he could eat only the very lightest of food such as raw eggs and milk.

The German retirement to this line in March 1917, was very carefully planned and carried out secretly. Only when an unusual lack of activity became apparent, did British patrols go forward and discover that the enemy trenches were empty. Corporal Wilkinson and several other men had been with the 10th Battalion Lancashire Fusiliers when this cautious advance to the New German Line took place, and they told us that the word soon went round to be very careful. Many booby traps had been arranged in the deserted trenches for the unwary, and trip-wires to hidden bombs had to be cut, and all dug-outs were approached and entered with great caution. Wilky told us how careful the signaller linesmen had to be as they laid new wires across this desolate country.

The Germans had turned the belt of country which they had given up, and over which the British troops had to advance, into a manmade desert. Trees had been cut down to block roads, houses in the villages had been blown up and demolished, wells had been contaminated, there were booby traps everywhere and there were delayed action mines at crossroads. This ruthless destruction, which the Germans carried out with their usual efficiency, limited the opportunity of the British to renew their 1916 offensive, and made even a cautious advance very difficult and dangerous.

It was from their strong positions in their Siegfried Line that the Germans launched their great spring offensive on 21st March 1918 with such spectacular success, and with such hideous losses on both sides.

Having retired in March 1917 to conserve manpower on a shorter and stronger line of defence, in March 1918, with a million men and 5,000 guns from the collapsed Russian front, they had overwhelming numerical superiority for their brilliantly executed attack.

THE BATTLE FOR GOUZEAUCOURT

Now, in September 1918, the Byng Boys were moving forward into position for their big attack on this famous fortification, The Hindenburg Line. This grim battle for the great German defence line to which they had now retired again, was preceded by an intense and massive bombardment by our artillery, which really sapped the German strength.

The 10th (Service) Battalion, Lancashire Fusiliers were to attack at Gouzeaucourt on the Hindenburg Line, at the base of the old Flesquieres Salient. This was not far from the position that the Old Tenth had held and retired from at Havrincourt only six months earlier.

During the night of September 17th-18th, we moved into position on high ground just short of a skyline crest. As soon as we got there the RSM sent for me and told me to collect about twenty men and lead them back down to the bottom end of the long communication trench up which we had all just toiled. I collected the men, told them to take off their equipment and follow me down.

This communication trench was exceptionally deep and also wider than any trench I had seen before, and because it sloped steeply down hill and the surface was rough it was hard going.

At the bottom there was a road where our transport had dumped many boxes of Mills bombs; several dozen two gallon petrol cans full of water; and a very large heap of picks and shovels. I then knew why I had been sent by the quartermaster on that salvage expedition.

There was so much to be carried that we had to make several journeys down and then uphill again before we got everything to the RSM, who was organising their distribution. Then we recovered our rifles and equipment and settled down to wait for dawn. While we waited, a young officer came up the communication trench, looking a bit bewildered. He had just been posted to the battalion and was reporting for duty. What a time to arrive, on the eve of a great battle! The RSM questioned him, gave him some of his own rations and told him that he could not report to the company to which he had been allocated until things were more settled. In fact the RSM was quite fatherly!

The night was very still. Considering how many thousands of men were now assembled in their places all along the front, it was uncanny. Then just as it began to get light, the silence was broken by the thump of a single gun firing behind us. Immediately, there was a tremendous roar of artillery as thousands of our field guns poured a ceaseless rain of shell over us into the enemy positions.

Some of us climbed up out of the trench and stood on the top to watch. We could see the ground ahead of us erupting in a long black cloud of smoke. The enemy positions were literally spouting smoke, soil, pieces of timber — probably bodies. Behind us was the ceaseless drumming of our artillery and over us, the roar and shriek of shells and the swish and flail of a veritable storm of machine-gun bullets. It all stunned our senses but we felt no fear.

This British barrage at Gouzeaucourt on September 18th 1918, was the most intense and concentrated I experienced; the crash and thud of multiple explosions was continuous. I have since read that more shells were fired on that day than on any other on the Western Front. The barrage was not prolonged, but it was accurate, controlled, overwhelming and unforgettable. Then it ceased, quite suddenly, as if every gunner officer called "Cease fire" at the same moment. There was silence, and then as we waited and watched, awed by what we had seen and heard, expecting the order to advance, something almost miraculous happened.

We saw grey clad figures emerging from the long pall of black smoke in front of us and as they got nearer we could hear them coughing as they groped their way through the acrid smoke. They stumbled towards us with their hands up; some wounded and all of them completely dazed. How had they possibly survived? The regimental police took charge of them and our first aid team bandaged some of the wounded. At this stage, the only casualty on our side, that I saw, was one of my regimental police. I say "my" because although a new provost sergeant had been appointed, to replace Sergeant Grendon, he was an "elderly" man who wore Boer War ribbons and was not fit enough to come up the line. His name was Nash and he was a real old soldier, more than twice my age. In civil life he was the landlord of a public house in Luton.

So I had to deal with the casualty, who had been hit in the seat by a piece of one of our shells which, as we used to say, dropped short. We never blamed our artillerymen. I said to him, "Lie down, face downwards, and let's see what you've got." We slit the seat of his trousers with a jack knife to see the damage, put on a field dressing and congratulated him on getting a real Blighty. We all hoped that it would be one, but he was mainly concerned that no one should get their hands on his souvenirs. These turned out to be a quite remarkable collection of cutthroat razors, which he had scrounged from the pockets of the dead over a considerable period.

He valued most those he had taken from the German dead, which were of excellent quality, having blades of special steel. I found two stretcher-bearers and sent him off down the steep communication trench, his two breast pockets full of his precious souvenirs!

Some men had a mania for collecting souvenirs; some had half a dozen wrist watches; others collected German revolvers. I picked one up myself once as we passed through a captured trench, but a few days later I got tired of carrying it and threw it away. Why carry unnecessary weight on active service, although it was quite attractive with an ivory butt.

MASSIVE BELTS OF BARBED WIRE

When we got the order to advance to capture the vast network of trenches and strong points of the Hindenburg Line, we had to find a way through many belts of barbed wire. These belts were quite unlike the pathetic lines of wire that we so hurriedly repaired at night near Bouzincourt in May.

The men who had erected these had done so in daylight, and with great thoroughness; they were securely fixed on iron stakes four feet high, and each belt of barbed wire was thirty or more feet thick. There were also concrete strong points that had been cleverly sited to produce cross-fire.

Our guns had blasted gaps and our tanks had gone through, but the PBI were able to follow only with difficulty. Some casualties from enemy machine-gun fire were inevitable as we had to cut our way through in some places. Among our dead on this wire, I particularly noticed "Gladys", a signaller whom I had known and liked for some months. He was a tall youngster, very slim, with incredibly blue eyes and flaxen hair, hence his nickname, which he never resented. As I passed through the wire, I saw him lying, still grasping, in death, his wire cutters; there was some talk of a recommendation for bravery, but there were so many who could have been recommended.

After passing through one of the thick belts of barbed wire, I advanced with others towards a clump of tall trees, and looking up, saw that among the trees was a steel structure about forty or fifty feet high, like a miniature electricity pylon. At the top of it was a metal platform on which could be seen several German machine-guns. Fortunately for us, the machine-gunners had already been killed, and lay at the foot of the pylon.

During one period when we were held up by enemy machine-gun fire, several of us explored one of the enemy trenches where there were many German dead. I looked into several of the large dug-outs and saw that again they were elaborately fitted up, with wire netting bunks in tiers and charcoal burners between them. Jerry had certainly made his Siegfried Line very comfortable!

THE ADVANCE QUICKENS

Once we had broken through the massive Hindenburg Line, the pace of our advance quickened. The whole front was on the move at last after four years. In 1916 and 1917, despite all the preparations; all the heroism and all the losses, the Western Front had been impassable; the machine-gun always had the last word. Now, in 1918, our field guns no longer dug in before an attack; they stood in long rows, wheel to wheel, with no cover for the gun crews.

Long lines of mules with panniers, three 18 pounder shells on each side, kept up the supply of ammunition. It was most impressive to see the whole front advancing; even our company cookers moved up with us, chimneys smoking, water-carts following.

A vast quantity of supplies in wagons and limbers followed close behind the advancing infantry except when they were engaged with the enemy. On one occasion, just after the battle of Gouzeaucourt, the battalion was issued with extra rations for forty-eight hours. They were brought up to us at night to a large farm and buildings in which we were assembling.

As usual, the RSM found me a special job; he put me in charge of these extra rations and I had them deposited by the police in a small barn.

Adjoining there was a very large one where hundreds of men lay on straw, waiting for the order to move at dawn. It was packed with men. The extra rations were brought up by a party of men led by Sergeant Brown, the brigade gas NCO from whom I had taken over in July as battalion gas NCO. Brown also handed over to me some rockets tied up in a long heavy package encased in waterproof sheeting.

I asked him what they were for and he said they were to be used, if necessary, to signal for an artillery barrage. I had heard of these rockets; they were popularly known as SOS signals, and I had been told that they were fired up into the air when the infantry required a protective barrage against an enemy attack. However, I was not at all clear what use could be made of them in our attack, and asked Lieut. Smith, our intelligence officer. He simply said, "Carry them along, Corporal, let the police carry them just in case they are needed."

A little later, Sergeant Brown entered the small barn where the rations were, and in the dark he stumbled over some wounded men who had just been carried in on stretchers. I could see that it had upset him and posted one of the police at the door telling him not to let the SBs bring any more wounded to that barn as we should soon be taking out the extra rations for distribution.

Then I went to see what was going on in the big barn; I could get only a few feet inside; it was so packed with men lying on straw. At the far end I could see a group of officers, studying their maps by candle-light. All was very quiet; there was little conversation; the men were making the most of these few hours' rest before the next attack. Then I heard a voice, pleading with the officers; it was a youngster whose nerve had broken, asking to be sent down the line. As I withdrew, feeling a mixture of embarrassment and pity, I could hear the boy's pleading voice and the reassuring voice of one of the officers.

SPECIALIST SERVICES

About ten days after our big attack at Gouzeaucourt, we reached a small village where we remained for several days, other troops having taken over the spearhead of the advance. All kinds of specialist services quickly appeared in the village, including an Expeditionary Force Canteen with a long queue outside; water-carts with a guard on them; the cobblers' and tailors' shop; and what some irreverently called the wooden cross wallahs.

I went to a barn in one of the farmyards, where I had my boots repaired while I waited, and as I came out again on to the road, I noticed that a long line of wooden crosses had just been put leaning on a wooden fence. They were freshly inscribed, the black paint was wet, and they were drying in the autumn sun and wind. I walked slowly past them, and noted that Captain Hamilton now had a posthumous MC, and that Lieutenant Gibbs was a captain.

These two officers, the company commanders of A and B companies, were sharing a dug-out a few weeks earlier at Fins when I went to them to warn them of the drenching of gas that we had had at the HQ Company.

I wasn't surprised to see Captain Hamilton's cross; I had seen him being brought down on a stretcher, obviously mortally wounded. He directed the stretcher-bearers to carry him to the adjutant, to whom I heard him make his last report on the situation at A Company during the Gouzeaucourt attack. Captain Milne could see how gravely he was wounded, and took his hand for a few moments while he listened, and then urged him to let himself be carried to a casualty clearing station.

Captain Gibbs was, I think, killed outright in the attack. I noticed that both these fine young officers were aged twenty-four and at the time I thought this was quite a mature age; in the circumstances of their young lives, it was. As for Captain Milne, he must have been over thirty!

Looking back now to those days, our attitude to and calm acceptance of death as a natural daily event, amazes me, but it was so common and so casual that it was almost unreal.

A COMPARISON OF THE TWO GREAT OFFENSIVES OF 1918

In the vital battles of great offensives, where hundreds of thousands of men are involved, the individual infantryman knows little beyond his own battalion front, but years later, when all the facts are known, the survivors of these battles can read the accounts of them. I have found it interesting to compare the German Spring Offensive which commenced on

21st March 1918, with the British Offensive which commenced on August 8th.

On 21st March 1918, when Field Marshal Ludendorff, one of the greatest military brains of the war, launched his vast and well-prepared offensive on a fifty mile front, he knew it was all or nothing. With America's entry into the war in 1917, Germany's last hope of victory was to strike at the Allies' weakest point, where the British line joined the French.

The attack was an eye-opener, and it all but succeeded, for with ruthless efficiency, Ludendorff had re-equipped his armies, reinforced by forty-four divisions and 5,000 guns from the collapsed Russian front, and had retrained them for a War of Movement. That was innovative after years of trench warfare.

With 192 divisions at his disposal, Ludendorff's armies advanced forty miles, threatened to capture Amiens and drive the British to the English Channel and then destroy the French at leisure. This, of course actually happened in 1940 (Dunkirk and the French surrender).

Despite the large amount of ground gained and the destruction of General Gough's Fifth Army, the great spring offensive failed in its mam object. Losses on both sides were immense, and though Ludendorff continued to hurl Army after Army at the Allies until midsummer, somehow each blow was parried or absorbed.

By contrast, on August 8th 1918, the British Fourth Army under General Sir Henry Rawlinson attacked on a forty mile front with 100,000 men; 534 of the new Mark V tanks; 2,070 guns, and 800 aircraft.

The blow which fell on the German Second Army, commanded by General von der Marvitz, on that famous August 8th, was totally unexpected and victory was swift.

Ludendorff called it the Black Day of the German Army, and it was undoubtedly the turning point of the war; the first of a never ceasing succession of hammer blows which three months later, on 11th November, forced Germany to surrender. The attack began at 4.20 a.m., and so great was the surprise, and so swift the penetration, that before 7 a.m. the 5th Dragoon Guards, thrusting nine miles behind the German line, had captured a train with reinforcements of 600 men and three batteries of guns. Until the German artillery and machine-gunners halted them, the British cavalry roamed almost at will.

By midday, the Australian and Canadian infantry were more than five miles through, and the French 1st Army, (General Debeney) on the British right and under Field Marshal Haig's command, joined in the attack. By late afternoon the Germans were desperately trying to stabilise their front, then nine miles in the rear of the original positions.

By evening, the German 2nd Army was in a state of disorder, with losses of 30,000 (16,000 of them prisoners) and over 400 guns captured. British losses in men were relatively light at 9,000 killed and wounded, (compared with 57,470 on 1st July 1916), but tank losses and casualties were high, with only 145 of the 534 being serviceable by nightfall. Tank losses continued to be high. Only eighty-five were still in action on the 10th August; thirty-eight on 11th August; and only six on 12th August. The RAF flying just above the battle to bomb and machine-gun the retreating Germans, also suffered heavily. Nevertheless the tanks and planes played an invaluable part in the deep breakthrough.

The Battle of Amiens was a masterpiece of military art in its shrewd conception, meticulous preparation, with surprise the key note. The irresistible elan of the troops brought swift victory in the battle which was the beginning of the end. From then on, the British Armies, for the first time in history, engaged and defeated the main enemy in a continental war in a succession of battles that have no comparison.

As Marshal Foch said "Never at any time in history has the British Army achieved greater results in attack than in this unbroken offensive."

INSPECTIONS BY GENERALS

These were very different from those to which we were accustomed during our training days in England. Then, there had always been a vast amount of spit and polish, followed by close inspections by our NCOs and by our officers. Only after this did we form up for the grand ceremonial march past which was then followed by a personal inspection by the general.

Here, in France, they took place quite informally and very unexpectedly as we were marching up towards the line, or returning from the trenches for a period of rest, reinforcement and retraining.

As we were marching, suddenly the command would be passed down the long column of marching men "March to attention! Rifles at the slope!"... "Come on now — pick up the step! Left, right, left, right, left!"... "Smarten up there!"... "You! Get your shoulders back and your head up!"... "Left, right, left, right, left!"

The PBI were never very impressed by their generals; we never saw them in the forward area. They were such a complete contrast to the fighting men; we in our stained and well-worn khaki, wearing steel helmets, carrying rifle and full equipment, 120 rounds of S.A.A. and all our personal possessions on our backs; they, mounted on their well-groomed chargers at the roadside.

There they sat, in their smart clean uniforms, adorned with red tabs, scarlet bands on their gold-braided service caps, brass buttons all gleaming, leather top-boots highly polished, proudly wearing their medals. They were well-fed, red-faced men with smartly trimmed white moustaches; men whose background was quite different from ours. Their training and their military experience as young officers was probably confined to peacetime soldiering in India, with possibly a little active service in the Boer War twenty years earlier as majors or colonels.

As we marched past and gave the eyes left to these "Brasshats" and overheard some of their remarks about us, we knew that they were very critical of the civilian army that they, the professionals, had been so unexpectedly promoted to command. Feelings were mutual, but on our part concealed. They so obviously thought we were not proper soldiers, and we knew that they were not real ones.

On one occasion, I was the object of severe criticism by my Divisional General. Just before we were ordered to march to attention, some of us had been smoking cigarettes as we marched at ease with our rifles slung by the strap over our right shoulders. I stubbed mine out and put it on my left ear, a common practice among marching troops, but not to be recommended on such an occasion as this! The eagle eye of the general spotted it as I turned my head towards him in the eyes left, and he sent one of his red-tabbed staff officers to deal with this, to him, very disgraceful occurrence.

The young dandy spurred his horse and came after the marching column, identified me and then rode on ahead to order my company commander to "tell that corporal to remove that cigarette from his ear." My company commander, Lieutenant Duckworth, stepped aside from the marching column, waited for me to pass, and then gave me a strong rebuke.

Brigadier Generals were in close touch with the battalions they commanded, especially during our attacks, but Divisional Generals and their staffs lived in a totally different world from the troops in the trenches.

There was a story of one be-medalled elderly staff officer who paid a very brief visit to the trenches one evening, and after a chat and a whisky with the CO was heard to say as he left the BHQ dug-out —

"Well, keep up the good work. I must be off! We've got roast pork for dinner tonight, and I don't want to be late for that!"

The troops felt like giving him three ironical cheers as he disappeared down the communication trench on his way to his well-earned dinner. Perhaps three loud grunts would have been more appropriate.

"E'eh lads, didst tha see 'is medals?"

THE OLD FRENCHMAN

One afternoon the HQ Company was approaching a small town through some cultivated fields on its outskirts. The men were moving forward in a long line across a turnip field. We were following up the advance and ahead of us we could see enemy shells bursting at the crossroads just outside the town.

We saw the colonel and the adjutant sit down with their backs to a large tree in the middle of the turnip field. They were looking at their maps. Since it looked as if we were not going on for the time being, we all sat down amongst the turnips and some of us cut one up to see if it was eatable — it wasn't.

Then some men walked over to the left to a farm, and I decided to go too. The farm was old and in bad condition; shell fire had destroyed some of the barns and other outbuildings. On the farther side a muddy road led towards the town. When I reached the back door of the farm, I found a small queue of men waiting, and saw inside an old Frenchman pumping up water from a well under an old stone sink; it was very primitive. Soon I moved into the stone-floored kitchen and as I waited my turn, I studied his old wrinkled face; grey hair sprouting out from under a peaked cap. Outside, on the road, enemy shells were bursting, some quite near, but the old man was completely unconcerned as he pumped up water for the thirsty troops. His twinkling eyes and stolid peasant patience revealed an uncomplaining acceptance of the war on his farm; life must go on; British boys were thirsty, so he filled our water-bottles.

CAMBRAI BURNS

As we continued the advance, we could see, for several nights, on our left in the distance, a huge red glow in the sky where Cambrai was burning. We could hear dull thunderous explosions as many delayed action mines which had been left by the retreating Germans either went off or were dealt with by the Royal Engineers. We spent one night in a grassy sunken lane, having been told to be ready to move at a moment's notice. I took off my equipment and sat with my back to the grassy bank, keeping everything I used within hand's reach in case we got the order to move off in the dark.

I don't think anyone slept that night, and in the early light of dawn we watched the huge slowly mushrooming smoke of mines, and heard the dull boom boom of explosions miles away to our left as Cambrai burned.

AUTUMN WEATHER

The weather in the autumn of 1918 was favourable for a war of continuous advance, and right into October it was still fine, apart from one period when we marched in the rain. The volume of military traffic moving forward turned the smaller roads into muddy tracks, and I saw many dead, both German and British, lying soddened by the roadside.

At one sharp corner on a hill, I particularly noticed the muddy body of a British soldier being repeatedly sprayed with liquid mud as the wheels of a long convoy of lorries turned this corner, passing within a couple of feet of him.

One day we passed through a sunken lane where many dead German troops lay, pockets emptied and inside out; evidently the souvenir hunters had been busy. There were a few British dead, and in passing I observed one British soldier lying, his thick glossy black hair still neatly parted, so unusual among the tousled heads of the majority. The silent dead, lay so still and some were as grotesque as dolls. I was fascinated by the German dead; they had such strange packs, made of hairy red horsehide, and their respirators were in leather cases too.

When fine weather returned it became colder, and leather jerkins were issued to us. They were sleeveless and we wore them on top of our tunics, adjusting the straps and buckles of our equipment to accommodate them.

The autumn leaves were blowing madly off the trees when we halted one day at the edge of a large wood where there were many dead, mostly Germans.

As we stood eating our food, Corporal Thomas put on a dead German's overcoat and a round German field cap with no peak. He entertained us for a few minutes with grimaces and guttural noises. We all laughed at his antics and congratulated him on his performance as a Jerry.

THE BIG PUSH CONTINUES

As the Front continued to move steadily forward, we found that the country east of the Hindenburg Line was mostly undamaged; it bore little resemblance to the countryside west of that great fortification. The war-torn wilderness of the 1916-1917 Somme battles was now behind us; no longer were we passing through shattered villages, ruined roads lined by tree stumps and fields pitted with thousands of shell holes.

Ahead were a number of small towns, some of which the Germans were to defend very strongly, to our cost; sometimes they tried to delay our advance by the use of poison gas.

One evening we were marching, in column of four, towards a small town which lay deep in the hollow of a river valley. Presumably our forward troops had already passed through, or we should not be marching in column of four. We could see shells bursting near a bridge over the river as we marched down a long hill, and as we got nearer, we could see that it was a pontoon bridge, constructed by the Royal Engineers.

Then word was passed back from the head of the column "Corporal Hodges to report to the head of the column." As I trotted past the marching men I could smell pineapple gas, and when I reached the officer leading, he said, "Now Corporal, when you say, I'll order the men to put their gas masks on. What do you say?" What a decision; I knew how many of them would "hate" me if I did, but as we descended lower down the hill, I could not do other than say that gas masks must be worn.

ATTACKS FROM GERMAN PLANES

During these last weeks of the war, with a mobile front, the 10th Battalion, Lancashire Fusiliers, if not actively engaged with the enemy, were always moving, following up the advance. Once we were marching in column of four on a very busy field track towards the front.

Suddenly we heard machine-gun fire, and saw a German plane diving out of the cloud, machine-gun blazing over the congested column of men, mules, wagons and horses. We had no time to scatter as we usually did on such occasions. About fifty yards behind us, an anti-aircraft gun, one of the new mobile type, was travelling in this column. Swiftly its crew drove it a few yards off the track, swung it round, and to our amazement, as the German plane wheeled round for another burst of fire at us, the very first shell from the gun, shot off its tail. We all stopped marching and watched this extraordinary sight, and then we cheered and cheered as the German plane crashed.

On another occasion, we were marching at night towards the front to take part in the next attack, as usual marching on the right side of the road. We were passing a long column of transport wagons coming back from the front. We heard explosions ahead of us as a German plane dropped small anti-personnel bombs. As it came nearer we realized that it was flying low above the track. We could see the column of men in front breaking up as officers and men ran off the track to the right. We all followed suit, flinging ourselves down about thirty or forty yards from the track.

When it was all over, we stood up, and for some reason that I cannot explain, some of us were laughing as we returned to the track, where we found both men and mules lying dead. We marched on, and soon we reached the forward area. The moon was rising as we left the track and moved in open order across a very large field of stubble, and here in the bright moonlight, field mice scampered in scores; one could scarcely avoid treading on them. Obviously this area had been cultivated, unlike the Somme fields, where no corn had been harvested during the war.

THE BATTLE FOR NEUVILLY

Right through October the Western Front continued to move forward as the British Army, now mainly composed of nineteen-year-old veterans and young inexperienced eighteen-year-old boys, with a leavening of the survivors of many past battles, struck blow after blow, forcing the Germans to retreat.

There were, however, some very hard and costly battles for towns, villages or ridges where the enemy, for various reasons, chose to make a stand. The capture of Neuvilly, a small town or large village standing on the far side of the River Selle, was one of these very difficult tasks. It was given to the 52nd Infantry Brigade, of which the 10th (Service) Battalion of the Lancashire Fusiliers was a part.

After the battle for Gouzeaucourt on the Hindenburg Line, the 10th had a short rest and were reinforced at Lesboeufs and Rocquigny and then moved on to Equancourt on 5th October. From there we moved forward to get into position for the attack on Neuvilly. We dug in along a sunken lane south-west of the town of Inchy on 8th October. On 12th October, the battalion took part with the two other battalions of the 52nd Brigade, in the first attack on Neuvilly. The village stood on high ground on the far side of the River Selle, and the houses overlooking the river were fortified with sandbags in the doors and windows.

The German machine-gunners had a clear view of the long gentle slope of the river valley, and, of any British troops advancing from over the crest, which was their skyline, from our positions near Inchy. For this reason all our attacks took place in the half-light of dawn. I took no part in the first attack, being with BHQ in the sunken lane behind the ridge. The 12th Battalion of the Manchesters attacked on the north side of the village, and the 9th Battalion of the Duke of Wellingtons on the south.

A creeping barrage by our artillery preceded them as they crossed the bridges over the Selle and advanced to the line of the railway beyond it to attempt to seize the high ground. A and B companies of the Lancashire Fusiliers followed the two battalions with the task of mopping up the village. C and D companies were to reinforce or take action wherever they were needed.

The Lancashire Fusiliers were in position at 4 a.m., and the barrage commenced at 5 a.m. The Manchesters crossed the river, stormed the high ground and began to consolidate, while B company of the Fusiliers began to clear the village of snipers at 6 a.m. Nests of snipers were bombed out, some were killed and some were taken prisoner. Everything went according to plan on the north side of the village, but not on the south.

On the south side of the village the 9th Battalion of the Duke of Wellingtons met heavy machine-gun fire, and were unable to reach the high ground, and A company of the Lancashire Fusiliers were also pinned down by machine-gun fire at the river, and suffered many casualties from snipers.

Then C company advanced and entered the village from the east and began to clear it of German snipers. Corporal Lester, with half a dozen men, entered a house through the back door. He shot two snipers as they tried to escape by the front door.

Then the back door was blocked by a sudden fall of masonry. Meanwhile the street was being swept by machine-gun fire.

Lester saw that a German sniper was causing heavy casualties to some Fusiliers in a house across the street, who were faced with a choice between crossing the death trap of the street, or being picked off one by one where they were. Exclaiming "I'll settle him!" Lester dashed into the street, though he well knew the inevitable result, shot the sniper and fell mortally wounded himself.

"To save their lives he sacrificed his own." These are the words which end the citation notifying the posthumous award to him of one of the finest of the eighteen VCs won by the regiment in the war.

During a visit to the battlefields in 1965, I found his grave and also that of my first platoon officer, Lieutenant R. S. Stott and other Lancashire Fusiliers whom I had known, in the military extension of the Neuvilly Communal Cemetery.

Meanwhile B company had practically cleared its side of the village by 8.30 a.m.; but later, the enemy infiltrated men back into it through a sunken lane and a very long railway arch. By midday the village was again occupied by Germans, and A company and C company and a part of B company were ordered to clear the village again. Jerry was determined to hold the village, and at 3 p.m. put down a heavy barrage and counter-attacked in strength.

The 12th Manchesters were forced to retire with men of D and B companies of the 10th to a position near the river. The Germans were prevented from crossing the river by men of all four companies of the Lancashire Fusiliers. At 5 p.m., A and C companies again cleared the village. At the end of this long day's attack and counter-attack, when darkness fell, the

Manchesters held the far bank of the river whose crossings were held by the Lancashire Fusiliers.

At 5 a.m. on the 13th October, the survivors of the four companies, A, B, C, and D were relieved after twenty-four hours of continuous fighting. They returned very tired to our positions behind the ridge near Inchy. The losses had been five officers and 182 other ranks. Two officers and fifty-eight other ranks and some machine-guns had been captured.

On 19th October, after rest, reinforcement and reorganisation, the 10th Lancashire Fusiliers returned to the battle for Neuvilly; this time to support another Infantry Brigade by using their Lewis guns at the bridges over the Selle. Prior to this attack, our artillery regularly shelled the German positions every day at dawn; and infantry dug themselves small pits close to the river during the hours of darkness.

Then, on the 19th just before the now regular time of our artillery bombardment when it was hoped the enemy was taking cover in readiness for it, the infantry rose up from their slit trenches in the half-light of dawn, they crossed the river, where by some miracle the Royal Engineers had placed pontoon bridges.

The HQ company followed up in support, and as we advanced, rifles and bayonets at the ready, enemy shells were bursting ahead, just as they had done in August when the 17th Division attacked the great Thiepval Ridge. We began to meet a trickle of walking wounded coming back. I shall never forget one young lad I knew; he came loping towards me out of the smoke of shell fire and the morning mist. Most of the wounded who could walk were hobbling back towards us, but not so this youngster; he was taking huge strides.

We met, exchanged glances, and he was gone, but as he passed within a couple of yards of me, I saw that his steel helmet was neatly sliced off on the left side. Blood was running down his face on to his gas mask satchel. It was soaked with it as he bounded past me, eyes staring and mouth wide open. Judging by the speed of his running, it must have been only a flesh wound, but I wondered how far he would run losing blood at that rate.

A little further on, I came to some severely wounded boys who were lying in a small depression of the ground; it was about the size of a golf bunker. As I reached them, one of them cried out for water, and I stopped to give him some. I was, at this period of the war, carrying two water-bottles; one of which was part of my battle order equipment, and the other, which I had found, slung over my shoulder on a long leather strap. It was a very nice one and had once belonged to an officer.

I knelt by the boy; he was very young and I was about to give him some water when our MO suddenly arrived with several of his first aid staff. "Wait Corporal," he said, "let me see him. No, no water; abdomen wound, I'll give him morphia." The boy was deathly white, groaning with pain and crying out "Mother, Oh Mother." As we left to continue the advance, he was lying quite still and I saw the M for Morphia, in indelible pencil on his forehead.

A GRIEVOUS LOSS

This second attack, though costly, was successful, and the little town of Neuvilly was at last in our hands. But, while Corporal Wilkinson was fixing up a signal station in one of the captured houses, a German shell came through the wall, exploded and badly injured one of his legs. I was in the street when he was brought out and then attended to by the MO.

Two men took him away on a light wheeled stretcher, and then as the news spread, a group of men gathered round the MO asking him if "Wilky" would be alright. He shook his head and said that he had a very bad wound in the calf of his leg. "I'm sorry I had to give him morphia," he said.

Next day we heard that he had died at the casualty clearing station. It was a grievous loss; no man in the Lancashire Fusiliers was more missed than Wilky; we often spoke of him when we were on the march. His unfailing cheerfulness and his pungent flashes of Lancashire wit were a tonic to us all.

I still remember an occasion when we were waiting in a sunken road until we got the order to move forward into a reserve trench. Men of another battalion passed close by and several asked the usual question "What lot are you?" This question was often answered in a humorous way by some wit, but Wilky reduced even the officers to helpless laughter on this occasion.

In the Spring of 1918, when the great German Offensive created a very critical situation, Foch, a French General, was hurriedly appointed commander-in-chief of all the allied forces in France. There was no time to set up a Supreme HQ and combined staff such as Eisenhower had in the Second World War. So General Foch never actually commanded the fighting armies, but he controlled all their reserves, and he decided when they should be used.

Among the British troops nothing was known of these great military and political decisions, except the fact that Foch controlled the reserves. So, when the question was asked "What lot are you?" and Wilky's answer was "We're Foch's reserves!" there were roars of laughter from both battalions.

Another old comrade killed in the capture of Neuvilly, on 12th October, was my first platoon officer in France, Second

Lieut. R. S. Stott. He was posthumously awarded the Military Cross for his selfless direction of trench mortar fire during the final and successful assault of Neuvilly. After Neuvilly, the whole front was constantly moving forward; we rarely spent two nights in the same place. If we were not in action, we were following up battalions that were, and then leap-frogging them into the next battle. New drafts came to the battalion to make up the numbers; no one was indispensable or irreplaceable; and I began to be regarded, and to feel, one of the old soldiers of the battalion that I had joined myself only six months earlier.

THE KALEIDOSCOPE OF WAR

Many of the boys I had known had now gone; only very occasionally did I now see and speak briefly to one of the boys who had come out to France with me. Three of them were Norwich boys — Griggs, Hoddle and Guymer, who were in the same hut with me in the big camp at Mansfield; they had been put into the East Yorkshire Regiment when we arrived at Calais.

One day, as the Lancashire Fusiliers passed through the East Yorkshires during a leap-frog, I spoke to Griggs, who told me that Hoddle was still alive but Guymer had been killed. Another day I waved and smiled when I saw Corporal Hammond, another East York, as we marched through a village, and he touched his stripes and waved back.

Usually, before an attack, the officers were called to an officers' meeting, to be briefed by the colonel and the adjutant. Following this, on their return, the platoon officers briefed the platoon sergeants and the various specialist sections — Lewis gunners, Mills bombers etc. — and boxes of Mills bombs were distributed.

The company cook was summoned and ordered to get tea brewed for say, 4.30 a.m.; on one of these occasions he overslept and there was no tea. Algy, the HQ company commander, was furious, and dismissed him from his job on the spot. Sometimes a rum ration was issued at dawn.

Once, as we were waiting for our barrage to lift from the enemy positions before we went over the top, a summer thunderstorm broke out.

Nature versus man were at their noisiest as the crashing peals of thunder rolled across the sky and were outmatched by the continuous thunder of our field guns behind us, and the roar of our shells screaming over our heads into the German positions. That was indeed an awesome and unforgettable experience.

Moving forward for an attack and getting into position, we pass rough fingerposts with messages like: Walking Wounded; POW cage; CCS (casualty clearing station).

One day when we were moving forward behind our forward troops, we came to a very deep trench; I could see men leaping over it before I came to it myself. As I leapt over it, I saw a British soldier hanging by his foot, having apparently been killed as he jumped across, and in falling back his foot had become wedged between the trench wall and some timber supports. His head was down nearly at the bottom of the trench, and his blood, all of it, in a crimson pool. As I saw this gruesome sight, I realised what the expression bled white means.

We reached another trench where many German dead lay. Others, some of whom were wounded and bleeding, put up their hands.

In these kaleidoscopic scenes I remember too the eerie silence of a newly-captured and deserted trench after our first wave had gone on. What shall we find as we turn the corners? More of his dead? Or some of ours? Once we ran right through a newly-captured village street without stopping, passing a German machine-gun and its dead crew. The street was littered with things as if a giant's hand had scattered them; steel helmets, bits of German equipment, water bottles, metal cups, rifles, machine-gun ammunition belts, German coal scuttle helmets, German packs with hairy red flaps made of horsehide and German hand grenades. These we always called tater mashers as they had a short wooden handle to which was attached a metal cylinder full of deadly explosives; sometimes three or four cylinders were attached to one handle. It was a most effective weapon, of which Jerry always seemed to have more than we had of our Mills bombs. I imagine they were much cheaper to produce too, but in those days Britain would produce nothing but the best quality.

All along this street the dead lay, like dolls, some in grotesque attitudes.

THE FINAL BATTLES

The Western Front, which had moved so little in four long grievous years, now moved forward daily, but the German troops still maintained high levels of both skill and courage.

When ordered to hold a ridge or a village, they were as difficult to dislodge as ever, invariably leaving behind their tough machine-gunners to hold us up and inflict casualties until they were outflanked or otherwise forced to retreat.

There were still some costly and bloody battles to win, but by the middle of October, the British infantry, now mainly youngsters of eighteen and nineteen were advancing far beyond that ravaged belt of country where the brutal and fruitless battles of trench warfare had raged.

For four years, the Line on the Western Front had moved no more than ten miles, despite the heroic fighting and the enormous casualties which had sucked the life blood of an entire generation of men, British, French and German alike.

In actual time, it was only six months since we boys had been sent so suddenly to the Western Front, but in our experience since the spring, so much had happened. The initial force of the German spring offensive of 21st March had spent itself by the middle of April. By contrast, the great British advance, which started on 8th August, maintained an ever widening and advancing front.

The sheer scale of this final Big Push was enormous; the follow-up of supplies, ammunition and Mills bombs; the battalions leapfrogging past one another, gave us a sense of purpose and a confidence which the men who fought in the earlier fruitless and bloody battles of 1915-1917 never experienced, despite their persistent courage and self-sacrifice.

Between 8th August and 11th November, the young British Army captured 188,700 prisoners and 2,840 guns, and sustained 350,000 casualties. By contrast, in the whole of the 1939-1945 war, the army's losses were less than those sustained in the fighting of 1918.

At Waterloo in 1815, the casualties were 10,813 killed and 36,195 wounded, out of 150,000 men engaged.

Compared with Blenheim, Austerlitz, or any of the great battles of the past, the vast battle of 1918 was like a slow moving picture, a movie in slow motion. Seven million men, Germans, Austrians, Italians, French and British in ceaseless battle from the Alps to the North Sea — not for an hour or two, or even a month, but for eight months.

AMONG CIVILIANS AGAIN

Now that we had broken through the massive Hindenburg Line, we were in open country without trenches, where the French towns and villages were relatively undamaged.

It was a strange experience, after months in trenches and fields, to pass through a town occupied by civilians. On one occasion when we were following up other troops who were in contact with the enemy, we halted in a main street of a town, sitting on the kerb for a few minutes' rest while waiting for orders. As we moved on down the street, I glanced into shop windows; it was a glimpse of another world; a far away world which we had almost forgotten.

Halting again in another street, some civilians opened their front doors and called out to us. We started talking and some coffee was offered to us on the doorstep of a house. As I was drinking it I felt in my haversack and produced some sugar. This caused a sensation for they had not seen white sugar for years, so we gave them all we had.

Then one of the officers called me and told me that we were actually going to spend a night in the town. He and I started enquiring for accommodation in barns and outhouses, and one old Frenchman showed us a very large barn with a boarded loft. I went up a ladder to see and shouted down to my officer "There's room for thirty or forty up here, sir." I spent the night up there myself and remember being awakened next morning by insistent enquiries below for Corporal Hodges and wondering wherever I was. The rations had come and I had to get up to take charge of them, and later, distribute them.

PRISONERS GALORE

We were now advancing over country abounding with small villages and large farms. I particularly remember a large farm which we captured soon after dawn one October morning. I have since identified it on a map as Bois de Boustres Farm. It had not suffered the severe damage that befell so many farms in the old battle area now well behind us.

The farm buildings were well built of red brick and extended all round a large central farmyard which we entered by an arched gateway in a high wall. As I entered, the Germans had just surrendered; about twenty stood with their hands up or clasped on their heads; others lay dead or wounded.

I went straight across the farmyard and entered a long open-fronted shed on the far side of the yard. It had a manger running all along the back wall, and on the floor there were half a dozen German dead and some badly wounded who had been carried there by their comrades during the fighting; there was one German Red Cross soldier attending to them.

My investigations were suddenly interrupted by the RSM whose voice I heard bellowing, "Corporal Hodges! — Corporal Hodges!" As I hurried out of the shed and across the yard, I saw that more Germans were pouring through the main gate where the RSM stood just inside the farmyard. They all had their hands up, and the RSM was pushing and poking them with his revolver into some sort of double rank. "Come on," he roared at me. "Get them out of here!" And added with a grin. "We're outnumbered in this yard. Lead on, Corporal, I'll make them follow you. Take em to the POW cage."

As I led this untidy looking double line of prisoners out through the gateway, I could hear the RSM's rasping voice counting them out, "Two-four-six-eight-ten—". When I was about fifty yards from the farm, I stepped to one side, motioned them to keep going, and looked back to see what I had got. I estimated that I had about forty prisoners, and at the rear, one Lancashire Fusilier. Seeing, about sixty yards away, another Fusilier driving another half a dozen Germans before him, I shouted across to him to join us. A few minutes later we were also joined by another small group, which to my great surprise, included a German officer.

I asked him if he spoke English, and he said "Ja, some English." So I took him to the front of the straggling column, and halted them all by raising my arms with rifle and bayonet held up. Then I told my three or four escorting Fusiliers to get them into column of four, and the German officer, catching on to my orders, shouted at them in German. I posted a Fusilier each side of the column, and one or two at the rear, and with the German officer at my side, gave the order to march.

INFERIOR GAS MASKS

It was a good thing I had them under better control, because the enemy guns opened up with gas shells. I ordered my men to put on their masks and Germans followed suit, but it was quite evident that their gas masks were not as good as ours. By 1918 the British naval blockade had caused a serious shortage of rubber. After the war, I brought home a German groundsheet which was wonderfully designed with innumerable metal buttons and strongly stitched buttonholes; but as a groundsheet it was inefficient because of the poor quality of the rubber or synthetic material used.

Coughing and spitting, the German prisoners followed me as I led them over the ground where we had fought early that morning, where the dead, German and British, lay as they had fallen. I felt some sympathy for the Jerries; to be shelled with gas by their own guns, and to have inferior masks.

THE ROADSIDE ESTAMINET

After a quarter of an hour we moved out of the area being

gased, and leaving the now deserted battlefield, we marched along a country road. I really had no idea where I was, not having seen this area in daylight; all I knew was that the front was behind me, and that somewhere I should eventually find a POW cage. We came to a lone house by the roadside; it was an estaminet, a three storey building with large shell holes in the walls, and a dangerous looking roof. It had evidently taken some punishment. I saw leading to it the coloured wires of some signallers, and halting the prisoners and escort I went to investigate.

Picking up the wires I let them run through my left hand and they led me to the cellar of the estaminet, where I found two or three signallers fixing up their kit. They were turning the cellar into an advanced Brigade HQ signal station, which indicated the speed of our advance, for only five or six hours earlier it had been in German hands.

I told the corporal in charge that I had about fifty German prisoners and asked him if he had any idea where the POW cage was. "Oh yes," he said, "its back in Poix du Nord, only a few kilos, Brigade HQ is there."

While we were talking several salvos of HE burst near the estaminet, and stumbling my way up the cellar steps, I was nearly choked with cordite fumes and fine brick dust. Peering along the road I could see no sign of my prisoners, and momentarily I was worried.

Then, through the cordite smoke I saw one of the escort; he had seen me and stood up. The rest were all flat in the ditch, taking cover from HE. "Come on!" I roared, bellowing in the style of the RSM, and much relieved to find that the prisoners had not bolted. "Fall in," I shouted, "and get moving."

PRISONNIER DE GUERRE

As we began to march, I said to the German officer, "The cage is in Poix du Nord, about another three kilos." He looked at me dubiously, and then asked "Vot ist carge? Vere go we?" "Oh" I said "Cage is where prisoners go, it's the POW cage." I could see that he didn't understand, and I said, "POW means prisoner of war — comprenez?" He stared at me, so I said "Prisonnier de guerre." "Ach" he said, "vous parlez français?" "Un peu," I said, "mais lentement LENTEMENT" as he started to gabble in French.

Our conversation, in a mixture of English, French and German, was decidedly slow and of limited comprehension. I tried again, and said, "You," and I touched his chest, "you Allemand prisoner, prisonnier de guerre, comprenez?"

"Nein! No! Not Allemand!" he said, indignantly "No! Non!" I looked at him again; he was certainly not the typical Prussian or Bavarian type, but I was puzzled by his vehemence. "No, nein, not Allemand! What are you then?" I was shouting as if more volume would compensate for his lack of English. "Ich Pomeranian," he said and told me the name of his city; it was on the Baltic Sea, but I have forgotten its name.

"So you are a Pomeranian?" I was only nineteen and it tickled me immensely, though I succeeded in not laughing openly. Inwardly I was chuckling. Pomeranian! That's a breed of dog!

POIX DU NORD

By this time we were approaching Poix du Nord and were meeting troops marching to the front. They were fresh and full of humorous quips; in a very different state from we Lancashire Fusiliers who had been on our feet in fighting equipment for about fifteen hours without food or rest.

We had marched up from the rear the previous evening, got into position, made an attack, and were now escorting prisoners who were as weary as we were. As these fresh troops passed us on the road, they shouted insults at the Germans, and one of them, seeing the German officer at my side, shouted as he passed "Make that b— b— Boche carry your pack!" I made no reply, and reflected that the nearer one is to the battle, the less hate there is. Some of these boy soldiers going up to the front had probably not been in action. I felt a certain strange kinship with my prisoners.

Entering Poix du Nord I led the prisoners down the main street, and seeing the brigade sign and two sentries at the arched gateway to a courtyard, I turned in and shouted to them to halt.

As I did so, the brigadier-general came out from a door on the left, looking I thought, clean, rested and well fed. I noticed he had no less than five wound stripes on his cuff; I had never seen so many before, nor did I again. He approached us and I saluted him. He asked, "Where is your battalion now, Corporal?" I told him that when I left to bring the prisoners we had just captured a large farm about five or six kilos from Poix du Nord.

He turned to the German officer, who saluted and received an acknowledgement in kind, and, to my surprise, started to speak to him in German. Then the brigadier produced a map, spread it out and asked the German officer a number of questions which he willingly answered. Turning to me again, he said, "When you have taken them to the cage, Corporal, come back here; I shall be going forward and you can help me contact your battalion." I saluted, and watched by a group of brigade HQ staff, including grooms and officers' servants, I called my party to attention and gave the order to march.

THE POW CAGE

Still not knowing where the POW cage was, I enquired of a warrant officer entering the courtyard at that moment. "Do you know where the POW cage is?" "Yes," he said, "it's the cattle market, just round the corner on the left." It was about 10 a.m. when I finally handed over the prisoners to the military police, who counted them, and to my great surprise, gave me a receipt for them as if I was delivering cattle.

The receipt was for one German officer and fifty-eight other ranks. I noticed that they detached the German officer from the rest, led him off into a building and expertly sorted the other ranks by regiment, penning them like sheep. They were only too ready to lie down on the straw in the cattle pens. For them the war was over.

I felt very tired and hungry as I returned to the courtyard, and was grateful for a can of hot sweet tea from the brigade HQ cooks. Soon the brigadier-general came out again; he was a strong well-built man, well over six feet tall, and he wore the ribbons of the DSO and the MC. I later discovered that his name was Alison.

"Right!" he said. "Let's go. Your men can follow with my orderly."

GUIDE TO THE BRIGADIER-GENERAL

We set off up the main street and out of the town. The brigadier was strong and fresh; his stride seemed about half as long again as mine and I had difficulty keeping up with him. His orderly, a cavalryman, carrying a lance with a small pennant, followed with my four or five Fusiliers.

When we reached the estaminet, I left the road and led him across country, following as nearly possible the route on which

I had brought the prisoners. The brigadier was really keen to get to the Lancashire Fusiliers and find out how far they had advanced; I was getting more tired, and when I glanced back I saw that my LFs had dropped behind the orderly. They were weary too, which was not surprising since we had had neither food nor rest for about sixteen hours.

At last, I could see, in the distance, the farm where the Germans had surrendered. "There it is, sir," I said. "My battalion is somewhere beyond that red brick farm, I don't know how far beyond."

He stopped, looked briefly at his map, and then at me. Possibly he realised that he had used up my last energies, for he said, "All right, Corporal, you and your men can make your way back to your battalion at your own pace." He smiled as he said, "I hope you've got a long way to go; thank you, Corporal, good luck!" I saluted, and off he went, striding towards the farm, followed by his cavalry orderly, bearing his pennant aloft on his lance.

When my four or five LFs caught up with me, we sat down, turned out our haversacks and pooled our resources, pieces of bread, a piece of cheese, a tin of bully beef, some broken pieces of army biscuits and a tin of cafe au lait. We shared it, ate every scrap, lit up and felt better.

After a rest, I said, "Well, we must get cracking, the brigadier seemed to think, and he certainly hoped it might be quite a walk before we find the battalion again. I wonder how far they've gone?"

So we set off to find the battalion and walked along a field track that we had marched along in the darkness of the previous night.

A DESERTED BATTLEFIELD

There was not a soul in sight on this deserted battlefield; the battle front had swept on and left the dead lying where they had fallen. We came to a group of nine Lancashire Fusiliers; they lay on, and just off, the track in grotesque attitudes, just as they had fallen when a direct hit from a German battery had caught them as they marched. We stopped for a moment or two to see who they were; I forbade any pocket rifling, but we took some of their iron rations, i.e. "bully", biscuits and tea in a white canvas bag.

Further on, we saw a British soldier, on this otherwise completely deserted area, coming out from a farm shed standing by itself half left from us. He pointed to the shed, and shouted, "Have a look in there! Some of the poor blighters in there need help badly." We went across to the shed, ducking our heads to enter by a low doorway. There was a manger along the back, and on the ground, lying quite close to one another in a row, were about twenty men. Some were British, some were German. Some were dead, some dying; about half were able to talk.

As I walked along the row of men, eyes in ashen-pale faces looked up at me. I spoke to several young Lancashire Fusiliers but knew none personally. It was midday and some of them had doubtless been there since dawn, or just after. We gave some a drink from our waterbottles, and offered to redress their wounds, but they said "No, we'll wait for the RAMC."

We promised to report where they were and left them; there was no more we could do. Often there was this gap of a day or more in a rapid advance.

Wounded men unable to walk to a dressing station were bandaged by the stretcher-bearers or by their mates, and left behind as their comrades pressed on to consolidate their position or continue to attack. Later, the ancillary services come forward, tend the wounded, bury the dead, collect weapons, ammunition, picks, shovels, petrol cans and generally tidy up.

MORE DEAD

We passed the farm from which we had escorted the German prisoners, and then after crossing more fields, began to approach a large village, I think it was Englefontaine. It had evidently been strongly defended, for as we passed through orchards of apple trees between us and the village, many tree trunks were scarred white by machine-gun fire.

Under the trees lay several groups of Lancashire Fusiliers; all dead. Amongst them lay a young officer; I went close to see if I knew him, but his face was so disfigured I could not recognise him.

Looking up, I saw one of my men trying to remove from the sleeve of one of the dead, a Lewis gunner's badge, and I ordered him to leave it alone.

I realise now that we were all mere boys of eighteen and nineteen, and how understandable it was at that age to covet a nice brass badge, even in those grim circumstances. I realise too, how hardened we had been forced to become in facing the awful experiences, then a part of our young lives. It was a common sight to see the dead lying with their pockets emptied, but I certainly intended to permit no looting of the dead by men under my command.

MORE WOUNDED WAIT

We made our way warily through the orchards, although we felt reasonably sure that this end of the village at least, was in British hands. When we reached the main street we were delighted to see our battalion cooks brewing up tea and cooking porridge. Collecting our ration, we looked round for a place to sit, feeling quite exhausted after being on the move for more than twenty-four hours. That night was spent lying on the floor of a street corner shop, in somewhat cramped conditions among a dozen wounded men. They had been given first aid, their wounds dressed and bandaged by the battalion stretcher-bearers, and now they were waiting to be removed to a casualty clearing station.

One youngster, whom I knew well, groaned with pain and had to be continually comforted and reassured. "Everything is OK, you're alright now, you've got a lovely Blighty and you're just waiting for an ambulance. You'll be moved down the line in the morning." The stretcher-bearer who had bandaged his hand told me quietly "They'll have to take it off, poor kid; the piece of shell has shattered the palm of his hand and the fingers are nearly detached."

I lay next to this youngster all night as he lay moaning with his hand swathed in dressings and bandages, and saw the blood still soaking through.

There had been other occasions when we comforted wounded men who had to wait. I remember a long night that several of us spent with a wounded signaller. This man often neglected to wear his steel helmet; in fact he never wore it if he could avoid doing so. A shell splinter wounded him in the nose and forehead, and his great fear was that he was blind. All night we crouched with him in a large shell hole, trying to comfort him and reassure him as we waited for the dawn, when we hoped it might be possible to get him down the line. As it became light he tried to lift the bandages off his head to see if he could see.

On some occasions our attempts to help men were soon over, as in the case of Greenoff's companion. After the shell burst that killed Greenoff, we saw him hopping on one leg and waving to us. Four men left our trench and scuttled across the one hundred yards between them and us. They brought them both in; Greenoff dead and the other lad crying, "I'm dying, I'm dying." We comforted him and tried to reassure him; someone spoke of the nice clean white sheets he would soon be in, but he quickly bled to death. Little could be done in such cases; every man carried a field dressing which consisted of a pad, a bandage and a small phial of iodine, but a bad wound needed more than we could do. Walking wounded could usually get to a dressing station and had a good chance of early attention, but those who were taken on stretchers to a CCS often had a long wait.

HIGH SPEED BUTCHERY AT A CASUALTY CLEARING STATION

One Northampton man, whom I met again after the war, told me of his experiences at the CCS to which he had been carried on a stretcher.

A very busy medical orderly came to him as he lay with many others waiting to be attended to, and after briefly examining his wounds, said "You'll lose your left eye and your right hand."

"Oh no, I shall NOT! I'm not having my hand off, I've only lost two fingers, and as for my eye, we'll see about that," said my friend. After being threatened with being charged for disobeying military orders, he finally resisted the threat to his eye and hand. When I last saw him, in the 1940s, apart from a bad scar near his left eye and the loss of the second and third fingers of his right hand, he was very fit. This example of the high speed butchery sometimes practised at a busy casualty clearing station where wounded men were arriving in large numbers, had a relatively happy ending.

A NEW RSM AND A NEW COLONEL

At dawn, after our disturbed night's rest, we heard the sound of horse transport in the streets of Englefontaine, and hoped for an ambulance for the wounded. I went outside, but saw only limbers drawn by army mules, bringing up more ammunition and supplies. I decided it was time we returned to our normal duties, and sent the men who had accompanied me with the German prisoners back to their platoons. When I reported to the RSM and gave him the receipt for one German officer and fifty-eight other ranks, he was very surprised. He said he had never before seen a receipt given for prisoners, but added, "It is all to the credit of the 10th Battalion to have these things acknowledged in writing. Typical of him!

That was the last time I saw him; he was posted back to the headquarters of the battalion at Preston, Lancashire, and replaced by RSM Cotton.

THE NEW CO

Our CO, Colonel Cotton, (no relation of course to RSM Cotton) also returned to England and was replaced by a much younger man, Lieutenant Colonel Torrens DSO, MC, who had, earlier in the war, been a junior officer in one of the companies of the 10th (Service) Battalion, and had at last as he said to the NCOs of the HQ company, "managed to get back to the Old Tenth again". Colonel Torrens was a handsome man, ambitious and forceful, another born leader of men. He told us he wanted to get back into the war again before it was all over. We all laughed, little realising the end was so near.

During the Christmas period after the war was over, Colonel Torrens acted as the Brigadier-General of the 52nd Brigade while Brigadier-General Alison was on leave. I was on duty as battalion orderly sergeant on Christmas Day 1918, and it was a part of my duties to accompany the battalion orderly officer when he led Colonel Torrens round the various places where the men were having their Christmas dinner. Many of the men were half intoxicated, and one of them lifted up his glass of vin blanc and said to Colonel Torrens "A Merry Christmas co you sir, and we all hope you'll get the brigadier's job." Colonel Torrens smiled and waved as he passed between the tables.

MORMAL FOREST AND BERLAIMONT

When we moved out of Englefontaine we began to approach the great Mormal Forest and then to probe into its shady depths. For a couple of days we were among the great trees of this large forest, but saw no sign of the Germans, except for some of their dead. We also saw some French civilians lying dead beside a handcart which was loaded with their possessions. Eventually we emerged from among the trees into the daylight, and then began to advance towards Berlaimont, which was on the far side of a wide canal with deep banks, the Canal de la Sambre à l'Oise. The canal proved to be a major obstacle to our progress; its capture had caused many casualties among the troops ahead of us.

BILLETING IN BERLAIMONT

Once again I was sent ahead with the advance party, one officer and five NCOs, one from each company. As we entered the town, from which the Germans had just been finally driven out, we saw frightened civilians coming up out of the cellars of buildings in the main street.

Many looked half-starved and ill as they stood forlornly on the pavements watching us march past. I noticed that there were no men or older boys, only old people and mothers with young pale-faced children. Later, I learned that the Germans had taken with them all the older boys for forced labour.

At a crossroad in the business area, right in the town centre, was a huge crater caused by a mine exploded by the retreating Germans. The Royal Engineers were examining the crater as we passed by and went on to explore the possibilities of billeting our troops in one or two of the factories in the town.

We split up and I went into a factory and saw that all the machinery had been destroyed by some form of explosion. I was very doubtful about using it for fear of delayed action bombs or concealed booby traps among the wreckage.

I reported back to the officer, and after some discussion we decided to put the battalion in some old warehouses and large old houses along the banks of the canal. On my way back to the outskirts of the town to guide the HQ company to their billets, again I passed the blown up crossroads, and saw that the REs had just stopped a passing pioneer company (older men in the Pick and Shovel Battalions, who wore a brass pick and shovel, crossed, on their arm).

The REs set them to work filling in the huge mine crater by the simple process of demolishing the damaged houses, offices and shops at the four street corners. Crashes and clouds of brick dust filled the air as I passed. This ruthless work was necessary to enable the huge flow of oncoming traffic to pass through the town.

At this late stage of the war the entire British Army seemed to be on the move, daily. Nothing like it had been seen before throughout this long war. It was a heartening sight for the British troops; even the company cookers travelled with the troops as they marched, tea and stew or porridge steaming. In Berlaimont I noticed that each building had a notice-board at the entrance, which listed with typical German thoroughness, the names, ages and descriptions of the official occupants. The best rooms, on the ground and upper floors, were for the German troops, while the French civilians were relegated to the kitchens and cellars. The town had been occupied for four years, and all the many public notices on doors or walls were, of course, printed in German, and usually contained the favourite word VERBOTEN.

JERRY'S LAST STAND

The Germans made one more stand in the fields beyond Berlaimont, and here my battalion suffered their last casualties. Sad to say, among them was my old comrade Wally Beale, who came from Brigstock to join the army with me, along with Tim Costello from Guilsborough; Jim May from Towcester; and Crouch, Swain, Thompson, Wells and Whitehead from Northampton.

I felt so sad about Wally's death; he was a simple country boy, always cheerful and good to be with. He had been billeted with me, Tim Costello and Bob House in Norwich, in February, and now, on 4th November, one week before the armistice, he was killed in the last battle.

ALLEMANDS PARTIRENT! VIVE LA FRANCE! VIVE L'ANGLETERRE!

The last village we captured was Beaufort (or Beaumont) which we entered very cautiously during the night of 10th-11th November, not knowing whether the Germans were going to try to hold it, and little dreaming that the war was so near its end. It was a very dark, cold night and the village seemed uncannily quiet as I led a group of men quietly down the main street. Then a door opened for a moment shedding light for a few seconds before it closed again. Then we heard a bucket overturn with a noisy clatter.

We halted, rifles and bayonets at the ready, thumb on safety catch and finger on trigger. One of my patrol said, "That was a civvy who kicked that bucket." Someone else said "He nearly did too!" And we laughed. The door opened again, and in the light we saw a man, standing at the bottom of a short flight of stone steps which led up to the house door.

At the door, two women stood with the light behind them, and as we moved into the light, they saw our uniforms and screamed "Les Anglais! LES ANGLAIS!" They kept on saying it, over and over again, as if they couldn't believe it. Then they beckoned us inside, talking excitedly all the time, "Allemands partirent! Vive la France! Vive L'Angleterre!"

It was a cold night and the room we entered was warm and cosy. They told us that the German troops had left the village during the evening, leaving a machine-gun rearguard at the far end of the village.

Some of our troops went on to the outskirts of the village, but found no sign of the enemy and returned to us. The women then opened an old oak chest and produced the French Tricolours and then handed round hot coffee to the British troops.

A noisy babble of Tommy Atkins French and village patois filled the room as we drank coffee, and they told us how they had kept the flags hidden for four long years. They unfolded them and spread them out excitedly on the table, babbling away about the Boche "Arrh! Les Boches". Their eyes sparkled and their faces were flushed with excitement.

Then the old Frenchman we had seen at the foot of the steps came into the house with a load of wood for the fire; it was obvious that these French villagers were in no mind to go to bed, they were far too excited, and no wonder!

AMAZING NEWS — UNBELIEVABLE NEWS!

Later that night, in the half-light of dawn, I was attending to various duties as orderly sergeant, when I was told some amazing news!

A despatch rider from brigade HQ rode into the village on his motor cycle and stopped to tell me that brigade HQ had just received a special message from General Headquarters to the effect that hostilities were to cease.

Later I saw the full text, as follows —

> Hostilities will cease at 11 hours today, November 11th.
> Troops will stand fast on the line reached at that hour.
> Defensive precautions will be maintained.
> There will be no intercourse of any description with the enemy until the receipt of instructions from GHQ.

The despatch rider rode on through the village, and in about half an hour returned and told me that he had seen no sign of Jerry. He said, "He's really bunked this time; the PBI will have a long march to catch up with him now." I laughed and said, "Well, perhaps they'll give us all motor bikes like you!" Actually, I was stunned by the news; I couldn't grasp it; I didn't know what to say.

As 11 a.m. approached, I left the village and walked back to some of our guns. The field across which I walked was littered with the usual debris of war. Especially noticeable to me were the groups of German rifles, bayonets plunged into the soil, with German coal scuttle helmets hanging from them by their chin straps. I had seen this many times before and knew that they marked the hastily dug graves of our enemy in the last battle, but now it came home to me that these graves were the graves of our former enemy.

It was now nearly 11 a.m. and our guns began to fire; I wondered what their target could be in view of the despatch rider's report; perhaps it was a symbolic gesture.

SILENCE ALONG THE BATTLEFRONT

At 11 a.m. the guns stopped firing, and a strange, almost uncanny silence lay across the battlefield. I was silent too, feeling no desire for any conversation with the gunners, who began to clean their guns and tidy up the gun sites. The occasion was too big, too poignant, for words, and I walked slowly back to the village, mind and spirit strangely numbed.

The weather was fine and cold and still.

I looked again at the German graves as I passed, and I thought of the relations of these men in Germany. I thought too of the many "Men of 18" who also would never return home to their families.

I thought of the first casualties in the trenches at Mesnil — Fox, White and Willard; I thought of Dunmore and Whitehead and the many others who had died, right up to the final ones, including Wally Beale.

I was trying to realise that it was all over; that I was alive and that I had a life to live. It was almost unbelievable. For seven months I had lived a day at a time, but now I could look forward as well as back.

Only seven months since we boys had been so suddenly drafted into the 10th Lancashire Fusiliers. How MUCH had happened in those 200 days and nights. From early April until July we were holding, deepening and strengthening poor trenches which were always dominated by an enemy holding all the high ground of the great Thiepval Ridge. From early August, just around our nineteenth birthdays, we became the spearhead of the new style British infantry with packs discarded, in fighting order, stripped to the bare essentials of an infantryman who was ready for action and always on the move — forward!

We had attacked the enemy in his stronghold; up and over the great Thiepval Ridge, and from then on, it had been attack after attack.

Attack and counter-attack at Flers, Le Transloy, Rocquigny, on to Fins Wood, the Hindenburg Line, Inchy, Neuvilly, Poix du Nord, Mormal Forest and Berlaimont. Now, suddenly, unexpectedly, almost unreasonably, it was all over.

POST WAR IN FRANCE

ANGRY FRENCHWOMEN

Getting back to the village, I found a crowd of angry Frenchwomen shouting excitedly outside the village church. I went inside and saw about twenty-five German soldiers, wounded, and sitting or lying on the floor. Evidently they had been collected there during the last battle and abandoned by the retreating enemy.

If I had not put a couple of our regimental police at the door of the church to prevent them entering, I feel sure the Frenchwomen would have attacked them; pent up feelings of four years occupation were at bursting point. The worst cases were later removed by British ambulances and the walking wounded were helped into a three ton army lorry; the angry cries of the Frenchwomen following them as they were driven away.

A LONG WINTRY MARCH

The despatch rider's prediction that we had a long march ahead of us before we saw Jerry again was not fulfilled. In fact, the 17th Division was halted where we were on November 11th, and neighbouring divisions took over our front as the British Army followed the defeated and retreating German Army.

The Lancashire Fusiliers soon began a very long march in the opposite direction, right back across the battlefields to Inchy, and then, before Christmas, to the small village of Vergies, near Abbeville. As we marched, day after day through the battlefields through which we had fought, we were able to see, in daylight and at leisure, the war ravaged countryside which we had previously seen only in brief glimpses from a trench or when fully occupied in an attack. This long march was an experience I shall never forget. The weather was cold and wintry. Every night we halted and slept in one of the empty war scarred villages. We all appreciated the regular nights' sleep and I was glad to be finished with posting gas sentries.

MEMORIES OF WAR

During this long march, and particularly during the ten minutes'rest each hour, men were saying to one another — "Cor! Do any of you remember when we held that trench." "Look over there, that's Havrincourt Wood, does anybody remember those comfy German huts we slept in when we were in reserve, just before his attack on 21st March?" "Yes, but look, that's the trench we held when Jerry came over." "This must be where we lost Captain Sankey when we attacked up that rise and met Jerry head on and had to retire." "Who remembers putting up barbed wire here? Blimey, this was no man's land when we were here last May." "Yes, and that's where Captain Jowett was killed, he was a good 'un." Actually, there was only one officer with us who remembered any of these scenes.

THE DEVASTATION OF WAR

We also began to appreciate the enormous damage that France had suffered in the four long years of war, and particularly during the Somme battles of 1916-1917. Even this was but a part of the enormous damage which ran like a huge 400 mile long scar, disfiguring a wide belt of countryside in north eastern France. I have since read some official figures "In northern France, a wide swathe of country was devastated; an area larger than Holland. Two and a half million people were displaced from their homes." "One million head of cattle was lost, 3,000 miles of railway were destroyed." "32,000 miles of roads were destroyed; 1,300,000 Frenchmen were dead." "Three million houses were destroyed; many villages whose name only survived."

We passed through many of these shattered villages; saw the desolation, ruined houses, blackened brickwork, broken timbers, neglected gardens.

These sad scenes evoked a mood of pity for the people who had been forced to leave everything they possessed. Around the remains of the houses was the ugly litter of war; shell cases, rum jars, rusty rifles, belts of machine-gun ammunition, broken furniture, piles of books, jars, bottles, tins, and everywhere, groups of wooden crosses.

It was a desolate scene. A deserted countryside with blackened tree stumps where once verdant woods had been. The fields were pitted with millions of shell holes and craters filled with green-scummed water. Right across this desolate scene long rusty belts of barbed wire curved like ugly snakes.

We saw very few French civilians; once we passed through a village where an old man was trying to mend a broken roof, and once when we were having our ten minutes' rest outside a large house, a French officer who presumably owned it was looking round. Within a few yards of what had once been his pillared portico there were about a dozen British graves, some of them bearing the names of Australian and New Zealand troops.

INCHY

At Inchy we were billeted in some disused warehouses with bunk beds made of timber and wire netting.

Some ceremonial drill was now the order of the day and ceremonial guards were mounted regularly. This meant much cleaning of our war worn equipment and polishing of brass, etc.

BRIGADE GAS NCO

One day Captain Smith sent for me. He had recently been appointed adjutant in place of Captain Milne who had left the battalion to take up a post in education. He told me that Sergeant Brown had left brigade HQ to take up a commission, and he wanted me to take his place as brigade gas NCO. I went to the 52nd Brigade HQ, only a few miles away and reported to the brigade major.

Here at brigade HQ there were obviously no duties for me to perform as a gas NCO, and I spent my time with other brigade NCOs who were similarly unoccupied. The armourer sergeant and I used to visit the nearby village in the evenings and listen to the village gossip in the local estimanets. We both spoke and understood some French, and between us were able to hear about the long German occupation. The villagers discussed those who had been willing to co-operate with the enemy for extra rations and how some of the local Frenchwomen had misbehaved and had been publicly disgraced when the war ended by having their heads shaved.

Then brigade HQ began to shed some of us who were virtually unemployed, and I was told to report back to my battalion. I reported to Captain Smith, who said, "Well, Corporal Hodges, there is nothing for a gas NCO to do now at battalion level, so you had better go back to your company."

"A" company was completely different from what it was when I left in July; the troops seemed very young; the only NCO I knew was Sergeant P. Walsh, who welcomed me back

288

with a grin. "P" was always a man of action and a few words. The company sergeant-major was new to me, as was the company commander. He had just come out to the battalion from England. I soon became friendly with Corporal Easterby, an older man who had been awarded the Military Medal for his leadership of young lads who came out to France to take part in the last battles.

VERGIES

Before Christmas we marched from Inchy to Vergies, where A company was billeted in barns and other outbuildings of a farm with a very large farmyard in the centre.

THE MIDDEN

In the middle of this large farmyard was a huge midden, with a solid crust of old dried manure; it was quite inoffensive, we just walked round it to and from our billets. Captain Rhodes came round one day with the CSM to inspect the billets, and when he saw the midden he ordered some men to clear it "Completely!" As soon as the crust was broken a penetrating odour pervaded the whole area, and the men refused to continue to disturb it.

MUTINY

Captain Rhodes was determined to have his way, which of course was usual when an officer gave an order; none of us had ever seen an order disobeyed. He picked on two of the men and said "Now, you two, pick up those shovels and get to work." After a nervous glance round at the assembled troops, they both refused. "Arrest those men and take them to the guardroom," said Captain Rhodes. One of the NCOs marched them off under escort in true military style, just as I and Beale and Costello were marched through the streets of Norwich when we overslept and failed to parade with the company.

This scene was repeated several times as other men refused to pick up the shovels, and I began to wonder when it would be my turn to march some men to the guardroom, or whether we would run out of NCOs! It was really a very serious situation, but there was an element of comedy about it too. Then the company sergeant-major, who was always known as Gladys Cooper, reported to Captain Rhodes that the guardroom was full! I was not surprised, having been sergeant of the guard earlier in the week, and knowing that the accommodation for the guard of six men and several prisoners was quite cramped. Eventually Rhodes stamped off looking shaken and frustrated. We never saw him again. He was posted to a job in education.

We all felt a bit shocked at this semi-serious, semi-comic minor mutiny. Never having seen an officer disobeyed before, we wondered what the outcome would be. However, the CSM, who had gone off with Captain Rhodes, eventually brought back the men who had been arrested and dismissed them to their billets. He then told the NCOs that Captain Armstrong, the Company Commander of B Company, had been to the guardroom, and had really read the riot act to the prisoners before releasing them. Armstrong was a tough officer who had risen from the ranks, won the MC and several bars, and he had no mercy on any kind of failure.

RHODES' SPECIAL COMPANY PARADE

Before the mutiny Captain Rhodes did one other stupid thing while he was our company commander. He sent for me one day, and told me, as the orderly sergeant, to round up every man in the company for a special parade. He gave me a list of the A company men whom he said were never on parade, and said he intended to have every one of them on the company parades. When I read the list of names I was not surprised that they never paraded, but, wearing belt and bayonet as orderly sergeant, I went to every billet in the village and rounded them up.

On Rhodes' list were clerks, storemen, cobblers, and some officers' servants, including my old mates Carpenter and Fisher, who had not worn their equipment since the armistice. One, whom I had never seen before, was officer's servant to the lieutenant quartermaster. Altogether I rounded up a motley collection of twenty-five to thirty men, and ordered them to parade, properly dressed, outside the company office at 9 a.m. the next morning.

When I marched this awkward squad to the field where A company was to parade for Captain Rhodes' inspection, the four platoons were already drawn up and in the charge of Gladys Cooper. Captain Rhodes had not yet appeared. As I marched them up, brought them to a halt, and then ordered them to dress by the right, the CSM's pungent remarks turned the air blue. "Hold your heads up!" he roared. "Pull your stomachs in. You look as if you are pregnant." Then, of course, inevitably he shouted, "Look to your front! You there! Look to your front! Don't look at me! I'm not Gladys Cooper!" Then he said to me, "Well, Corporal, I don't know what Captain Rhodes will think of 'em when he sees 'em, but I know what I think! Pah! Soldiers!"

BATTALION ORDERLY SERGEANT

During the period we spent at Vergies I was twice on duty with the battalion orderly officer (BOO) as battalion orderly sergeant (BOS) for a period of twenty-four hours. These duties which were new to me, were varied and involved various inspections of all the huts and billets, the cookhouses and latrines and the ceremonial guard. As we entered each hut, barn or cookhouse, it was my duty to precede the BOO and shout "Stand to attention! Orderly Officer's inspection!" One very cold night I went round with the BOO to every barn and billet and assisted him to dish out the rum ration. Before he dismissed me he insisted on giving me an extra large rum ration. "Go on, Corporal, take more than that, here, let me pour it." How I reached my own billet I can't remember, but next morning I found that I was only half undressed. On Christmas day I again performed the duties of BOS, and the BOO said several times as we went round that I was the only sober NCO in the battalion. The last duty of that day was to accompany the battalion orderly officer to the guardroom, turn out the guard for his inspection, and then we all stood to attention while the guard bugler blew the last post; and so to bed.

SERGEANT OF THE GUARD

Another unfamiliar duty I had to perform was sergeant of the guard for twenty-four hours at the guardroom. I had no experience of being in charge of a ceremonial guard, having been simply a private the last time I was a member of a battalion guard back in England.

Being warned for this duty, I attended the changing of the guard ceremony at 4 p.m. the previous day, to observe, and especially, to estimate the number of paces for the various manoeuvres needed to bring my new guard into position exactly opposite the old guard lined up outside the guardroom.

The guardroom was a corner shop at a street junction with some awkward angles, and it was essential to know the number

292

of paces available, as I gave my orders to the new guard as they were marching. I also memorised all the orders I should have to give, for the first time in my life, while under the eagle eye of the regimental sergeant-major and a crowd of onlookers who had nothing better to do than watch, criticise and spot any flaw in the ceremony.

I returned to the farm buildings, mustered my section and chose six of the tallest. Lancashire Fusiliers were not noted for tall men, in fact, at five feet ten and a half, I was known as the big corporal. I told them to start cleaning their equipment, rifle and bayonet, and if necessary to borrow better items from men not detailed for the guard. They were all busy cleaning and polishing that evening, and next morning I paraded them outside, drilled, criticised and rehearsed the various manoeuvres they would have to perform at 4 p.m. We were, of course, excused all the other duties and parades that day, and by degrees I managed to get them quite enthusiastic about a good performance.

THE CHANGING OF THE GUARD

At 3.30 p.m. I marched my guard, with leather shining and brass gleaming, to BHQ to be inspected by the battalion orderly officer of the day, and then marched them through the streets to the guardroom to arrive precisely at 4 p.m. The orders and manoeuvres all went well, and by 4.15 p.m. I was in charge of the guard for the next twenty-four hours; changing the sentries ceremonially every two hours. The whole guard turns out to be inspected by the battalion orderly officer once by day and once by night, and also on the first occasion when the commanding officer of the battalion passes by, or when any other such senior officer does so. At 4 p.m. the next day there was another similar ceremony of changing the guard and another NCO and six men took over.

DEMOBILISATION BEGINS

About ten days after Christmas, demobilisation began. As the battalion had in its ranks a number of ex-coalminers, these were the first to be demobilised so that they could get back to the production of coal in Britain. Soon the battalion began to shrink in size, and then men other than miners were included in the lists. As orderly sergeant, one of my duties was to read out the names of the men who were to report next morning at the office at BHQ for demobilisation instructions. On the evening of 22nd January, when reading the names aloud in the various barns and billets in Vergies, I found my own name on the list. Within a day or two I was on my way with a party of about fifty men, marching along the snow covered roads to Rouen, sixty miles away.

THE JOURNEY HOME

We left Vergies on a Sunday morning and I arrived home in Northampton the following Sunday evening, a journey of eight days. The weather was cold; sometimes snow fell as we marched from rest camp to rest camp along the snow covered roads.

By the road sides, hundreds of men belonging to the Chinese labour companies, whose job was keeping the roads clear of snow and slush, grinned at us and made all sorts of gestures as we marched past. At the rest camps, which we reached every evening after a long march, we queued in long lines with thousands of men from other battalions for food and drink. Moving slowly forward in long queues, we would come to a trestle table with large stacks of clean white plates; something we had not seen for a very long time!

We took one and also a cup, and then moved on to a hatch where we were each given a large piece of bread. At the next hatch, a piece of cheese, at the next some bully beef and so on, until, with a steaming hot cupful of tea we sat at long trestle tables! Something we also had not done since we left England the previous spring. At night we slept on wire netting bunks until reveille, and then after a wash and shave in the huge wash-houses, we sat down to hot porridge, bacon and beans or sausages. It all seemed so civilised.

Daily we fell in with hundreds of others to resume the march to the coast along snow covered roads. At one of these rest camps, I met Pelly one of the nine Acton boys, formerly a friend of Basher Gordon. What a surprise that was to us both. Pelly had been wounded in the head; he showed me the deep groove in his scalp where a German bullet had ploughed through the skin on the crown of his head. He was now one of the many orderlies in this rest camp.

RECRIMINATIONS

The orderlies in the rest camps were either British soldiers, who like Pelly were recovering or convalescing after hospital treatment for wounds, or they were German prisoners.

On one occasion, several of these German prisoners whose duty it was to clear the long trestle tables after meals, were trying to sell various useful articles they had made out of scrap metal. They had obviously used much ingenuity and skill, but their attempts to sell these articles for a few francs to British troops who had only recently been their enemy, were not always well received. One angry corporal on my table was furious, stamped on their goods, swore profusely at them and threatened them with violence if they did not get out of his sight. I felt for both sides in this altercation; the prisoners who were using their skills to obtain a few francs to improve their lot, and the British corporal who could not forget his dead comrades, killed by the Germans.

Many years later, in 1961, my wife and I were on holiday at Benidorm in Spain. At that time Benidorm was still a small village, quite undeveloped for the tourist trade. All the other guests in our hotel were German, and we talked freely to several who spoke English; a young couple with a baby, and an older man who had lost a leg in the Second World War.

He used to undress on the beach, unstrap his artificial leg and hop down to the sea. We saw he also had a deep scar in his back. Also in the hotel was a woman whose husband never returned from the winter campaign at Stalingrad. She was living in Berlin during the period when the Royal Air Force bombers went every night, and the American Flying Fortresses bombed Berlin every day. Her baby died in the air raid shelter through lack of air, and she said "I thought I would never smile again, but I did, and I do." A very brave woman. I felt privileged to hear her tragic story and see her fine spirit.

In Vancouver I met another German lady who told me what her life had been from the days when Hitler took control in 1933. Meeting with these two ladies I realise that, grievous as has been the lot of many British people in both World Wars, we have never suffered invasion, civil war, starvation and ruthless dictatorship, or lost home, savings and loved ones to the extent that many Germans, Poles and other Europeans have experienced. The human spirit is unquenchable despite the worst of man's inhumanity to man.

NEARING THE COAST

As we marched nearer the coast, the accommodation deteriorated, and one night we had to sleep in bell tents, with snow piled up all round. There were, however, wooden boards on the frozen ground and we were each given four army blankets, so despite the freezing weather outside, our young bodies soon created warmth and we slept soundly until reveille. At this camp we had to fetch our food and drink to the tent, and I remember saying to Jim May as we arrived at the tents with our blankets, "You bag a place for us in one of the tents while I take our billycans and see what I can get." Some time later, after queuing up, I returned to the candlelit tents in the dark, along the slippery duckboards through the slush, shouting "Where are you Jim?" as I carried one billycan full of hot tea and another full of berghu, with slices of bread and cheese balanced on top.

Incidentally, the great Spanish Flu epidemic was raging at this time, but we soldiers knew nothing about it until we reached home and heard of the many people who had had it and how many had died.

MEDICAL INSPECTIONS

When we reached Rouen we marched to a hutted camp near the River Seine, and spent many hours in queues waiting for various medical inspections by medical officers. We were given various small paper certificates which declared that we were free from lice or scabies or various other ills. During the long waits in the cold between various inspections, French children came along the queues, crying "App-ulls! Shocolarts! Zigarettes! Merci, M'sieur, deux francs. Orranges! Appulls! Shocolarts! Zigarettes!"

Eventually, we boarded a small paddle steamer for the journey down the winding River Seine to Le Havre. It was very cold and many hours since we had had any food or hot drink, and we spent the time lying huddled in groups on the deck or stamping up and down in the light snow that was falling.

LE HAVRE

It was a dark cold night when we disembarked at Le Havre and marched to a rest camp. Snow was now falling heavily, and it was evident as we queued at a large gate in the docks area that we were not expected. By degrees, the hitherto disciplined troops began to sound more like a howling mob as they stood outside the closed gates and demanded admission. Eventually we were admitted and queued for a meal, and then some of us went into a large YMCA hut, where we found, in addition to the fighting men on their way to demobilisation, other men who were often contemptuously called Base Wallahs. They were serving in some capacity or other at the large base camps, and some of them obviously spent their evenings in the YMCA trying to make a few francs by gambling.

There were the Crown and Anchor wallahs, the Pontoon professionals and the Souvenir salesmen. When one of these souvenir wallahs tried to press his wares on me, I was exasperated and was really mad with him. "Look!" I said, "here are two sound arms and two strong legs that have survived the war. Now? What have YOU got to match THEM among all your souvenir rubbish?"

There were also the Housy-Housy wallahs, crying "Who says a buckshee card?" This game is now called "Bingo". There was even a one-armed billiards champion, who offered to take on anyone for a stake of ten francs. I was quite pleased to leave this Vanity Fair when we were ordered to fall in and then marched through the snow to the docks.

At midnight on 31st January 1919, we were on the quay, thousands of us, all ranks, all regiments, waiting in the snow in long queues to go up the gangways to two ships bound for Southampton. As I stepped off French soil, I felt a deep emotion. I STILL could hardly believe that I was going HOME.

> Breathes there the man, with soul so dead,
> Who never to himself hath said?
> This is my own, my native land!
> Whose heart hath ne'er within him burned,
> As home his footsteps he hath turned
> From wandering on a foreign strand?
>
> *Sir Walter Scott.*

The next ten hours was spent packed in the hold of a very smelly Norwegian cattle ship. Up on deck it was snowing heavily and it was bitterly cold, so we spent the long hours alternately being nearly frozen on the deck, gulping fresh air before returning to the foetid atmosphere of the hold below, where we lay on dirty straw used previously by horses.

SOUTHAMPTON

Early next morning, at first light, we passed the Isle of Wight and saw two British naval destroyers, taking on board the troops from our sister ship, the *Naragansett*, which had gone aground!

After passing up Southampton Water, we disembarked at a dock, and before we boarded the waiting train for London, we were given hot drinks and sandwiches by some English ladies who had a canteen on the railway platform. They also gave us some FRUIT!

All this unexpected hospitality; fruit indeed!… and the sight of a REAL train instead of cattle trucks, created a sense of unreality. We boarded the train, took off our equipment, and put it up on the RACKS! We stacked our rifles and SAT DOWN on soft seats and tried to believe it was true!

POST WAR IN ENGLAND

ENGLISH FIELDS AND FARMS

When the train left, and we emerged from the docks area, we had our first sight of English fields and farms; at first so strange and different from the French landscape we were used to, and then suddenly so familiar, so lovely and heart-warming.

We stared out of the train windows, taking in every detail, satisfying our long suppressed hunger for England, home and beauty. We feasted our eyes on posters with familiar advertising signs and slogans; and as we neared London we passed close by the gardens of houses by the railway. We waved to children and anyone else who noticed the train at level crossings; and as we slid smoothly along into the heart of London, one man actually pointed out the house where he lived. We marvelled.

PURFLEET

From London we went by train to Purfleet on the Thames Estuary, where the final demobilisation procedures were to be undergone. Perhaps endured is the right word, for the camp was literally bursting with troops; there were long queues everywhere. The camp was staffed by young Welsh Guards, who directed us to some huts, told us where to queue up for blankets, where to get a meal, what to do, where to go.

After getting some food and a hot drink, I tried to sleep in one of the wooden huts, but found it impossible; the floor was too flat after all those months of active service in the open. I was quite pleased when a staff sergeant aroused everyone at 4 a.m. and told us to start queuing again.

Outside, lights were on everywhere, a hive of ceaseless activity; new troops marching into the camp, others marching out. We queued at the door of one hut after another, in each of which clerks at tables filled in various forms and did all the paper work of demobilisation for a never ceasing flow of men.

FENCHURCH STREET AND EUSTON

When at last we had been given all the certificates, instructions, booklets, railway warrants and everything else the authorities thought we might need, we boarded a train for Fenchurch Street Station. From there we walked through the streets to Euston Station, accompanied by London street urchins who amused us by offering to "Carry your kitbag, sir!" We laughed at their cockney impudence and gave them a few francs. It was now Sunday morning, and being Sunday, the trains were few and packed with troops when they left for the north.

NORTHAMPTON

I arrived at Northampton Castle Station, at about 9 p.m. on Sunday, the 1st of February, 1919. My father had met all the previous trains from London, and was waiting for this last one. I said goodbye to Jim May, one of the nine boys who had joined the army with me in July, 1917 in Northampton. He had the difficult task of finding some means of getting to Towcester, nine miles away; I have never seen him since.

There were no trams running in Northampton on a Sunday night, and my father and I walked the three miles home through the dark cold streets. The wartime black-out was still in force and there were few people about. At this time, everyone thought of the armistice as a cessation of hostilities, not as peace. Demobilisation meant, not discharge from the armed forces but merely a transfer to the army reserve.

In fact, our demobilisation papers, which were finally contained in a strong linen envelope, contained the following order

"In case of EMERGENCY, you will report for duty, IN UNIFORM, at the Headquarters of the LANCASHIRE FUSILIERS, at Preece Heath, Preston, Lancs."

HOME

As we entered home, my father shouted "I've got him!" My mother and my younger sister came running to meet me. What a moment! My older sister and her husband had just left for their home, thinking that I was not coming home that night.

We had so much to talk about that it was late when I went upstairs (!) up two flights of stairs to my old bedroom and tried to sleep in a bed!

ADJUSTMENT TO CIVIL LIFE

Next day I gave my mother some sugar coupons; they were part of my various demobilisation papers; I had never seen such things before. At first, my mother was delighted "Oh, sugar coupons!" Then she looked doubtful and said, "But I don't suppose I shall be able to get the sugar." "Why not?" I asked in amazement. "Well, there is very little sugar in the shops, and they wouldn't give ME extra sugar for these" she said. "EXTRA sugar" I said, "I'm entitled to my RATIONS." So off I went, searching for sugar, and returned in triumph with several pounds, which, my mother said, I had been able to get because I was a soldier!

This was a strange world to me; rations were rations, whether they were in short supply or not. In the army I had always shared fairly whatever was issued by the quartermaster-sergeant; sometimes three to a loaf, sometimes four or five, according to the trench strength and the casualties.

Here, in civil life, the issuing of rationed foods was apparently both complicated and devious. I have never forgotten that other world, the Western Front, a place apart, unimaginable to a civilian. Not only were the sights, smells and sounds all different from civil life, the SPIRIT was completely different.

Mud, duckboards, shell holes, trenches, sandbags, barbed wire, dug-outs, shattered tree stumps, dead mules. These were some of the sights. The sickly smell of dead mules, the fumes of cordite, the smell of phosgene lingering in shell holes, the acrid smell of burning rubbish, the mouth-watering smell of bacon frying … these were some of the smells.

The crump of shells bursting, the chatter of machine-guns and the song of a lark high in the blue sky … these were some of the sounds.

Laughter, witticism, dry humour, real comradeship, everything shared, good or bad … this was the spirit in this uncomplicated world, free of unessentials, life lived a day at a time with the threat of death common to all, of whatever rank.

I have always been grateful that I was old enough to go out to the front in 1918, and share those experiences.

TWENTY-EIGHT DAYS' LEAVE

I was one of the first demobbed soldiers to arrive in Northampton. This was due to the 10th Lancashire Fusiliers being dispersed earlier than most battalions to allow those who were miners to return to the pits and ease the coal shortage, and also because the 17th (Northern) Division, of which my battalion was a part, did not follow the defeated German Army to the Rhine.

Despite all the delousing on the way home, I still felt very itchy and unfit for civilised society. My khaki uniform was stained and worn, but my belt shone, my buttons gleamed, and my tunic bore the colourful insignia of my regiment, brigade and division. On my epaulettes I wore the green and black tabs of battalion gas NCO with the brass fusilier bomb and the brass letters LF.

On the upper arms above my Corporal's stripes, the Battalion sign, an oblong yellow flash and the 52nd Brigade sign, a green square 52, and above these and just below the epaulettes, the 17th Divisional sign, a white morse dot and dash on a red background. My mother said it was quite colourful.

The weather in February 1919 was still cold; lakes and rivers were frozen and I spent some of my leave skating on the flooded moors at Kingsthorpe.

NEWS OF OLD FRIENDS

During my service in France, I had heard of various casualties among my old school friends, neighbours and acquaintances. I knew that Jimmy Knight, my old cross-country running friend, had crashed in a plane during training in Egypt; and then I met his sister, who told me that her mother could not get over his death at eighteen years of age. She told me that her mother spent hours just sitting and weeping in his bedroom and could not be comforted. I told my mother about this and she said "Oh, I don't know what I should have done if you had not returned, but I couldn't have been like Jimmy Oldham's mother; she went into all the shops telling everyone my son's killed."

Then my father began to talk about several other boys who had been at school with me, and had been killed. Two of them, both young officers, had been killed in action on the Somme, before I went there.

One was Norman Beale, who my father told me he had spoken to at the Castle Station when he was returning to the front from leave. The other was the only son of Councillor John Woods, an ex-Mayor of the town. I remember him best when we were fellow full backs in one of the house elevens. He had been killed in action in July 1916, at Ovillers in the Ancre Valley, which my battalion had captured in August 1918.

I said, "Yes, dad, they are only two of the many thousands of young officers like them who have given their lives in this war." Now that it was all over, the enormous waste of young lives began to hit those of us who had been in it and had necessarily become hardened to the casualties.

SURVIVING FRIENDS

Surviving friends began to return home during my twenty-eight days' leave. The first was my special friend Griff. He also was a corporal, in the Gordon Highlanders, and we walked round the town together for a week or two as we had done in our schooldays. Since he had run away to join the army in 1916 at the age of seventeen, his old employers who were local solicitors, didn't want him back, and Griff certainly had no desire to return to legal work in an office. So he had decided to accept his colonel's offer of sergeant's stripes and sign on for three or four years service in the Sudan. Actually he spent thirty years there, first in the army and then in the Sudan civil services.

My next friend to come home was Bert Chapman, who joined up with me, but had been sent to another training camp and another regiment. We also walked round the streets and parks talking of old times and war experiences. Bert told me that his older brother, Harold, was missing and since this was at Ypres, we knew that there was no hope of his survival. His mother was very sad and I had several conversations with her about the lack of any news of Harold. She asked my advice about dealing with a man who had called on her several times, purporting to be a friend of Harold's and also showing her what he said was Harold's cap badge. I advised her to have no confidence in such a story, and told her that little was known of the men who had disappeared in the Ypres salient and were officially listed as missing. I also warned her to give him no money, or believe a word he said, and I told her that men at the front wore steel helmets, not service caps with regimental badges.

OLD GRAMMAR SCHOOL FRIENDS

Then I met another demobilised soldier, H. A. White, who was a prefect at the grammar school during my time there. We had a very long conversation, exchanging news of many of our old friends.

I learned that Jarman, my old rival for first place in the weekly form order in the lower fifth had been killed. Also Hall, who sat next to me in that form (Hall, Hodges, Hope, etc). We laughed as we recalled the occasion when one of the masters, Mr Hincksman, was drilling a squad of the school cadet corps outside the classroom where Hall was playing the piano during his music lesson. Hincksman, said to him next morning in the Form Room "How can I get a squad to concentrate on my orders while you are playing sentimental music? In the Gloaming!" We began to exchange news of others who were with us at the Northampton Town and County School from the time the new building was opened in 1911. We knew that Beavan Pitt, Sid Hanafy, E. Nightingale and A. G. Grose had been shot down on the Western Front while serving in the Royal Flying Corps (later the Royal Air Force). We knew about H. W. Hayard, a 2nd Lieut., 6th Northants — killed at Thiepval, 1916. Ernest Mace, a 2nd Lieut., 6th Northants — killed at Thiepval, 1917 and W. L. McColl, a 2nd Lieut., 6th Northants — killed at Ancre Valley, 1917. I knew that my friend C. S. N. G. Beale, a 2nd Lieut., 7th Northants was killed at Guillemont in 1916.

Others who had been killed that we knew about, were:

R. H. Garrard, 2nd Lieut., Kings Royal Rifles.

P. H. Laughton, 2nd Lieut., Royal West Surreys.

A. G. S. Naylor, 2nd Lieut., 7th Northants.

A. E. Owen, 2nd Lieut., 7th Northants.

H. A. Redhead, 2nd Lieut., 6th Northants.

H. S. Skillington, 2nd Lieut., 1st Northants.

A. B. Tebbutt, 2nd Lieut. Norfolks.

B. A. Streeton, F. R. S. Adams, A. Shaw, A. T. Speight, F. Cleaver, R. Cleaver, F. Boyson, M. Boyson, H. W. Boyson, P. R. Orgill, R. B. Bishop, H. E. Tresham, S. Wooding, K. Hammond.

Two of the masters at the school when we were there were killed — R. B. Hincksman and J. L. Urquhart. Also Sergeant George Bayes, 1st Northamptonshire Regiment, who used to train us in the cadet corps. Even though we knew that most of the prefects and most of the NCOs of the school cadet corps had been killed, we did not realise how great the full toll was. In 1924 a war memorial tablet in honour of the fallen boys was unveiled in the school hall. It contained the names of the ninety-one boys and three members of the staff, from a school which opened a new building in 1911 to accommodate 400 boys.

CHILDHOOD FRIENDS

Every time I met another demobilised serviceman whom I knew, I heard of others who had been killed whom I had known in childhood. Arthur Allbright, Billy Miller, Bill Savage, Dicky Lovell, Bill Waters, George Tipler, Billy Smith, "Colonel" Rigby, "Bloater" Wright, Jim Hutchins, Oliver Stevenson and two others who were inseparable when they were at junior school with me "Rocker" Brown and "Fatty" Tanser.

Among school friends who had survived, several told me about their older brothers who had been killed. Fred Amos had lost an older brother whom I remembered well because we both used to have violin lessons from the same teacher. Dick Hollowell and Jack Foil, near neighbours and old school friends had both lost an older brother. Reg Tomalin, who lived next door, had lost his older brother, Bert, a very talented violinist. He had died in Italy during the world influenza epidemic of 1918. Fred Amos, who was also serving in Italy with the Northamptonshire Yeomanry as a bugler, sounded the Last Post at Bert's military funeral.

PRISONERS OF WAR

Then one day I was delighted to meet Stanley Day, a special friend of my childhood; we used to collect cigarette cards and swop them to make up sets. Stan had been a prisoner of war since 1917; he was one of those who had rushed to join Edgar Mobbs' company in 1914 when he was nearly seventeen. He went to France with the 7th Northants and took part in the battle of Loos. Then he volunteered to become a stretcher-bearer and had been awarded the MM for bravery. During our long conversation he told me it was pinned on his chest in the square of Albert. Then his battalion had taken over some trenches near to the coast at Nieuport. It had been a comparatively quiet sector until the British took it over from the Belgians, their policy being to live and let live. The British policy was almost invariably to stir things up, strafe the enemy, give him a bloody nose; and this often brought a strong retaliation. Stan confirmed this when he said, "You know, Fred, what the British are like. As soon as we took over, there were new roads and new railways under construction, huge dumps of all kinds of war material. And you know Jerry, too, he soon spotted all this activity, and he took appropriate action. He made a strong raid down the coast, wiped out two platoons of Kings Royal Rifles, and got behind the Northamptonshires, encircled them, cut them off and took most of them prisoner. About half a dozen got away by swimming."

It was interesting also, to hear of the experiences of others who had been taken prisoner in the German spring offensive of March, 1918. A neighbour named Greenhough told me that the massed waves of advancing Germans swept past his battalion on either flank and encircled them. He said some of his mates tried to run when they realised what had happened, but they were ruthlessly mown down by the German machine-gunners. Greenhough did not have a bath or any change of underclothes from then until after his release in November. He then weighed only ninety-eight pounds.

Two of my church friends told me how they were taken prisoner. The exhausted and depleted battalion of one had been retreating for days and nights without sleep or regular food. They were out of touch with any other British troops and were trying to snatch a few hours sleep in a wood when very suddenly they were surrounded by German troops and captured in the middle of the night.

The other man said that his battalion was just behind the front resting in some very large dug-outs dug deep into a hillside, when the German attack began an 21st March. They were actually asleep on the wire netting bunks when the German advance trapped them in the dug-outs and they had to surrender without a fight.

Another old grammar school friend, Walter Tresham, was not old enough to join the Royal Flying Corps, or Royal Air Force, as it was then, until the summer of 1918. He was hurriedly trained as an observer with map reading, use of an aerial camera and how to fire a Lewis gun from an aircraft. He and his pilot were forced down in the closing stages of the war, because the Lewis gun jammed, due to the round pan of bullets being carelessly loaded by ground staff. Walt told me that the German pilot realised what had happened and that he could easily have shot them down. However he circled them and pointed down. Walt's pilot started to go down, and eventually saw a small green patch below. The German pilot again circled, and pointed to it and followed them down to it. They were taken to a Bavarian town where revolution had broken out. Walt said that he saw no German officers in the camp to which they were taken and the place seemed to be run by a German corporal! This makes me think of Hitler, but he hadn't been heard of then.

Another childhood friend, Vivian Lucas, who lived opposite at the chemist's shop, came home on fourteen days' leave. I asked him why he had not been demobbed, and he told me that after a wound and hospital treatment, he had been drafted away from his former unit for some very strange duties. During the war, men had been buried by their comrades, if it was possible, but now that the war was over, the bodies or remains were being collected and reburied in war cemeteries.

Vivian's job was to assist in the recovery, not of those marked by a wooden cross, but those with no marking. I asked him how this was done and he said that these bodies were revealed to the practised eye by the shallow hollows in the soil. This was not only an unpleasant task; it was potentially dangerous since the battle areas were full of unexploded shells and hand grenades. I asked Vivian about his two older brothers whom I had known in our childhood; I used to help them put up the sunblinds outside the chemist's shop, hooking them up above the shop windows and attaching them to wooden posts in sockets at the kerb.

They had both volunteered early in the war and had been sent out to the front to reinforce the 1st Battalion of the Northamptonshires after only a few weeks' training. Now I learnt that Alfred had lost a leg, and that Noel, whom I had known well at the grammar school, had survived, but was now suffering from mental shock. He lived only a few months after this.

Then one day Billy Swaysland, another school friend of our third form days, came home on leave from hospital wearing Hospital Blue. He was having treatment for a disease he had caught in the middle east. There were no antibiotics in those days and he died a few months later.

Crouch, one of the boys who joined the army with me in July 1917, came home on crutches, one leg missing. Smith, an old form mate in the lower fifth, returned with one arm, as did a near neighbour whose name I forgot. Arthur Swan, another close friend, younger than me, returned home from hospital after extensive dental treatment and facial surgery. He did not go out to the Western Front until nearly the end of the war, but had no sooner arrived when a piece of a whizzbang hit him in the cheek. Bumper Wells returned to the town after recovering from a bullet wound in his thigh. His was also a very short spell in France, not going out until August 1918.

As demobilisation proceeded, other friends reappeared in the town, Johnny Fox, Reg Morton, Wally Gross, Billy Houghton, Frank Hicks.

Jack Foil returned from the Navy, another friend from the Royal Naval Division. All my friends were glad to be home again and finished with the armed services, except Jack Bradley, who had risen to the rank of company sergeant-major at the age twenty-one and signed on for further service.

SOMETHING MISSING

As I spent these twenty-eight days of my demobilisation leave, walking round the town, in the parks, and visiting the familiar places of my youth, I was conscious of something missing in the spirit of the people. It may have been partly due to the fact that for 18 months I had been exclusively with other young men, and here in Northampton in February 1919, the only young men were we men just back from the war.

The town seemed very quiet, and many people seemed depressed; there was something missing, the vitality of youth, which had never flagged in the army, whatever the conditions. There seemed to be an atmosphere of apathy, or was it shock? Was it the communal grief for the many sons that the town had lost? War changes the spirit of a people.

In 1914 there had been a light-hearted spirit, ill-informed and ignorant of the realities of war. The popular saying was "It will be all over by Christmas".

In 1915 there was still a certain arrogance, and unjustified confidence. It was felt that the war would be over when our new army, Kitchener's Army, went to France, although the casualties suffered at Aubers Ridge, Neuve Chapelle and Loos were a shock.

In 1916 the reality of the war came home when the horrific losses on the Somme were published, but the false optimism still remained to a large extent among those not bereaved.

In 1917 the false optimism died with still more losses at Arras, Cambrai and Passchendaele, where men were sent continually to fight in swamps of mud, filth and slime. In such conditions the wounded could not be evacuated, and men actually drowned or sank in the mud and slime. The final weeks of cold and drenching rain, under constant and accurate German shell fire, saw the lowest point of morale on the Western Front.

In 1918 the rigid (or tight) discipline of the regular army had gone. Its members were either dead, captured, or fit enough after wounds, only to train the young soldiers of eighteen. The Crusader spirit of Kitchener's volunteers had also gone, so many of them were also dead or disabled. The enormous losses, and the repeated merging of the survivors of fine spirited battalions, men who had volunteered together and trained together, had broken up the old spirit of comradeship. The new young Boy's Battalions, though only half-trained, brought to weary survivors a fresh injection of spirit, and morale rose as victory came in sight.

In 1919 demobilisation brought survivors home to a civilian population suffering from delayed shock and war weariness.

I began to realise that the war had taken its toll of civilians as well as the soldiers, sailors and airmen. The battles of Aubers Ridge and Loos in 1915, the long drawn out battles at Ypres and Passchendaele, the grievous losses on the Somme from 1916 to 1918, and at the Dardanelles and at other fronts where Northamptonians had died — what a toll it was!

I found it difficult to talk to some people and was often conscious of the sad glances of bereaved mothers, some of whom looked at me with a strange intensity.

I realised too that there was an unbridgeable gulf between those of us who had experienced at first hand the realities of war, and those who were civilians living in their own country free from enemy occupation, and who had only been able to read censored reports of the battles and conditions of the war. Some of the things we had experienced they would never be able to understand, and so we couldn't talk about them, except to one another. This book may, in part, help to bridge the gulf.

My employers were short staffed and keen for me to resume work with them, and so on 24th February 1919, I put away my uniform and became a civilian again.

"MEN OF 18 IN 1918"

Marshal Foch said —

"Never at any time in history has the British Army achieved greater results in attack than in this unbroken offensive."

Winston Churchill said —

"Disasters, disappointments, miscalculations and the grievous price paid by the soldiers, never affected the confidence of the British Army or its will to win the war. Despite the losses of 1915, 1916 and 1917, the now very young British Infantry of 1918, by continual attack, from the Somme to the Selle, overcame the brave resistance of Germany's diminishing military strength, and spared mankind the further slaughter of the unfought campaign of 1919."

The British Infantry of 1918 *was* very young, but it must be remembered that the Western Front had, in 1915, 1916 and 1917, literally swallowed up the generation of men born in the 1880s and 1890s.

Consequently, by the spring of 1918, when the great crisis came, men were in short supply in Britain. Britain was producing only about 200,000 male youngsters of eighteen each year, and these "Men of 18" were the best and the only material available to rebuild the battalions that were virtually wiped out in the so nearly successful German spring offensive of 1918.

When we joined the depleted battalions that had lost most of their officers, NCOs and men, killed, wounded, missing or captured, we were indeed only boys dressed as men, but we matured very rapidly into fighting soldiers. Those who survived to nineteen became our prime assault troops in an unbroken offensive that did indeed turn near defeat into final victory.

No longer laughing boys full of weird enthusiasms after we had been blooded. We rapidly became experienced for the simple reason that so much was expected of us.

I am privileged to have been born in the summer of 1899, and so to have been eligible to be one of the "MEN OF 18 IN 1918".

REFLECTIONS BY THE AUTHOR AT
AGE 88 ON WHEN HE WAS 18

I am often awake now in the early hours, and sometimes my thoughts go back to an area of northern France which is still known to the British as the SOMME. There are few of us left now who know that comparatively small area of France as well, if not better, than our own local countryside. The name of every village and wood was deeply engraved on our young memories.

For four long and tragic years, British men, and eventually British men of eighteen, lived in, fought in, and defended that part of France as loyally, fiercely and stubbornly as if it had been British. I also think sadly of the many I knew who are buried there in the War Cemeteries which are so carefully tended. I think of the tragic waste of promising young lives in that generation of men who were born during the latter years of Queen Victoria's long reign.

In 1914, they faced a universal obligation to die for their country, and they accepted it quite simply. Few of them had any knowledge or experience of what is involved in "going to war on a foreign field". In this ignorance and innocence, the sheer glamour and glory of war, of wearing a uniform, of joining the regiment of one's choice, was very attractive.

Lord Kitchener asked for 100,000 volunteers, and the response was overwhelming. The vitality of youth, and the sense of taking part in exciting events outshone any thought of the grief and sorrow that was certain to accompany such a mainly purposeless waste of so many lives. When I look back to 1914, I realise it was one of the hinges of history on which many changes turned.

It seems almost incredible now that a sports loving non-military nation such as Britain then was, should so light-heartedly take on a well-trained militaristic nation such as Germany was then. The British people had tremendous enthusiasm for the war, but no experience of war on a continental scale. We possessed only a small well-trained army of professional soldiers, and we had no means of equipping or training a large army.

For months there were no uniforms for the enthusiastic "Pals battalions" (We'll all go together) which were suddenly recruited in many towns. These dozens of battalions of raw recruits, most of whom regarded the experience of answering "Kitchener's Call" as an exciting kind of picnic from which they would be home again before Christmas, were battalions in name only. They had no trained NCOs, and were commanded by elderly retired officers, to whom were allotted only two or three regular army NCOs, who trained the recruits, in their inadequate civilian clothes, in marching, physical exercises and squad drill.

Eventually, the requisite number of NCOs emerged from those who possessed qualities of leadership and the right temperament, for to be an effective NCO one needs to be a bit of an actor. The Commissioned Officers were, in those early days of the war, often appointed by the Mayors of the towns in which these battalions were raised. They were drawn, from the upper and middle classes of those pre-war days, some of them having had a basic military training in university, public school and grammar school cadet corps.

The creation of this new army of volunteers was typically British, an ad hoc, do it yourself army of enthusiastic patriotic amateurs, who were both physically and mentally better than the rigidly trained regular army who had been recruited from a limited type. It was basically an improvisation, democratic in spirit, full of confidence, but oblivious of the realities of training for war against professionals.

I remember two of many humorous incidents. In one, a squad of raw recruits was being taught to number off and form fours. They treated this very necessary procedure in the movement of troops as a huge joke, and their response to the order to Number! was One! Two! Three! Four! Five! Six! Seven! Eight! Nine! Ten! Jack! Queen! King! They then roared with laughter and the recently appointed NCO, who gave the order, laughed with them. The other incident happened when a newly-appointed young officer strolled up to and spoke to his colonel without saluting him. "Oh!" he said, when rebuked, "I didn't know that officers had to salute anyone."

On 1st July 1916, 97 of the 143 volunteer battalions of Kitchener's New Army, who had signed on for three years or the duration, were sent, ill-trained and inexperienced, into battle north of the River Somme. They faced a well-trained and now war experienced German Army of professionals on a twenty mile long front, stretching from Gommecourt southwards through Beaumont Hamel, Thiepval, Ovillers, La Boselle to Fricourt. The result is well known, not the glorious victory expected, but the greatest losses ever sustained by the British Army. Another result was that the names of many French villages and woods became well known in Britain, chiefly by the many who had lost a son, a husband or a school friend on the Somme.

I have vivid memories of those ruined villages and devastated woods, because I was one of another new army, also only half-trained; the boys who were suddenly called upon to be "Men of 18" in the spring of 1918. By this time, the Somme had its own history, but to us, everything was new and exciting, although, after two years of shelling in many attacks, the whole area looked old, much older than its two years' history.

There was neither time nor opportunity for anyone to teach us how to take our place in this scene of feverish activity and improvisation. We were soon very conscious that it was a time of high crisis in which the single aim, at whatever the cost in effort and lives, was to stabilise the front and plug the great gaps made in our defences.

So, inexperienced half-trained boy soldiers were very quickly welded, with the survivors of battalions fresh from a fighting withdrawal, into new platoons, new companies and new battalions. We were then sent forward to man and defend an unstable, and in some cases, a non-existent front. In the words of Field Marshal Sir Douglas Haig, which were read out to us, we were to "fight to the last man; there must be no more retirement".

Within days, three of the boys with whom I had trained in the 53rd Young Soldiers Battalion, were killed in the front line by blast from a trench mortar. There was not a mark on their bodies as we buried them; just some singeing on their uniforms. Blast creates abnormal pressures or vacuums in the organs of the human body, and this can cause ruptures and haemorrhages in the brain and spinal column.

Within weeks, many more of the boys were dead, as the Germans shelled and trench mortared us from their dominating positions on Thiepval Ridge, where they could see every movement we made. They constantly threatened to renew their full-scale offensive by probing our defences by night with various types of trench raids in which more boys were killed or wounded or taken prisoner. They never again broke through our improvised defences in that devastated area of confusing 1916 and newly-dug trench systems.

The German well-planned massive Spring Offensive was initially a classic victory; an eye opener to the Allied Generals. When this ruthless non-stop attack was finally stemmed, after horrendous casualties on both sides, its main objective had not been achieved. Their plan had been to deeply penetrate the British front by well-rehearsed new tactics and overwhelming manpower.

This they did. They failed, however, to capture Amiens, and they failed in their plan to roll up the shattered line by further strong attacks northwards to the French coast, and so win the war.

On August 8th the British Army commenced their final non-stop offensive which brought more than four years of war to an end.

The "Men of 18" who had survived to their nineteenth birthday, were no longer inexperienced boys, and took part in attack after attack from the Somme to the St. Quentin Canal and on to the River Selle and finally to the River Sambre de L'Oise Canal at Berlaimont.

Victory, total victory, came suddenly, on November 11th. We could scarcely believe it then, and I have often thought about it since. How did we win that war? Not because of our superior military arts and skills. We were quite unprepared for a long continental war.

British civilians had to learn how to fight and win that long war by bitter experience, by trial and costly error. The German generals had prepared themselves and their troops for years. At the age of twenty, much more mature than eighteen, every German commenced two years training and was recalled for a month each year while on the reserve. They were ready for instant mobilisation when required.

Nor do I think our victory came solely by the dogged courage and will to win at whatever the cost of our untrained civilian army. I believe victory came because of qualities which are much deeper, which spring from strengths which stem from traditions which have been built up through, and inherited from past centuries of British history. Traditions of duty, of self-sacrifice, which I personally witnessed in ordinary men. These native qualities, reinforced and activated by the regimental traditions with which we were imbued, always surfaced in a crisis. Through these traditions the British war time civilian army possessed a powerful impetus which was the mainspring of ultimate victory. I can never forget that time when a generation of ordinary men played their part in a scene where death always hovered, but was ignored.

I remember strangely beautiful scenes — in the still hours before dawn, standing sentry on the fire-step, when the moonlight transformed the ever mysterious no man's land from its aura of fear to one of stark beauty. I also noticed the stars, which as a civilian I had not noticed. I had great pleasure in wild flowers, which sprang up in most unexpected places — on parapets and in old shell holes.

My perception was very sharp and active in those days, even in the most appalling conditions or violent scenes. I noticed what was going on around me, and also the varied reactions of both officers and men.

I still remember faces and places, and incidents tragic and comical. One day, Corporal Thomas and I transformed an officers' latrine. It had been made for officers by the troops of a battalion we had just relieved. This posh structure was, in our opinion, far too good for that purpose, and we coveted it as a shelter for the night for ourselves — this was during a period when we were never two nights in one place. "First of all," said Thomas, "we must mackle up something for them," and that is what we did. Then we dug out about a foot of soil to make our temporary home sweet and habitable.

As soon as we had moved in, along comes an officer, looking for something! I shall always remember the puzzled look on his face when he found the latrine he had previously seen and noted, now occupied by two corporals who politely directed him to the clearly marked officers' latrine further along.

On another occasion, Thomas and I took possession of a very cosy dug-out which the Germans had made — it even had a door! Along comes the RSM and he wants it, bless him, so we moved on. Further along this earth bank, several men were digging a large hole in the bank to accommodate a large wardrobe which they had brought from the ruins of a nearby house.

Along comes a runner, rifle slung on shoulder, cigarette in mouth. He was a perky soldierly man, his tunic, which displayed a Military Medal, was very tight on his broad chest. As a runner, carrying messages between companies, he was often exposed to shell fire or sniping. He stopped, he stared, he took a few more puffs on his cigarette and continued to watch the progress being made to get the wardrobe into the hole in the bank. Then he said "Ee'eh! Ar doarn't knoarr. Some folk, seems, only coom oop t'line to meeark th'sells comfut-arble!"

He was typical of that generation of men who played a vital part in a unique and unrepeatable period of British history.

The last survivors are now coming to the end of their long lives. I am now the last of ten who lived in the same district of Northampton for many years. As the years have passed, and one by one my fellow soldiers came to the end of their lives, I began to realise how unique, how unrepeatable had been the experience we had shared so long ago.

It was a period of British history which is so totally alien to the present day and age, that any account of it reads like grotesque fiction. We lived in a world completely isolated from our former life as civilians, although only a few miles distant across the channel.

When the survivors returned to civil life, their experiences of war were too stark and their memories too powerful and too intimate to share, except with those who had also experienced them. For more than ten years, no books were written about the war.

My last visit to those horrifying, yet fascinating scenes of war, stirred me to write. I saw the whole scene and my own experiences from the distance of time. I had had a graphic view of the 1918 scene while it was happening, but the passage of time has enabled me to get the overall view into perspective.

With many others who have written, I am very aware of the awesome losses incurred in the War Games played by the generals, but I also realise that the individuals who were mere pawns in the mass performances, achieved a special maturity of spirit. They were indeed a unique generation. It has been said that their faces often reveal something of it.

So I began to write, first to get it out of my system as it were, and second, to record and share some of that period of our history with others.

I have tried to convey the dogged courage, the unquenchable spirit, the stickability and the earthy wit of the infantryman at war, who, though he was a mere pawn in the plans of generals, yet remained an individual who also served ideals; and for those ideals, faced death daily at some chance or mischance of war with courage in the line of duty.

A BIOGRAPHY OF THE AUTHOR

The author was born with his twin brother in 1899 in Northampton, England, educated at Northampton Town and County School (now the Northampton School for Boys) which was founded in 1541 during the reign of Henry VIII by the town mayor Thomas Chipsey and others including Lawrence Washington a county resident and ancestor of the first President of the USA. In 1914 at the start of World War I young men were called to the armed services thus reducing the staff of many businesses. The local company supplying coal gas for domestic use and street lighting asked the school for a bright teenager for their finance department. The headmaster sent the author aged 15 who subsequently spent his professional career there becoming Chief Cashier. He always regretted the premature end to his education.

In 1917 at the age of 18 the author was automatically drafted into the British Army and arbitrarily placed in the Lancashire Fusiliers whose men had been decimated by recent German offensives on the Western Front in France. Again, the author's training ended abruptly when his cohort was rushed to the Front Line as young combat soldiers to stem the German advance. He remained in battle lines until the end of the war in November 1918. Initially a Private, his abilities were soon recognised and he was promoted in rapid succession to Corporal, Battalion Gas NCO, Orderly Sergeant and acting Provost Sergeant of the Regimental Police.

He was fortunate to survive. After the war he returned to the same firm, married at age 25 and raised a son and daughter. During the Second World War, being too old for military service, he served as an Air Raid Warden during German bombing raids. He retired early at 60 and supported by his wife Elizabeth Olive (neé Hawkins) embarked on a second career that included gardening, painting, travelling, speaking, writing and mentoring their 11 grand- and step-grandchildren. His public speaking was initially rooted in his lively Christian faith and he was respected locally as a Bible teacher. However, his traumatic experience of war as a sensitive teenager left indelible and accurate memories although he never spoke of them. They generated a deep conviction that the political and military mistakes that killed many young men of his generation and blighted life for millions must not be repeated. He felt compelled to record for posterity what he had witnessed. So, at the age of 80 he enrolled in a typing school learning on a manual machine in a class of teenage girls. Without any notes he then typed from memory the manuscript of this book.

The book led unexpectedly to invitations to lecture in schools, military units, and cultural centres on his experiences in the First World War. The BBC then discovered him as a living witness of that War and invited him to speak nationally on radio and television. The media then realised he was a fluent and interesting raconteur able vividly to describe the social and economic scenes of the early 20th century and he became a participant in many TV documentaries. He also produced audio recordings for his grandchildren describing the vast social changes he had witnessed since the Victorian-Edwardian era. His natural and modest stance and the fact that he was then in his 90s added to the merit of his contributions. He was awarded the French Chevalier d'Honneur by President Chirac along with the few surviving British soldiers who had fought in France 1914–1918.

He and his wife continued to live alone until they were both 100 when they moved into a Senior Home. At the age of 102 after 77 years of marriage they were identified as the oldest, longest married couple in the UK. The TV crew interviewing them in the Senior Home asked for the secret of their long marriage. Their answer was 'Love'. A few days later, the author died peacefully in his sleep. His twin brother had died at 6 months of age. Shortly after his death, the BBC morning show 'Breakfast' interviewed the author's wife asking whether she wanted her husband back. "Oh no" she said. "He is now with Jesus and at his age that is far better". The interviewer then asked her to define "Love" which they had earlier said was the special ingredient of their long marriage. She answered briefly "Love is giving, not getting". The BBC received so many affirmations they rebroadcast the interview at home and on their World Service.

John Hodges,
Executor of F. J. Hodges Estate
June 2021.

APPENDIX I

The recorded casualties of the XXth The Lancashire Fusiliers
Killed in action:
The Regiment
726 Officers.
12,916 Other ranks.
Total: 13,642

Killed in Action:
The 10th (Service) Battalion
41 Officers
891 Other ranks
Total: 932

In 1914 there were 8 battalions.
In 1915 there were 26 battalions.
In 1916 there were 24 battalions.
In 1917 there were 22 battalions.
In 1918 there were 8 battalions.
In 1919 there were 3 battalions.

Decorations awarded to the Regiment:
Victoria Crosses: 18
DSOs: 80
Military Crosses: 448
DCMs: 290
Military Medals: 1273
Mentions in Despatches: 617
Foreign Decorations: 180

APPENDIX II

The instruction and training of men who were sent on a course to the Vth Corps Gas School included:

1 — TYPES OF GASES USED BY THE ENEMY

TEAR GAS

This affects the eyes only, and the extreme effect causes temporary blindness. It smells like a mixture of rubber solution and horseradish.

TEAR GAS AND ASPHYXIANT GAS

This affects the eyes first, then closes the glottis. A smell of varnish or, if weaker, sharp cider.

ASPHYXIANT GAS. GREEN CROSS. CHLORINE

A yellowish-green gas, foggy when the air is damp. Smells like chloride of lime. A very active poison when there is only 1 part in 10,000 of air. Effect — the actual destruction of the lungs; will knock a man out in five minutes if he is exposed to 1 part in 10,000.

PHOSGENE

Four times heavier than air. Has a mouldy decayed smell. Two parts in 10,000 will knock a man out in two minutes. Acts on the blood, lungs and heart. No chance of recovering owing to delayed indirect action. Forms a compound with the blood, which then will not flow; this causes heart failure. If stronger, acts on all three — blood, lungs and heart; kills at once.

MUSTARD GAS

This affects the eyes from temporary soreness to total blindness. It affects the skin, causing blisters on the moist skin of the armpits, chest and thighs. If the skin is splashed by the liquid wash it off immediately if possible, using plenty of soap. If clothes are splashed, get them off immediately. The liquid blisters the skin even through clothes if still worn. A small stock of clothing — uniforms and underclothes — was available for me to allocate to men whose clothing had become impregnated by long exposure to a Mustard Gas attack. The effects are most persistent, having the actual effects of burns. The effects of breathing Mustard Gas range from a sore throat to the complete destruction of the lungs. If possible gargle with Soda BK Solution, of which the Gas NCO should have a small stock. The Service Box Respirator MUST be worn even while there is the slightest smell of garlic — the smell of Mustard Gas.

BLUE CROSS

This is not a gas, but a solid, so it has to be used with HE. Becomes a gas when exposed to the air, and is very effective because it contains elements which cause coughing and sneezing, the eyes to run and the throat to smart. All this is very unpleasant, but the gas is not lethal.

2 — THE DUTIES OF GAS NCOs

These were very extensive and important, and included the regular posting of Gas Sentries on a twenty-four hour basis, the regular inspection of the gas masks of 800 Officers and men, and the responsibility of ordering gas masks to be worn.

In the continual war of movement from 8th August onwards, I had only one opportunity to call together the four company Gas NCOs to give them a short revisionary lecture.

This I did with the authority of Lieut. Smith, the Intelligence Officer, during a short period in reserve at a Nissen Hut Camp recaptured from the enemy. One morning while the companies were busy training, I visited them and asked each Company Commander to release the Gas NCO for this occasion. I then summarised their duties thus:

1. Regular inspection of service box respirators (SBR) of all officers, NCOs and men.

2. Test the inlet valve by short sharp breaths through the mouthpiece and observing if rubber moves up and down. Check for rust of box by pressing each rib of box.

Examine joint of box and flexible tube. Check joint at correct angle.

Examine flexible tube — elbow. Check correctly wired on and taped.

Examine elbow soldering and joint of elbow mouthpiece.

Examine mouthpiece — that ring is present.

Examine nosepiece. The clip and that muslin is present.

Examine facepiece, especially the triplex eyepiece.

Examine elastics and tape. Check safety pin is present.

Test outlet valve. Place hand over inlet valve, breathe in; no air should go in, and suction should be felt on the hand.

Check haversack or satchel, that nothing else is present except string, anti-dimming and card. Check sling and stud.

Condemn any masks found damaged or faulty by writing "Condemned" on the card kept in the satchel containing the SBR, and sign name and rank.

3. Post and instruct gas sentries.

4. Report location of dud gas shells, and look for markings on base caps.

5. Report to officers when a gas attack starts. Give progress reports, and when certain, report ALL CLEAR.

6. Treat shell craters which exude gas — sometimes later, when weather is warmer.

A NOTE TO THE READER

If you have enjoyed this book enough to leave a review on **Amazon** and **Goodreads**, then we would be truly grateful.

The Estate of Frederick James Hodges

Sapere Books is an exciting new publisher of brilliant fiction and popular history.

To find out more about our latest releases and our monthly bargain books visit our website:
saperebooks.com

Printed in the USA
CPSIA information can be obtained
at www.ICGtesting.com
LVHW070042290224
773075LV00031B/632